Aunt Lillian Told Me to Keep Laughing

"*a memoir*"

Rosalie Bott

iUniverse LLC
Bloomington

AUNT LILLIAN TOLD ME TO KEEP LAUGHING

Author Credits: Roberta Roth.

iUniverse books may be ordered through booksellers or by contacting:

iUniverse
1663 Liberty Drive
Bloomington, IN 47403
www.iuniverse.com
1-800-Authors (1-800-288-4677)

ISBN: 978-1-4917-1720-2 (sc)
ISBN: 978-1-4917-1722-6 (hc)
ISBN: 978-1-4917-1721-9 (e)

Library of Congress Control Number: 2013921918

Printed in the United States of America.

iUniverse rev. date: 12/30/2013

CONTENTS

To My Lymphedema Soul Mates

PREFACE

What does it feel like to be a patient? How does a patient cope with the bad news? How do you move on after treatment? My book explores these issues through my many experiences. I consider the medical community an extended part of my family. Frequently I am in the unique position of giving my doctors information about medical conditions that go beyond their own specialty. My desire is to share this knowledge both with the public and medical professionals.

PART ONE of my book on **ADVICE** is purposely written first. My goal is to give practical information to those experiencing difficult medical situations and is geared towards cancer and lymphedema patients. It is my intention to help a patient survive their ordeal and navigate their personal medical issues immediately. Much of the advice is usable by anyone with a hospital or doctor appointment, facing a trauma, surgery or waiting for test results. Practical suggestions are given based on conclusions from my own experiences and directions passed on to me by the medical community. Let my experiences be your inspiration to survive and my suggestions give you the motivation to help yourself.

PART TWO is a very real accounting of my medical, environmental and personal life and their effect on me from childhood until now. These incidences continue to permeate many of my decisions and attitude throughout my own history giving me the strength to recover and cope through illnesses. When cancer and lymphedema patients congregate together they generally refer to this part as **MY STORY** and share our personal experiences with each other.

Some of my experiences are quite graphic in nature. They are not to scare you off but to let you know I survived each incident and am still laughing.

The greater majority of people in the medical field, doctors, nurses, support and clerical staff, etc., are really wonderful and excellent at their jobs. They will do everything they possibly can to help you, the patient. Though perhaps unintended, there are always exceptions to the above and they may be insensitive to a patient's needs for their own reasons or ill-equipped for their job. To many of them that is exactly what it is, a job and not a really suitable one at that. Their communication skills may be lacking. Some jobs may empower them and they feel they do not have to listen to you. You are the patient and it's incumbent upon you or someone with you to be alert at all times as to what is needed for your condition and recuperation.

Your attitude is one of the most important aspects in any recovery. The medical community can do just so much. The rest is up to you. If you are able to joke under horrific circumstances, you are on your way to acceptance of your condition and the healing process.

My father's family seemed to go through life by laughing. As my Aunt Lillian told me on several occasions, "Don't forget you are a Bott and the Bott's always laugh!"

Laughing is great for lymphedema. It helps to keep your lymphatic system moving. Smiles and laughter work better than screaming and yelling even when you do not speak someone's language. If you are still waking up in the morning and breathing, smile and be happy because you have lived to see another day.

ACKNOWLEDGEMENTS

I want to thank my physical therapist Mani. I shared many of my experiences with her through hours of lymphedema massages. She encouraged me to put everything down on paper.

A thank you goes to the entire lymphedema department of St. Augustus and especially Kate who has been instrumental in providing us with programs to keep our spirits up and our bodies moving.

A special thanks to all my doctors for their encouragement in writing my book.

I want to thank all the people who have passed through my life giving me hope, help and support including doctors, their support staff, teachers, friends, strangers and even some relatives. Many of them unfortunately are not with us anymore but I hope somehow they knew the positive impact they had on me.

I am indebted to my grandsons Donny and Larry for helping me with their computer skills. You deserve a big hug, kiss and special thank you for making it possible to getting my book out to where it is needed.

I must especially thank my husband who gave up computer time for me to write this, for being my chauffer when necessary and mainly for being my best friend.

*Names may have been changed in certain circumstances but the experience has not been altered.

INTRODUCTION

Everyone on our planet has access to information, from the caves in Afghanistan to the citizens of the developed world. We are inundated with information on a constant basis yet so very few people are familiar with lymphedema.

Electronics in our era alert all of us to new medical information as it is happening. Not all of the information is accurate but the consumer is exposed to knowledge about diseases, medications and treatments. One medical issue never acknowledged is lymphedema. Most doctors and many others in the medical world are not necessarily trained to recognize lymphedema. It is often a misdiagnosed, unrecognized, and mistreated side effect from the treatment of breast cancer and surgical scarring blocking our lymphatic system from doing its job.

Disputes abound with diagnoses and treatment. I am using my book as an introduction to lymphedema for those who are hearing the word for the first time, the medical community to expand upon their knowledge and acceptance of the condition, insurance companies for payment of compression bandages, sleeves and equipment, therapy with no cut-off date for treatment of the disease, recognition by the media of the millions who suffer with this ailment or the reasonable fear of developing it and encouraging those who deal with cancer to promote lymphedema as one possible side effect of breast cancer treatment. Lymphedema at an early stage may be manageable with proper treatment but your lifestyle is forever changed.

Once you are diagnosed with lymphedema extreme care must be taken to avoid infections that may result in erysipelas or cellulitis both life-threatening conditions on their own if left untreated.

Enjoy something every day in your life and be grateful you are still breathing.

PART ONE

ADVICE

Chapter 1

IMMEDIATE ADVICE

I have now reached the ripe old age of seventy even though I can't quite believe it. I do wear shorts in the summer and my husband tells me my legs are still a turn on. I'm glad some part of my body looks okay. That does not mean my legs don't have problems, they do. I will continue to think of myself as younger though readily admitting my years on this earth. Getting to this point took pain and effort.

My extensive involvement with doctors, hospitals, and the medical community from my childhood to the present puts me in a unique position of offering advice, encouragement and inspiration for others to move on. My coping skills and tenacity in dealing with my continuing issues may be of personal value to you but why wait for a concluding chapter if some of my ideas can help you now?

My Medical Journal

As my medical challenges keep occurring my knowledge is expanded about each one but I can't remember them all without a system. Acknowledgement of the fact I am not a computer and cannot type in key words to find answers, I formed my plan. My medical journal is kept on one page of my computer with a list that includes medications, medical conditions, allergies, blood type, surgeries, dates and who to contact if necessary.

Doctors and hospitals love my medical journal. They scan a copy into my file on their own computer system and my record is made up to date each time the doctor sees me. The journal is also a terrific substitute for filling out long forms for each visit. I just write on the doctors forms, "See Attached." The list becomes a *Reader's Digest* of my life giving new doctors an immediate sense of my medical history and is easily updated. As my medical list continues to grow I've had to change the font size on my journal or what I call my cheat sheet. One of my doctor's might eventually tell me he or she needs a microscope to see the writing.

My physicians list is long too. I've categorized the doctors by their specialties, along with their names, phone, fax numbers and addresses. I keep this list up to date as well and attach it to my cheat sheet.

When a repeat of an unusual medical problem arises I make sure to tell the doctor how it was resolved in the past. Many doctors have not seen some of my issues with other patients and it's incumbent upon me to inform them of successful past treatment.

My daughter suggested I email her every time I make changes to my lists so she will always have the updated version. It doesn't take much to lose all your work. Think of a virus or just hitting the incorrect key on your computer. Poof! All your hard work has disappeared. Forward your lists to someone you trust.

Medical Reports

Be organized. I keep a file folder for every year with all my medical tests and reports in it. Not every doctor or hospital will fax a report to every one of your doctors. Always ask for a copy for yourself. Past surgical reports are especially important for any new doctor you may see and you will have them right at your fingertips.

I started a new file even though it duplicates some of the above. It's categorized by illnesses e.g. breast cancers, kidney cancer etc. Many specialists are only interested in one particular category. My solution was to put all the reports for one area together. This also is a quick way to get the information you need without going through each year.

If you have the capability of scanning your reports into your computer use the same headings as above by medical category and year. Paper and storage can then be kept to a minimum. Always remember that a doctor's original signature must appear on all test results and reports. Your information can be printed out as needed.

Petroleum Jelly

Heloise's panacea for all your household problems is "vinegar." My favorite is "petroleum jelly."

My gynecologist suggested I put a slight film of petroleum around the outside of my vaginal and rectal area to prevent irritation. I remember doing this for my girls when they were babies but never considered it for myself until she mentioned it.

I have shots in my eye on a regular basis for a retinal occlusion leaving my surrounding skin red, irritated and swollen. Unable to prevent salty tears that ensue after every visit, I use a slight layer of petroleum jelly where the tears might fall. It really works. My skin no longer burns from the salty tears I cannot control while preventing the area from additional redness, swelling, and irritation.

I put petroleum jelly on my top lip and under my nose when I have a cold or my allergies act up. Irritation, soreness and redness from frequent blowing are lessened.

As I learned from meeting many other cancer patients, problems with a dripping nose affects them when they are on chemo. I suggest putting on a thin layer of petroleum jelly under and around your nose and on the perimeter of your top lip as well.

Another hint for use of petroleum jelly is to put it on your hands and under your nails before you put on gardening gloves. Not only does it help to save your nails, it makes for easier clean-up, is a barrier from a sharp branch piercing your gloves and acts as a preventive measure for the lymphedema of your hands.

Petroleum jelly is also a skin softener. Rub some onto your hands before going to bed and wear white protective gloves over them during the night. Your hands will feel smooth and silky by the morning.

Whoever thought a hint for a private area of your body could help with other parts too? Just use a fresh jar or tube of petroleum jelly for each area. Label each jar or tube if necessary.

Salt

Remember if you have lymphedema to avoid salt at all times. I've learned to cook without it and use substitutes for flavoring. No one has complained about my cooking to my face and in fact they ask for seconds. I've been told to avoid soy. It's salty and somehow interacts with female hormones. Soy seems to be added to almost every packaged product. My doctors have advised me to stay away from Asian foods because of the abundance of soy. I do miss having Chinese food every once in a while.

If you notice additional swelling in lymphedema areas, consider what you have ingested. Your food may have contained salt. The advice given to me is to drink plenty of water. I also notice a weight increase after a salty meal. Restaurant prepared soup is notorious for an over amount of salt and sodium.

It's irrelevant what the top chefs' say on TV. Ask for no added salt when ordering in a restaurant. Restaurants provide salt on tables for patrons who insist on using it. It's not necessary to add salt for every ingredient in a dish. Many chefs use several different types of salt to make one item. They're probably hoping someone from a TV food program will walk through their door. Why else would sea salt, kosher salt, regular salt and pink salt from a far off land be necessary for one recipe?

I would love to have it out with one of these chefs. It would be interesting to see a reading of their blood pressure. No one has yet admitted theirs and certainly no one has admitted to having lymphedema.

Odors that are essentially chemicals are absorbed into your body when they are placed on your skin. I was told to avoid all perfumes, body washes and colognes for that reason. No one yet knows the long term effects on our own body's chemistry.

Appearance and Other Thoughts

Do not let your appearance keep you at home. Enjoy the time you have left no matter how you perceive yourself in the mirror. I quite literally would have lost years of my life if all I thought about was my appearance. No one can see all my scars under my garments. I am qualifying this comment to say I make sure I am clean, wear laundered clothes, and dress as best as my body will allow. Try to remember a cardinal rule in fashion. The hint came from my clothing buyer aunt. The tighter the clothes are on your body, the more the jelly rolls will show. Those with lymphedema are told to avoid tight clothing. It impedes the lymphatic system from working properly.

Liquid bandage is a necessity for me in dealing with the repercussions of lymphedema. It's is a way to avoid a long term relationship with a bandage. If a wound is small, wash it well with soap and water immediately; pat dry with a clean tissue or paper toweling and apply liquid bandage. I'm referring to a tiny puncture wound similar to a prick from a needle or pin without irritating the surrounding skin.

Bandages that are covering a new surgical area and must be worn and changed by yourself daily can do a number on your skin. If you slightly change the adhesive direction with each new application some irritation can be avoided. Be cognizant if you see major rashes and swelling and feel very itchy on the adhesive site, you may be allergic to the bandage. Contact your doctor A.S.A.P. Better yet, ask the doctor on the day of your surgery to only use non-allergic bandages or the viability of other options such as staples and surgical glue.

Suntan Lotion is an absolute necessity when you leave your house. The strongest type you can find is the best. You want to avoid burning. Sitting in a car with the sun shining through the windows can give you a burn.

Hats with wide brims should be used when you are out in the sun. Try a straw hat. Keep it on your head by punching two holes opposite one another in the fold area. Thread the ends of a yard of grosgrain ribbon into each hole and tie under your chin. If you are concerned about the hat unraveling around the holes, use clear nail polish around the openings and let the polish dry before threading the ribbon.

Sunglasses should be worn outdoors to protect your eyes, even during the winter months. If your glasses are prescribed make several copies of your prescription and make sure you take one with you when you travel. Accidents happen and you might need to replace them on vacation. I learned this the hard way. The wind in Aruba was so strong my sunglasses were blown into the water and were never found.

Ice Packs instead of heating pads should be used when you have pain or swelling. Avoid very hot showers and baths. The heat can cause your lymphedema to become worse. Don't join your spouse or lover in a hot tub. There are plenty of other ways to make life interesting!

Hot Drinks may be soothing but if you are drinking it from a paper or a Styrofoam cup make sure to stack a few cups together first. The heat is too hot for a lymphatic person to hold in a hand.

Blood Pressure taken on an affected lymphedema appendage is typically a no-no. My cardiologist and internist take my blood pressure on one of my affected arms without pumping up the cuff very tightly. There is no way I will let an aide even try it. Several of my doctors have stated they can't hire competent help yet these are the people delegated to take your blood pressure. If you are lucky enough to have one unaffected side direct them there or wait for your doctor.

Ask if they've ever taken the blood pressure of someone who has lymphedema. Usually they do admit to the truth. Perhaps they are capable of taking your blood pressure on your thigh or ankle. Don't panic if your blood pressure is high and was taken in those areas. The higher reading may be due to the further distance from your heart.

The new watch type blood pressure devices that are placed on your wrist never register correctly for me. I think that they should go back to the factory and be redesigned.

A First Aid Kit is an important item to put in your purse or pocket. Keep a few bandages, a small Neosporin and a few alcohol pads with you in a small sealable plastic sandwich bag. You never know when you might get a cut. Replace the alcohol pads at the beginning of every month. They tend to dry out and new ones will be ready for your use.

Disposable Serving Items such as paper plates and cups, plastic utensils and foil pans should be used for parties. They make life easier and you've earned the right to use them. An assortment of patterns is available for every occasion. I gave my good China to my daughter and have yet to regret it.

Disinfectant Liquid or Wipes should always be kept with you. You never know when you may be in a place that lacks soap, water and towels.

Jewelry may have to be converted to other pieces if they were worn on an area now affected by lymphedema. An engagement ring can be made into a beautiful piece and placed on a chain worn around your neck or made into a pin. Even the time portion of your watch can be made into a neck piece with the removal of the band. Hang it on a chain around your neck upside down. When you lift it you will be able to read the time.

Wigs that are of manmade fabrics do need special care. Heat is to be avoided. The one thing I learned the hard way is not to go near a heated oven. The steam destroyed the front of two of my wigs. I'm seriously considering wearing a hat when I have company and avoid a wig altogether. The other alternative is only to serve cold food.

Tattoos should be avoided. The dyes used are chemicals entering your blood stream and lymphatic system.

Crutches cannot be used on the side of a lumpectomy or mastectomy. You might have to switch to a walker. Be sure to let the doctor know why a crutch is not a viable option for you.

A Cancer Support Community is one of the most valuable tools you have. Make use of it. Not only will you meet people who understand but you will learn about the newest treatments and medication for your cancer. Cancer patients share cancer information. Cancer is not a competitive sport. Find one in your area through your doctor, closest hospital or the American Cancer Society.

Self-pity must be relegated to the side lines as soon as you receive notification of cancer. You need to plan for your treatment and recovery.

Bills show up in your mailbox almost immediately after a hospitalization. Some doctors may hand you the bill as you leave their office or ask for payment before treatment. Don't be afraid to ask if payments can be made on a monthly basis instead of a lump sum.

Appropriate Treatment

One time an orthopedist gave me a cortisone shot in my lymphedema hand. We initially disagreed but the doctor convinced me, "I deal with lymphatic patients all the time." Not only was he wrong but I suffered the consequences for his decision. I ended up seeing my oncologist in the hospital. He agreed not to admit me if I sat at home for three days with my arm up and stayed on antibiotics. I watched a few good movies but the rest barely passed what could be called entertainment. It's hard for me to sit still and this was a form of torture. I suffered and still have a scar proving the shot. I will win the next argument with any doctor attempting to do the same thing to me. If you have lymphedema, you must take charge of what is appropriate treatment for yourself.

Do not give up. Live for each day. You are your own best advocate. Stay in tune with how your own body works. Check out any noticeable differences from your last self-exam. Above all keep a sense of humor.

CHAPTER 2

GENERAL ADVICE

Stress

Knowing full well that stress is bad for cancer stressful fighting in this day and age is a necessity. You must fight in order to live; fight to control pain; fight with insurance companies if you are denied coverage and insist on the safest option for your condition and the right to have more than one opinion. Enlist a family member or a friend to fight for you if you need help. Write down your wishes and give it to someone you trust.

Family seems to take the top prize for stress in dealing with my cancers and all the other extremely serious medical issues I've encountered throughout my life. It is much easier said than done to stay away from people who cause stress but within your own family you may not always have that choice. It was and still is absolutely not possible for me to avoid all my family.

I have gotten the opposite support from some of my relatives who should have been giving me the most help. The best and only thing I have been able to do is push certain relationships to the back of my mind for a period of time and then deal with them once they resurface. I have learned not to count on these offending people for anything but instead concentrate on those who can help, including strangers.

My husband Ben is obviously the one I count on the most since we are married. But I am the one who must seek help when it is needed and participate in activities to take my mind off unhealthy situations. Only I really know what works for me. Take control of your condition and find something to work for you.

Someone you love may have an addiction. They are not the ones to be around at this time. You will only be doing yourself harm. Do not let them take you down their path. Insist they get help and into a recovery program. Keep them out of your life until they are willing to take care of their own problem.

I will admit to being jealous of those who have very large, loving, supportive siblings and children but have learned I am not alone. We learn to be more independent, self-reliant and perhaps earn the title of survivor. I have heard the expression numerous times, "What doesn't kill you will make you stronger."

We tend to ask ourselves, *"Why are we the ones who have to keep being so fortunate? Perhaps the 'wealth' should be shared around a bit more."* Then again those who haven't gone through our many experiences will have a harder time dealing with a serious problem later in life.

Anger

For me anger and stress are part of the same package. If you can find something that works for one, it often will work for the other.

Cancer patients are told to keep their anger in check. Anger basically is not healthy for anyone. Two to five days is usually my limit on my anger. On a rational level I'm fully aware I am the one being hurt the most by my anger. In some cases the person who made me angry couldn't care less or they wouldn't have done it in the first place. Therefore the only one I really am hurting is *me*.

I must talk my anger out with someone and then I can get back to doing the things I enjoy most. The sooner I come up with an alternate solution for something that triggered my anger, the faster the anger goes away or at the very least helps me cope with it.

If your anger is caused over and over again by the same people, the ideal situation is to avoid them. It's not always possible. I have been given several suggestions that might help. Tell yourself:

"You are not paying rent. You cannot stay in my head for free."

"I'm slamming a door in your face."

"I have a wall around me and you are not entering."

Practice is needed to make any of the above statements work. Choose your favorite or make up your own with the same basic theme. Continued repetition of the same thought may eventually work.

Cancer Diagnosis

Are you angry about a cancer diagnosis? Turn the anger to your advantage. It will be the start of your getting well. Ask yourself "What is the best way to take care of my cancer?" Don't know where to start? Call one of the doctors who received a copy of the test showing your diagnosis. Don't like their recommendation? Ask another doctor if they know someone else who can possibly help you.

Call one of the hospitals famous for treating cancer patients. Even if the hospital is inaccessible to you, they can tell you the protocol for your diagnosis. They may even be able to recommend a doctor in your area or at the very least a hospital near you who could answer your questions.

Get on the computer. Make use of the internet. Check with the affiliated hospital of a doctor you may have found. My oncologist told me to look up physicians for their credentials but avoid comments from laymen for a diagnosis.

Acceptance

Still in the *"Why me?"* stage, accept what you absolutely can't change. If lifting is out and bowling is no longer possible or you can no longer play tennis, find something else to do. Use your imagination. Stay open minded. You might find something you never considered or even heard of before and grow to love it. Do not give up!

Angry about meeting people who have been in your life but now avoid you because they don't know how to react to your cancer diagnosis or deal with your new restrictions, find others within the cancer community. You will find they too have been through the same thing as you.

Seek out a support group for those who have gone through or are going through a similar type of medical diagnosis. You will feel relieved to be with people who understand. An exchange of information is one advantage but the emotional benefits are priceless. Often a facilitator such as a psychologist is on hand if extra help is needed. Exchange phone numbers with members of the group. You can keep in contact with each other if you need to speak to someone between meetings. Attending a support group is not shameful. You need all the help available to get through a very difficult period of time. A caregiver has a different perspective on your medical condition from yours and emotionally they are in a different place. As a patient a cancer support group can ironically be a *lifesaver*. You are helping your caregiver by helping yourself.

Life is not going to be the same once you've been given a cancer diagnosis. In most cases it doesn't matter how long ago your original cancer was diagnosed and resolved. Every doctor worth their medical degree will ask about a past cancer diagnosis. They will go into a heightened mode to see if there is a reoccurrence. You will be spending more time in doctors' offices for check-ups and tests.

A neighbor of mine says she forgets about her cancer. "It was so long ago." Yet I met her buying prosthetic bras. There is always a reminder from treatment but you can choose to resume your life instead of dwelling on it or let the anger associated with cancer take over your life.

Break-ups

A more in depth discussion of family relationships is necessary since they play such a huge role in the battle against cancer. Several of my doctors have told me stories about some of their patients' horrible relationships with close family members. No privacy laws were broken since names were never disclosed. The point of telling me their stories was to validate what I related to each one of my doctors. The pain emanating from these disastrous relationships can be worse than dealing with cancer itself. When you have more than one of these relationships the pain intensifies even more and you have to decide if a permanent break with some people is in your best interest.

After hearing, "You're always sick" by a friend after a mastectomy, it was time to sever the relationship. In the case of a close relative saying the same thing, the situation had to be handled differently on my part. The relative is involved in my children and grandchildren's lives and cannot be permanently tossed away. I need to take care of me! I just have to get over each unfortunate encounter.

Change

Sometimes a change in your behavior, reactions and responses might bring about a more acceptable change in someone else. A perfect example is a situation I had with my mother. She was alone and lonely. We often spoke on the phone several times a day. During one call she asked how I was. I admitted to not feeling too well. "You're always sick." I was taken aback by her response. I was taking care of her to the detriment of my own health and the statement really hurt.

There was only one way to resolve the issue though it was a very big stressor for me. "I'm great," was my answer every time we spoke.

After a few weeks of my *great* response my mother said, "You're hiding something from me."

I reminded her of what she said.

"I was repeating what was said to me about you. Make sure you tell me everything," Mom insisted.

Accommodation

Accommodating someone may not always be in your best interest. There comes a point when your frustration is so great it is doing you harm. I lost many hours of sleep, cried uncontrollably, did just about everything I could to accommodate one family member. I was advised to let him go by shutting him out of my mind. The stress was terrible for my own cancer situation. I was "To let G-d take care of him."

Encounters

One of the most unavoidable encounters you can have often surfaces on special occasions when you will be in the same place with offending people. I made a conscious decision not to miss my own children's or grandchildren's special milestones in order to avoid them. My mindset is to be polite. I cannot control other people's behavior.

It often takes several days to recover from one of these unpleasant encounters even if nothing has passed between us. Being deliberately snubbed doesn't better the situation. I absolutely refuse to miss out on important and memorable affairs. Speaking to my husband or someone else regarding the incident is usually the start of getting my life back on the right track again.

Unfortunately some sleep is always lost but once I involve myself in other activities and go back to my routine the latest incident starts to fade away.

Lies

If there is one thing I absolutely cannot tolerate, it is lying. Do not lie to me. I don't react well and in fact may go crazy when I find out the truth. I was once very, very naïve and it took me a long time to acknowledge I was lied to. It still may take me time but I am certainly faster in putting two and two together now.

People have lied to me too often and I have inwardly beaten myself up for believing those lies. The end result is my questioning and doubting everything that is said to me. I cringe inside hoping I'm not being told by family or friends that they lied to me for my own good. I want to make the decision not them.

I don't want to be lied to by doctors. I want my problem told to me and then we can work on solving my medical issues together.

I do not want family to lie to me for any reason because they are assuming my response to a question. I still have a mind that is working albeit slower than it used to. I am still a capable human being with plenty of doctors to vouch for my competency.

Caregivers

If you have someone who is a caregiver make sure they are in the loop at all times. They won't know exactly what you are going through in your mind and body but they can help you make some decisions and suggestions when you may not be very rational at a particular moment. Sometimes it's the most minor thing that sets you off and you may need someone else to put the incident into perspective for you.

Unsolicited Advice

Stay away from people who tell you they know better than you because they saw a television show, read about it on the computer or knew someone who may have had the same condition. This is not supportive or constructive advice. We are all individuals affected by many other factors than the general rule of thumb. Go over many of things you may hear about with your doctor. He is the one you should trust. Otherwise find a new doctor, one you can talk to.

Bring a list of questions for your doctor to your next appointment. Leave a pad and pen near your bed in case a question comes up during the night. Memory doesn't always work if your doctor leads you in another path of conversation. Take a pen with you to write down the answers. This will prevent you from getting home and realizing you forgot your doctor's response.

Fear

Fear is something we all encounter with a diagnosis of cancer. The waiting period alone to find out our test results is enough to make us nervous wrecks. After you follow through with finding a doctor, hospital and your recommended course of treatment, make a plan, write it down, give a copy to someone you trust immediately. Put your copy away and forget about it until the call comes for action to be taken. You may be able to speed up your treatment but there is always a period of time when you must wait.

I've learned the best thing for me and what I recommend to everyone is to keep busy. I reiterate, "Join a support group." Do not sit home and continually think about your diagnosis. You need a breather. Take a time out to give your mind and emotions a vacation.

Go to a park and let trees and flowers wrap around your body to give your mind a massage. Concentrate on how beautiful natural things can be. Your surroundings may help give you the will to face what is coming next and the incentive to get better. Use your mind to photograph what you see. You can drum up the images when you are feeling down later on. Take a deep breath. Breathe the smell of fresh air or the scent of the ocean. It can be relaxing even if you never appreciated the outdoors. Give it a try.

Watch young children playing in a park. You don't have to worry about feeding and clothing them or changing diapers. Just enjoy their antics. Laugh with them. Imagine what they will look like when they grow up and the careers they will have.

If you have children or grandchildren spend time with them. Immerse yourself in fun activities. Take the children to a funny movie. Laughter is contagious. If the children laugh so will you.

Read the comics in the paper. Look up jokes on the computer. Exchange email addresses with everyone you know and ask them to forward jokes but avoid anything that is serious and depressing.

Take up a craft or hobby to occupy your time. Concentrate on it. Visit a craft store to get some ideas. Often people are available to give instruction. Take advantage of their help.

Start a document on the computer or write in a diary about the fun things you've done in your life. Skip the depressing thoughts and concentrate on those experiences that made you laugh and happy. Read uplifting books not sob stories or those discussing your medical condition.

Let your inner inhibitions out by drawing or painting. You do not have to be a Monet or Picasso to express your feelings and don't worry about not being able to draw a straight line. It's absolutely unimportant and unnecessary. Fill up your paper with colors and shapes that appeal to you.

I was recently reminded of the fear when entering a hospital and being asked if you have a *"Living Will."* I have no idea or do I care to know if it is a Federal or State law or just a hospital's regulations. It's totally irrelevant. I probably was afraid the first time I was asked too. It's only a precaution.

Think of keeping a flashlight on hand if the electricity goes out. It's not used until absolutely necessary. Provide a *"Living Will"* without panic and put it away with your plan until needed. Your town or hospital may be able to provide a form or have an attorney draw one up. Have your *"Living Will"* prepared immediately after your diagnosis if you do not already have one. Then you can be free to continue with your vacation.

Cancer Detection

People are familiar with the motto "Early detection is the key to survival." Routine tests and self-examinations are the most common forms of the discovery of cancer in the early stages. More and more frequently cancer is being discovered by accident before any symptoms are apparent. Treatment of one problem often leads to the discovery of cancer cells or a tumor in another area of your body.

Surgical treatment of an unrelated medical condition produces scar tissue which in turn affects the lymphatic system. Our body parts are connected and it is a compelling case for specialists and surgeons to view us as a whole human being.

Pain

One of the most important pieces of advice I have been given along my journey through life is cancer works in a certain way. If the pain is intermittent it most likely is not cancer. This thought has helped me calm down. Every day I seem to have a new ache and pain. I need to remind myself I am getting older and have many scars. The aches and pains may just be from aging and arthritis. The thought does help to relieve some of my fears.

Do not hesitate to ask your doctor if anti-anxiety medication is indicated. Help yourself by making this period productive. Build up your strength with a healthy diet and exercise. Keep a positive attitude.

PART TWO

MY STORY

CHAPTER 3

MY BEGINNING

Now onto my history that has shaped so much of my advice.

Cigars and Cigarettes

Until I married my early years were spent growing up in a small apartment choking on cigar smoke. Cigars were the *in* the thing for men and Groucho Marx was the model of the day. A cigar was always in between a man's fingers or in their mouth. Repercussions from the smoke may have contributed to my developing renal cancer and a sample of my blood was taken for a clinical study.

Occasionally my mother smoked a cigarette claiming, "It calms my nerves." The additional smoke was so awful I was forced out of the living room. There were very few places for an escape and I often ended up sitting on the pot in the bathroom with the door tightly shut.

Advertisements and movies with sexy women and macho men luring people to smoke was the attraction of my fellow students in junior high encouraging us to light up a cigarette. Peer pressure caused me to experiment twice but one puff each time dissuaded me from taking up the habit. I took no pleasure in choking.

Smoking has been attributable to many forms of cancer and I for one am very glad it is banned in public areas. Unfortunately no one enforces the law in most places requiring smokers to stay a minimum number of feet away from a building. Hence you still have to walk through a thick cloud of smoke to enter or exit a building.

Smoking is banned on planes but not on Amtrak trains. There is a separate smoking car but it is useless if the smoke accumulates into other areas of the train. In my estimation smoking should be totally banned on any form of public transportation.

Antibiotics

Growing up I had all of the childhood illnesses yet I seemed to have many more colds. Allergy tests confirmed I should stay away from almost everything in our natural environment including trees and grass. Smoke was never mentioned though it became quite obvious it could be added to my allergy list.

I was frequently put on antibiotics as a child and as I've aged my body has built up a resistance to many of them. The result has been allergic reactions causing problems during needed surgery, recovery with some diseases and infections in a lymphedema site. I now have a disease specialist to handle my antibiotic problem.

Art

I have always been artistic and creative naturally. Art is my refuge. It helps me forget my pain and anxiety. When I was young my creative space was under the kitchen table. No one bothered me until we had to eat or it became too dark to see. There was a long period of years in my life when time, responsibilities and lost faith in myself kept me away from this activity. Even though observers enjoy looking at my finished project I am now aware art is my *drug of choice*.

My art work has evolved not just with age but with my medical conditions. I've switched from oils to other mediums since my first mastectomy. Every brand of pastels I picked up in one store was plastered with stickers saying they were found to be cancerous in rats. Pastels packaged in California had similar warnings printed on the boxes. Perhaps if my renal surgeon knew I painted he would have given me the advice to avoid using toxic oils and pastels after my renal cancer.

I was trained to mat and frame my art work but again my body prevents me from doing so. Aside from my back problems causing a lack of strength in my arms and hands, one misstep with a knife in a lymphedema area could cause a devastating problem. My resentment towards paying for something I was once capable of doing myself has changed. Even though it is an indication of how much I've deteriorated there is a positive side. I can still paint and draw. My senses have also been heightened and it shows in my work.

Environment

Fighting and tension were part of our daily living. The confines of a small apartment contributed to the atmosphere.

Our apartment building was heated by radiators throughout the building and fueled with coal during my very early years until the owner eventually converted to oil. The super shoveled the coal down to the basement after it was unloaded onto the sidewalk. The street was filthy black and we coughed as the dust from the coal rose from the pile with each shovelful.

The D train went through the tunnel in front of our building. A large grate covered the tunnel opening. People threw discarded wrappings, cigarette butts and anything else that fit through the holes of the grate into the space below. Garbage either disintegrated or built up but I do not recall the area ever being cleaned.

Gas fumes from all of the cars and buses travelling along the wide thoroughfare of the Grand Concourse contributed to smog with the constant smell of exhaust from their engines. New York City in general was and still is very congested. Tall buildings prevent a minimum of sunlight to shine through to the streets and prevent air circulation.

One of the schools I taught in definitely contained asbestos and was repaired during a summer recess. I'm sure many of the other schools I attended as a student had asbestos removed from the walls and ceilings as well. My first year of high school took place in a building that was used as a civil war hospital. The last two years of high school were completed in a building not much younger than that one. What unhealthy secrets did those walls contain? Lead paint was used in all my schools until laws were passed forbidding its usage.

My first home had a two lane highway behind it the first year we moved in but was very shortly widened to four very heavily travelled lanes afterwards. Traffic frequently came to a standstill and the fumes from idling cars and trucks entered our backyard.

Water has been contaminated with chemicals and dyes discarded into streams, rivers and oceans. Consumers flush unused medication down their toilets. The refuse seeps into the underground water and pipes and eventually makes its way into our waterways. Known carcinogenic cleaning products are still selling in stores and they too find their way into our water system. Labels may read *"Discard as recommended,"* but not everyone heeds the warning. Many people in my community refuse to recycle. The chemicals compromise our health and yet we cannot survive without water. I don't believe any manner of filtration does a thorough job to make our water really safe enough to drink. Additional chemicals are supposedly added to alleviate the poisons in recycled water. *Does anyone know the long term effects of those chemicals?*

If the environment is having an effect on our weather conditions *why shouldn't it be considered a factor in cancer?* Certainly the environment must have played some role in one or more of my cancers. Three of my immediate neighbors located next to my first house developed cancer and died.

Food

One of my doctors unexpectedly asked me, "Do you think the food we eat has a relationship to cancer?"

"I can only give you my opinion and I don't think any food is totally safe to eat or drink. Too much of any one item is probably not healthy and that includes sugary products."

Chemical additives are added to processed food for a longer shelf life. Other food is genetically engineered. Even home grown fruits and vegetables are affected by chemicals when they are sprayed to keep the plants disease free. The water we use to keep the plants moist contain chemicals and the soil is most assuredly somewhat contaminated. Animals are given hormone shots. Milk has additives. Perhaps that is why breast cancer has become so pervasive in our society.

"If the big shots and researchers in the medical community do not know for certain and disagree with one another, who am I to say there is a correlation between the two?" The doctor nodded his head in agreement.

I once went to an interesting lecture at Gilda's Club, a cancer support community. The gentleman who spoke was of Asian descent and was involved in the medical field.

He posed two questions to our large group.

"What do you think is the best food for you to eat if you have a cancer history?"

"At what point in the meal do you eat it?"

Everyone answered "*salad*."

"*We eat it as a first course or as our whole meal.*"

He disagreed. The Asian diet calls for our digestive system to be opened up with a hot liquid such as tea first. Then a starch and protein follows. Next to last is salad and then the meal is finished off with another cup of tea.

All of us in attendance were surprised to hear salad was almost relegated to the backburner. I use this as an example of not everyone being on the same page. My breast surgeon and gynecologist advised me to, "*Avoid Asian food.*"

We can pocket all the information we are given and decide for ourselves what works for us and our condition. I certainly would choose my doctors' direction before submitting to this lecturer's diet.

I do believe the man-made changes in our environment through cigars and cigarettes, chemicals, exhaust and improper disposal of medication, dyes, lead, asbestos, human waste, etc. contribute to cancers and the exposure may have led to a few of mine. There really is no safe haven. Wind and storms blow pollutants from one area to another, rivers flow into the oceans and the tides move polluted water. It's an endless cycle.

There is one other argument to explore. The growing population must be fed and in general the life span of people is longer than ever. Chemicals are responsible for that development too.

CHAPTER 4

MAMMOGRAPHY INTRODUCTION

I would be negligent in not mentioning an experience I encountered while living in Massachusetts for one year. I was thirty-one years old.

I was due for a check-up with a gynecologist. We recently moved and I relied on new friends for referrals. One was a nurse and recommended her gynecologist. I made an appointment and travelled miles to see him.

At the time there was much forested land in Massachusetts. If you did not live in Boston proper you drove long distances for everything. From a New York City girl anything you couldn't reasonably walk to by foot was considered far. There was plenty of thinking time between the doctor's office and home.

My aversion to the doctor began as soon as he walked through the door. I don't know why. He was oil to my water from the moment he entered the room. Things didn't improve when his exam started from the top of my head. When he reached my eyes he proclaimed "You wear contacts and they aren't good for you." *When did this gynecologist become an oculist or ophthalmologist?*

By the time he reached my breasts I knew something was going to be said and he certainly didn't disappoint me.

"When did you have your last period?" he asked. He followed the question up with a very scary declaration.

"You have lumps all over your right breast. Return after your next period and I'll see if your lumps disappeared."

There was absolutely no sense of warmth or caring in his cold tone of voice.

My next two weeks were nerve wracking and I didn't relish seeing this gynecologist again. My period was over and I went for my appointment. The doctor immediately went to my right breast.

"The lumps are still there and your breast must come off. Make an appointment with my secretary for the surgery. I'll take your breast off next week."

The one thing I was positive of, *this doctor would never touch me again.*

"I would like another opinion." It was the first time I used the terminology.

The gynecologist slammed the door as he left the room.

This was the era when breast cancer was first going public. Happy Rockefeller and other famous people were front page news about their breast cancers. Apparently many doctors decided to get on the bandwagon and lop off their patients breasts. It was a good money making business and I had just dealt with one of those doctors.

It really is debatable how I safely drove home, unnerved, with tears streaming down my face. I remember going up and down hills in wooded areas and not passing many cars. A well-known women's hospital in Boston popped into my head. I called my ex who was in his Boston office and asked if he could get a recommendation for me. The phone rang shortly afterwards.

"Pack your bag. You have an appointment with Dr. Bart in New Jersey tomorrow." Dr. Bart was my gynecologist before we moved.

I sat in Dr. Bart's office watching him as he stared at the business card I handed him from the gynecologist in Massachusetts. "The card doesn't say the gynecologist is a surgeon. Did you have a mammography?" It was the first time in my life I ever heard of a mammography and he wrote the word down on a prescription pad for me.

"I'm setting you up for a mammography immediately and want you to see a breast surgeon. I'm also going to examine you."

By the time Dr. Bart came into the examining room my two other appointments were set. The breast surgeon appointment was for later in the day.

"You can leave for your mammography right after my exam." Dr. Bart paid particular attention to my right breast even though he checked my left as well.

"There is a very tiny nodule moving all over the place." He felt for at least one other nodule and that one was even tinier.

"This often occurs when women have dense breasts. It does not necessarily mean cancer. The breast surgeon will probably have a hard time doing an aspiration for a biopsy but I don't want you to rely just on me."

I was sent off for my first mammography. The breast surgeon had the results of the mammography by the time I saw him that afternoon.

"I don't feel anything alarming but I will try to do two aspirations just in case." As my gynecologist predicted the tiny moving areas were difficult to locate.

"You really have nothing to worry about. I originally came from Massachusetts and practiced in Boston. I'll give you a name of a reliable gynecologist," the surgeon said.

We moved back to New Jersey before I saw a gynecologist again. I retained my right breast for another thirty years going faithfully for a mammography every year. Eventually I was saved by a mammography two different times.

CHAPTER 5

THE CAR ACCIDENT

Two years after getting married my daughter told me she was pregnant and I couldn't have been more ecstatic. Donny was almost nine months old when my daughter called early in the morning on a hot and humid day during the first week of August 1998.

"Mom, can you come out to help me?" Mindy asked. She was living in Long Island at the time.

After spending an enjoyable day with Mindy and Donny it was time for me to leave. Sundown was approaching and I didn't want to drive in the dark. Traffic was very heavy on the Expressway and I carefully tried to make my way on. I waited for an opening and finally saw one. Then I noticed two men sitting on the back of a car. The trunk was pulled down in lieu of a seat and their legs were dangling off the back. I refused to get behind them and waited for another opening. My chance came within a few seconds and I slowly made my way to the middle lane.

Nearing Shea Stadium the highway split into four lanes. I had to stay left. The men sitting in the back of the car were in front of me and I again wanted to avoid them. I slowly moved to the far left lane without a problem. My car was too cold and I shut off the air conditioning, choosing to open the driver's side window part way.

I was in the lane for a few seconds when the van in front of me jolted to a stop. I quickly applied my brakes and stopped only a few inches behind the van. I was talking to myself. *"Thank G-d my brakes worked and I didn't hit the van."* Next I felt a big bang in the rear of my car and was aware of myself being pushed forward. My eyes must have shut because I didn't see but felt the impact at both ends of my car.

The front of my car was crunched up and smoking. I was determined to get out of the car before it blew up. My seat belt wouldn't release and the car door refused to open. My body was in excruciating pain. I must have been screaming like a maniac. My fear was concentrated on the car blowing up.

A young man appeared at the window and I screamed, "Get me out."

The man used his hand to unlock the driver's side door and pulled until the door finally released. Another young man stopped to help and the two of them lifted me out of the car. I couldn't stand. My right leg was blowing up like a balloon and looked as though someone was pumping air into it. The pain under my left breast was increasing by the minute. I needed my bra unhooked and was embarrassed to ask the young men.

One of them called 911. The other man let me use his phone to call my husband Ben and Mindy. My son in-law, Jack was doing a residency at MRN. There was no way to avoid a hospital but I only wanted to go to a facility where someone knew me. I heard a voice. *"County Hospital is the closest."*

I remembered a beach lounge chair in the trunk of my car. "Can one of you please take out the lounge chair in the trunk of my car?"

I was lying in the fast lane of a highway with all the traffic swishing by. The noise from the traffic was deafening and the constant whizzing of the cars from the opposite direction was a fear unto itself. The pain felt as though it was eating me alive. My leg continued to blow up and the area around my left breast defied description in terms of pain yet I was still too embarrassed to ask either young man to release my bra.

A young female passenger from the van came over to me and stood at the end of the lounge chair. I begged her to open my bra and showed her the problem. She turned around and returned to the van. There was no way she could misunderstood my request because of my hand movements even if language was a barrier.

"Please help me!" I continued to yell as she walked back to the van.

The driver of the van came over. "I'm leaving. The van is not damaged and no one is hurt."

I yelled at him above the traffic noise, "You can't leave. I'm injured."

All of this was to no avail. Everyone including the driver piled back into the van. The police arrived. The van wasn't going anywhere.

I tried convincing a police officer I wanted to go to MRN.

"It's up to the ambulance drivers. They go to the nearest hospital," was the response from the officer.

"If you don't me taken to MRN I'm getting off the lounge chair and walking across the highway to land on the other side." We both knew this was absurd.

My car still hadn't blown up. The officer said the car engine has a device built into it to prevent a blow up from occurring. I watch too many auto chases with Ben on TV and in the movies. Interestingly enough the airbag never deployed.

The officer brought me my pocket book. He looked in the trunk of the car, "Most of the damage is there. Your car is totaled." I never would have guessed the rear of my car was worse than the front.

The EMT drivers put a collar on my neck, transferred me to a gurney and put me in the ambulance. The young man who hit my car kept Mindy informed. He was the man who released the door of my car. The second young man was riding a motorcycle and stopped to help. I saw him with his helmet. There was no way to say thank you and I have no idea of his name.

CHAPTER 6

MRN

I was taken to MRN and Jack was at the emergency entrance. My first wish was removal of my bra. The pain was excruciating and it was a toss-up as to what hurt more, my leg or under my breast. Jack left and I kept hearing my name over the loud speaker.

"Rosalie Bott please come to the front desk."

Beside my pain the thought of how nonsensical this scenario was. I arrived by ambulance on a gurney from an accident at the emergency entrance and I'm being called to the front desk. I was lying in the hallway. No one came over to me.

I finally spied what looked like a nurse and called to her. "My bra has to be removed." I started to help.

"The bra has to be cut off," she said and left to get a scissor.

Thank G-d! Someone in the hospital finally did something for me. My name continued to be called. Jack returned. "The emergency rooms are all filled. You'll be put in a room as soon as one opens up."

Eventually I was taken to a room in the emergency area that contained all the linen for the department. I was ordered to *change into a gown* as the garment was tossed to me by an aide. No one helped. Changing was far from easy while lying on a gurney in excruciating pain.

No one gave me any privacy. Men and women went in and out of my room taking linen. These people were not on staff. They were with other patients. I was forced to undress and put on the gown in front of them. These people had absolutely no qualms about walking in and out of my room without so much as an *"excuse me"* and no one on staff stopped them.

It was as though I didn't exist. *How would they have felt if someone did that to them?*

After what seemed like an extraordinarily long period of time a doctor came into the room. He was probably a resident.

"Get off the table and stand." Amazing! My leg looked like a huge balloon with a deep cut down the middle. No x-rays had been taken to see if it my leg was even broken. The doctor didn't even examine me to see if there might be a problem and yet he was telling me *to stand up.*

The doctor repeated his demand several times for me to stand even though I protested. Somehow I pulled myself up and held onto the gurney. His phone rang. "I'll be right back." He never returned. I hoisted myself back onto the gurney.

A man entered. "I'm taking you to x-ray."

Films were taken of my leg and Jack appeared out of nowhere. "I'm taking the films to be read."

Jack returned shortly afterward with what he considered good news. "Your leg is not broken. I arranged for you to have your own room since you must be kept overnight."

I was transferred to the room and remember nothing more about that evening because pain killers knocked me out.

The next morning a young man entered my room. "I'm taking you downstairs for a CAT scan of your body."

In the radiology lab I was transferred to a cold metal table. The technicians weren't really interested in me. They were busy conversing and laughing with each other. I was disturbing their conversation.

Once the test was over I was to be transferred back to my room, only I had an accident. I didn't think my back had been hurt in the car crash but later found out my spine definitely was injured. I expelled urine without feeling it but was aware of what happened. My gown and body were soaked as well as the metal table. The guys were preparing to transfer me to the gurney.

"Can you please clean me up and give me a dry gown?" I asked. They were not happy but then again neither was I.

I was transferred back to my room. Another young man entered.

"You're going down to surgery. Your leg might have to come off."

I couldn't quite absorb the whole thing. The surgery had something to do with a blood clot that could travel up to my heart causing a heart attack or stroke. I hadn't even seen a doctor except for my son in-law only he wasn't my physician and the doctor who abandoned me in the emergency room. *Who is calling the shots?* I asked myself.

Ben entered my room and I informed him my leg was coming off. Mindy appeared next. Then an R.N. came into the room to take me to the O.R. I was now dealing with the loss of my leg and was very frightened.

I needed everyone's support. The nurse pulled the gurney into the elevator. I couldn't believe what was happening to me and perhaps neither could Ben or Mindy. I wanted to hear my wounds were a *temporary setback* and I would be okay but was not hearing those words from anyone.

We reached the O.R but no operating rooms were available. Mindy and Ben were told to leave. Mindy left but Ben followed the nurse pulling the gurney.

I was taken to a large holding room with many people. Each gurney area was divided by curtains. Ben was directed to take all my belongings home.

Ben questioned a doctor standing in the aisle of separated gurneys. "Can you tell me how long the wait will be? I won't return to New Jersey if the surgery will be in a few hours. I'll wait in another area of the hospital instead of going home."

The doctor replied, "Look at all the patients ahead of her."

Ben kissed me good-bye and went back home.

A doctor came over. "What is your pain level?"

"10+++," I answered.

"I'm giving you a shot to put you out since the surgical waiting time is going to be very, very long."

My bed was near a window and the next time I awoke it was dark. If I didn't move at all the pain in my leg went down two pluses. Someone came over and saw I was awake. There were still many more patients ahead of me.

The doctor came over. "Give her another shot and put her out again."

This time I awoke and the pain had settled down to a ten in my leg. No one examined the rest of me.

"What time is it?" I asked a nurse.

"It's 6:00AM."

I still had my leg and had gone through fourteen hours without having surgery since my arrival in the holding area.

The doctor came over to me. "I'm having you put out again. If things go well by the end of the morning you won't need surgery." *I would really be keeping my leg!*

The next time I woke up it was near 11:00 AM and I was being transferred to a room. I only had my leg because so many people were before me and no operating rooms were available. We should all think about rushing to be first on line. Aside from all my other problems I could be missing a leg for the rest of my life. This was one time almost last in line was an advantage.

The next room was for the rest of my stay. I never saw or spoke to my roommate. Her bed was by the window and the curtains were always drawn. Every once in a while an attractive woman in her late twenties or early thirties came to see her. She never acknowledged me.

Jack visited me every morning before starting his rounds. Ben came in the afternoon. One day I told him not to come.

"Stay home and rest. We'll speak on the phone."

I never saw the doctor and had absolutely no idea of what was going on with my conditions. It was quite obvious I had more than one to contend with. I also was not allowed off the bed so the bedpan became my constant companion. Once I was able to get someone to bring in the bed pan I had to wait quite a while to relinquish it.

No one told me the results of my tests though I continually asked. "*Your doctor has to tell you.*" I protested but never saw a doctor and no information was forthcoming.

One afternoon Ben arrived at the hospital after picking up a copy of the police report. A man was on line in back of Ben picking up the same report.

"I'm going to sue your wife's pants off. My van is badly damaged and all my passengers were injured," he threatened.

I asked Ben for a description of the man. He was the driver of the van who was preparing to leave the scene of the accident. If this man high tailed it out of the accident site faster he wouldn't have been able to get the police report. The police showed up and the van driver was required to stay. The driver definitely spoke to a lawyer.

Our auto insurance agent said the last person who hits a car causing a chain reaction is responsible. Not to worry. If I received anything from a lawyer pass it on to my insurance company.

I received a letter a few weeks later and passed it on to the insurance company. I hope the guy driving the van was proved a fraud. Suggestions were made by a few people regarding the fact the driver probably was driving illegals back and forth from work and that is why he wanted to leave the scene of the accident. The man must have found an attorney who would somehow get around all of that. Unfortunately for both of us the young man who hit me was driving his mother's car and she only had the minimal amount of insurance. My claim eventually had to go under my own insurance policy.

As I was languishing in the hospital Ben called late one afternoon apprising me of the fact I would be going home the next day. I wanted to know how he found out when no one would tell me anything. He was bringing me a set of fresh clothes to go home in.

"Do you want a bra?" he questioned.

I passed on a bra. My left breast was sore, swollen and black and blue. Absolutely no one had addressed my breast or other extremely bruised and swollen areas of my body. Ben said he would notify my internist who would probably want to see me immediately. It was pretty obvious I needed follow-up care.

All of a sudden I became very frightened about getting into a car again. So much so I started to panic. An aide came to help with the bed pan and called the nurse. She decided a psychiatrist should see me but it probably wouldn't be until the next morning. He could prescribe something to calm me down.

"At least you will be able to get home," she said.

The next morning the bathroom called my name but I was not allowed to use it. An aide brought me the bed pan again. I questioned the wisdom of using a bedpan if I had to get up to go home.

"You have to use the bedpan. Those are our orders."

How can was I go home if I hadn't been off the bed in almost a week?

Lo and behold my doctor came into the room. I thought she was going to stop and speak to me. She was going to see my roommate. I stopped her. "My husband told me I was going home today."

Her response and attitude left me floored. "So go home."

"I haven't been off the bed," I said.

"Get off the bed."

"My doctors in New Jersey are going to need the reports and test results from the hospital."

"There is nothing to report."

"But I had tests."

"There is nothing to report. I have a very sick lady to take care of," and walked away as though I didn't exist.

My roommate's daughter entered the room and sat on a chair between our two cordoned off areas. The doctor was in with her mother.

I managed to get off the bed without any help to go to the bathroom. I succeeded but was very wobbly. As I came out of the bathroom my roommate's daughter rose from her chair to help me. She noticed I was about to fall over. I was grateful for her help as she supported me on my way to the sink adjacent to my bed.

I felt a tap on my shoulder and almost jumped through the ceiling. So much for psychiatrists! The psychiatrist had many students with him. Instead of speaking to me, he turned to them and said, "She has PTSD. That is why she jumped."

I probably did have PTSD but the water was running and I was looking down. I didn't hear anyone enter the room. I think this would be a normal response from anybody but I guess he had to show his students his big shot diagnosis.

He spoke to me for a few minutes. "I'll speak to the psychologist you previously saw at home." He gave me a prescription for sedatives and ordered one for me before leaving the hospital.

CHAPTER 7

RENAL CANCER

Ben arrived and I changed into my clothes. I was given a sedative and waited for my discharge papers. The papers showed I was to call the surgeon if my leg got worse. No other instructions. We drove home.

I was looking forward to my own bed after all that time in the hospital but first called my internist. He was on vacation. One of his partners said, "You should be seen immediately."

We got back in the car and went to the doctor's office. My bed had to wait.

The doctor who saw me stated, "I can't believe how swollen and black and blue you are all over your body. Did anyone in the hospital address your wounds?"

"*Only my leg!*" I brought the discharge paper with me to show the doctor.

"Ice should have been put on the swollen areas of your body at the very least."

"Your wounds aren't cleaned out." She proceeded to clean all of them putting bandages on those she wanted covered.

"You have no fever and miraculously you don't have an infection. Continue with the same sedative you were given and I'm prescribing some pain medication. See an orthopedist next week but give some of the bruising a chance to subside."

She recommended I see my gynecologist about my left breast which Ben was now calling a purple eggplant.

"I'm putting in a call to MRN to try and get your test results."

I spoke to Jack. "My doctor really wants the reports from my tests. "Could you possibly pick them up?" He was unaware all my medical issues had not been addressed at MRN.

When my orthopedist saw me he was stunned with my extensive bruising. "I'm demanding the results of your tests from MRN."

I gave him the doctor's name who said there was nothing to report. "I'm going after the reports in spite of the doctor in the hospital. I have a vested interest in you."

My orthopedist knew me for years and had been involved in four of my spinal laminectomies. "In the meantime, I'm sending you for a whole body nuclear test, physical and occupational therapy." My nuclear test came back negative.

I took my orthopedist's advice and made an appointment with my gynecologist. "You are too bruised to have a mammography. Wait for some of the bruising to dissipate."

A few weeks after the visit to my gynecologist I received a letter telling me to pick up my file. He was retiring. Each time my insurance plan was changed I had to switch doctors. I really liked this gynecologist and never bothered to revert back to my old doctor when I went on Medicare. I decided to return to Dr. Bart but he was no longer in the office. I sadly found out later he died. I made an appointment with one of the other doctors in the practice.

I was taken into an examining room and given help undressing and putting on a gown. My body was so sore and swollen I required assistance. My breast was noticed. "All the girls talk about a breast looking like yours after an auto accident from wearing a seatbelt. None of us have ever seen it." The aide exclaimed. A few seconds later my breast was on display for a whole group of women. I should have charged a fee to look at me. *The circus charges to see freaks!*

My new gynecologist was supportive and gave me the same advice as the other gynecologist. "Wait until some of the bruising heals and go for another mammography."

Ben took pictures of me. If all the people in doctor's offices couldn't believe what I looked like, then the auto insurance company might also like to see the mess. It might help in getting my medical bills paid. I was already paying deductibles on bills promptly sent out by MRN. I knew an attorney would have to be hired. The psychiatrist sent a bill higher than my auto insurance deductible. I called his office and was informed, "The doctor doesn't take insurance." We paid the bill. The psychiatrist was paid again by my auto insurance company. He refused to return either check.

I continued physical therapy as well as occupational therapy but no one could get me out of the funk I was in. I was having a problem with my elbow and it was a toss-up as to who should take care of it. I had an occupational therapy appointment the next day. I called my orthopedist. I can drum up in an instant the exact circumstances of the call.

A cleaning girl was working in the dining room. I could see her from the kitchen. Ben must have been near me to get by my side as quickly as he did. One of the girls who knew me very well stated, "Dr. Fried wants to speak to you."

Something wasn't right. Dr. Fried never got on the phone. He had a very angry tone to his voice.

"I just received the report from MRN along with your x-rays. Why didn't you tell me you have kidney cancer?" Perhaps he thought I was holding something back from him.

"There must be some mistake."

In a slightly more subdued voice he asked, "Was so and so your doctor?"

"Yes."

Ben was at my side now. The cleaning girl stopped the vacuum and was staring at me.

Dr. Fried now spoke with a more supporting voice. "I'm sorry to be the one to tell you that you have kidney cancer. Do you have a urologist?"

"Is there one in my internist's office?" I asked.

"No but I will call you back in a few minutes."

The few minutes felt like ten hours and I think it was only a few seconds. The phone rang and the same girl who answered originally offered the whole offices support. Dr. Fried wanted me to come to his office A.S.A.P. They were making a copy of my report. Dr. Fried spoke to a urologist in his building. He was going to see me immediately. Six weeks passed and Dr. Fried said I had to be seen.

I left the cleaning girl in the house alone, a very unusual move for me. Ben and I drove to Dr. Fried's office. I picked up the report and films and went down the hall to the urologists' office.

I went in by myself for what I thought was going to be an exam. Instead all I had to do was leave a urine sample and read about wiping yourself from front to back. Ben came in and we met with the doctor. He was young and had bitten nails. *No doctor was going to operate on me with those nails. If he was so nervous that he bit his nails, what did he do in surgery?*

Ben and I were taken aback with this new development. I wasn't recovered from the auto accident and now I was dealing with kidney cancer. The surgeon said, "Six weeks have gone by and you need another CAT scan to see how much the tumor has grown. When a tumor is in the kidney it is malignant." My tumor was in the left upper pole and my adrenal gland also had to be removed.

His girl made an appointment with Ledges Hospital for the CAT scan. A follow-up appointment was made with the doctor ten days later.

I was well aware that Dr. Fried was furious at the surgeon at MRN at this point. He had a hard time understanding how any doctor could be so negligent.

I went home to find a message on the machine to call the National Kidney Cancer Association. Ben had called Mindy to apprise her of the situation and she was doing her bit. I called up and a man answered.

"Are you calling for the patient or are you the patient?"

"I'm the patient." Surprising myself by accepting the fact I had cancer.

"Welcome to an elite group!" he said.

"Why?"

"There are only one hundred kidney cancer patients alive in the U.S.A." My day hadn't been scary enough and now I had to live with a proclamation of doom.

"Where do you live?" "You have the best hospital for kidney cancer within your reach."

I responded with, "Tremore." He surprised me by mentioning another hospital.

"Do not go with any surgeon who does fewer than twenty-five surgeries a year."

The next day Ben had an appointment with a doctor and asked her opinion. She would go with Tremore.

I called Dr. Fried. "Could you recommend someone at Tremore for another opinion?"

"I originally wanted you to see my friend but he wasn't in the office. I really don't know the man you saw." His friend had just taken him into his practice. "I'll call you right back." Dr. Fried gave me the name Mogani. There was no phone number. Dr. Fried's friend, a urologist, said he would use Dr. Mogani for himself. "Call the hospital for his phone number."

I called Tremore and was transferred to Dr. Mogani's office. I was told to come to their clinic on Tuesday.

I was planning on keeping my appointment with the original urologist in order to get the results of the new CAT scan. I called his office and the surgeon spoke to me. The results were back and he would see me in his office the following Monday. That part was now perfect since I was seeing Dr. Mogani the following day. The fastest way to get out of depression from one thing is to move onto something worse and that is exactly what kidney cancer did for me. My auto accident funk was over.

Ben went into the office with me and we were told the tumor had grown since the first CAT scan. The doctor already made arrangements for me to have the surgery in Ledges and all he needed me to do was donate six pints of my own blood. *This guy has to be kidding,* I thought. You're not even supposed to donate more than a pint every six or eight weeks if you're healthy and he's telling me to donate six pints in two weeks. I kept looking at his bitten nails saying, *no way are you going near me* to myself.

"How many surgeries do you perform in a year?"

"Five or six," he answered.

Thank you to the man from the National Kidney Cancer Association. I kept envisioning the bitten nails and doubted if the surgeon did four surgeries a year.

"I'm going to seek another opinion at Tremore." The urologist wasn't happy but gave me a copy of the report from the new CAT scan.

Ben said exactly what I was thinking. "He probably does three or four surgeries a year if that many."

The next day we went to Tremore and I was issued a card as a patient. Either I had visited or been a patient in numerous hospitals but nothing compared to this place. I waited in the clinic's waiting room until my name was called. A resident saw me and asked a myriad of questions. I brought all the reports and films. "Dr. Mogani will be in shortly."

A knock on the examining room door announced Dr. Mogani's arrival. He was a very calm self-assured man but absent was arrogance and superiority. He was a delight. He reviewed my paper work and the films. "You need to have another CAT scan at Tremore, a chest x-ray, and blood work."

"Surgery is absolutely necessary. You also have many other people to see before your surgery."

"Do you want to wait until the bruises on your body heal some more?" I wanted this poisonous thing out of my body as soon as possible.

"Your adrenal gland must be removed. Your tumor is on the left upper pole of your kidney and is adjacent to the adrenal gland." "Your rib will have to be removed for access." This was something the other surgeon never mentioned.

We settled on October 5, 1998 even though the day was a Jewish holiday. Dr. Mogani was going on vacation and it was the last day he could do surgery until he returned. I refused to wait any longer. The surgeon at MRN messed up so badly my chance of survival was better if I didn't allow the tumor to grow any larger.

Dr. Mogani didn't mention donating blood but I did. "You don't have to donate anything. If you need blood which I don't think you will, the hospital has safe blood," he said.

I told him about the other surgeon asking me to donate six pints of my own blood. "I'll write a prescription for the donation of one pint to make you feel better. I'm sure it won't be needed."

Ben and I spent the whole day going from place to place in the hospital as well as in the city in order to get ready for my surgery. I went back the next day for additional appointments. We went through what seemed like tunnels in the hospital to go from one area to the next. In one office I was asked, "How was your tumor discovered?"

I answered. The lady pulled out a folder from her desk drawer. "It is against New York State law not to give the reports from tests to the patient when they are requested."

The folder had an application to file with the New York State medical oversight committee. "You can wait until after your surgery to fill them out."

"Make sure your doctor(s) attach their complaint and findings to the application." This was not about money but about inappropriate conduct by a physician.

I donated a pint of own blood. My blood could not be used for anyone else because of all my medications and medical conditions. If it wasn't used it would be destroyed. My blood was destroyed.

All my blood work was completed and I was given a set of instructions for my preparation the day prior to surgery. My last appointment of the day was to Dr. Mogani's internist. The doctor had a huge collection of ducks all over his office. The ducks were very unimportant to me at the time but made an impression on Ben. Instead I recall rain and waiting for cabs to go back and forth to the hospital. We were both drained from the whole day.

The next day I returned to the hospital for the CAT scan and chest x-rays. The CAT scan technician noticed Dr. Mogani was doing the surgery. "You're in excellent hands and if I had a problem, Dr. Mogani is the one I would trust with my life."

One doctor at Tremore advised me I would be put in a very bad position for my back. There was nothing that could be done about it. "Your rib will be coming out for the surgeon to reach the kidney. You won't be able to wear a bikini again." I hadn't worn a two piece bathing suit since I was seven when I didn't fill out the top. I didn't think this would be an issue at all and had my first laugh since the nightmare began.

I was given a breathing device to use for practice until the day of surgery. I had a collection of them at home from my laminectomies. Nevertheless I went home to practice knowing I was a *poor* "breather."

The prepping for my surgery took a few days. I went off some of my medications and started on others. I was warned one of the medications would turn my stool black. When the color changed I became aware my cancer was not a dream; it was real.

The morning of my surgery Ben and I left the house much earlier than we anticipated. Neither one of us was able to speak because of extreme anxiety. Water always calmed me down and the day before we drove to a lake. I sat and watched the water trying to ease my fears. I pretended I was still looking at the water as we drove to the hospital.

We were in the waiting room when a large family entered. They came from South Carolina and stayed at a hotel the hospital arranged for patients and their families. "We won't let our mother have surgery for cancer at any other hospital. The cost and trouble in coming to another state is worth it," one family member stated.

I heard my name called and even though I had brought my signed paper work for my medical care Tremore had their own. One of the people from South Carolina signed as my witness. My name identification bracelet was put on my wrist.

I was finally taken up to a changing room and turned everything over to Ben. The only thing I had on was the hospital gown and slipper socks. I was put on my gurney in the pre-op area. The usual going over my history, medications, allergies, taking of my blood pressure and having my I.V. inserted in my arm was done. Since this was pre-lymphedema there was no problem getting an I.V. started.

A female minister came over to me. She introduced herself and noted it was a Jewish holiday. "It isn't possible for a Rabbi to be here. The Christian prayer for surgery is the same as in the Jewish faith." She put her hand on mine and said something to the effect, "Please G-d take good care of her and keep the surgeon's hands steady." I had tears in my eyes when I thanked her but became fully aware that I was now in a very dangerous situation.

Afterwards I was rolled out into the hallway. Ben kissed me. "I'll see you later." I don't recall anything after that until I heard foggy voices around me.

Everything was blurry but I noticed a big red ball in front of me. As things became clearer I saw the red ball was my mother's wig. She was close to the foot of the gurney. Ben was at my side. The pain was excruciating. I said something in jest knowing it wasn't possible. "I need Dr. Snider and acupuncture badly." Dr. Snider was my neurologist and acupuncturist. The method helped me get through many instances of excruciating pain.

I was taken to my room. Ben went with me. I heard my mother say something about my brother but I didn't see him. Apparently he came up from Delaware to take my mother to the hospital and went home.

I was wheeled into my room, saw a window and was happy. The happiness was short lived. I was transferred to my bed with the window behind me. I was facing the hallway. I learned the reason within a few days. I had many surgeries by that point but was never hooked up to so many contraptions. Their connections seemed to be coming out of every part of me. I had a pump for pain. It was useless. I was cut in half with staples holding me together. The worst pain was coming from my back. Absolutely nothing helped me.

My roommate was leaving the next day. She was pumped up to go home.

I didn't sleep throughout my whole stay in the hospital. I never thought that sort of thing was possible. The pain was horrific. I clung to the railing on the bed to try to get through day and night. I know the sleep deprivation was real. A nurse came into my room as I was dressing to go home. All beds faced the direction of the hallway for a reason. We were continually monitored. The nurse said, "It's noted on your chart you never slept."

At least twice a day I went to another floor for an x-ray of my lungs and CAT scans. I was in extreme pain and remained on a gurney in the hallway as I waited my turn. All of my equipment went with me. Once in a while another patient and I would speak. I was now enrolled in the world of cancer patients and I was one of them.

The third day of my stay a nurse told me I was getting off my bed. "*How?* I asked myself." A few minutes later my daughter Toni, and her husband,

Phil entered the room. Phil sank into a chair in the corner of the room and either wouldn't or couldn't look at me.

The nurse returned with a wheelchair. She proceeded to unhook my machinery. I thought the wheelchair was for me. Instead all of my contraptions were either put on the seat or hooked up to the chair.

I couldn't get off the bed. The pain was so excruciating it prevented my body from moving. I had no energy. *All of my insides were taken out of me and were sent somewhere else.* How else could I explain the way I felt?

Somehow the nurse and Toni got me up. I held onto the back of the wheelchair and managed to get into the hallway. My knees were buckling and I was about to give up. Toni wouldn't let me.

As in spinal surgery once you make the first turn, the next one gets easier. I did better about getting up the next time. I eventually did so well I managed to get up and down the elevator myself. I saw a *Succah*, best described as a temporary tent, outside the door from a crafts room. It was set up for the Jewish holiday. No one was in either place.

I walked the meandering hallways holding onto the wheelchair still filled with all my contraptions. My pain hadn't diminished all that much but I plowed ahead because I was starting to get some strength back. I picked up additional speed every day. The bathroom was still a no-no and I was not eating regular food.

My mother was a very hardworking volunteer for a cancer group for years. As president of the group she was invited to Tremore once a year for an award. Every year another award was hung up on a wall in her apartment. Mom presented a check to Tremore on behalf of her organization at a reception held for all the volunteers of the hospital.

Mom salivated waiting to taste the brownies served at the reception. They were the best she ever tasted. Her friend worked at Tremore and sent her home with some leftover brownies each time. I never tasted them but heard so much about them I was determined to try one if I was ever allowed to eat again. Ben went into the cafeteria every day to buy me one. He never saw them.

My room didn't stay empty very long after my first roommate left. My new roommate entered looking fully composed, sophisticated, well dressed and very well maintained. I believe that would be the last time she would ever be seen that way. We did speak a little. She was very sick and stayed up much of the night coughing. Her days were not much better.

One morning I was on the verge of falling asleep when a cheery young woman walked in the room. She was a family friend. In a very loud booming voice she began to entertain my roommate. It was 4:30 AM and the friend decided to visit my roommate before going on duty at the hospital. Whatever sleep was possible for me was totally lost.

The same day my mother's friend came to visit me. Mom told her I was a patient. "Would you prefer to change your room? Your roommate is very ill and I can have you moved." I declined. Numerous hospitalizations netted me many different types of roommates and some were unpleasant. My present roommate was at least nice and I hoped to be discharged shortly. Why bother?

I inquired about my mother's favorite brownies and how Ben searched for them every day. She laughed. "When there is a big event an outside caterer provides the food. The hospital doesn't serve brownies." The only thing I was looking forward to during my horrendous ordeal wasn't available.

"I'll send some home for you with your mother." It was the first week in October. The reception wasn't until May or June of the following year.

I told Ben what happened with the brownies. After a quick laugh he said, "I'll buy you some after Dr. Mogani says you can eat." I changed my plan to a fresh black and white cookie.

I had one unpleasant incident in Tremore and that is the first time I realized why the hospital beds faced the hallway. I was on the phone and the conversation went south very quickly upsetting me tremendously. What was said was threatening and I couldn't handle it. I became hysterical. Immediately someone came into the room and asked me what happened. "You can do nothing about it. You have no control over what other people say."

At Tremore someone watches you 24/7. "You have to calm down. It will affect your health and your only remaining kidney." She left my bedside and very shortly afterwards a psychologist walked over to me.

"What happened to you to go into such a state of distress?"

I repeated the words of the threat.

"You are not in a position do anything about it and now is certainly not the time to handle the situation. You have to recuperate first."

After my fifth day in the hospital a nurse handed me a special menu for solid food. I could order the food for the next day. I had a hard time getting excited about oatmeal and gelatin.

The next day's menu was better. I was allowed to have a soft egg and a muffin for breakfast. Before the meal was brought in one of the doctors came to examine me. "You can go home after all your staples and machinery are removed if you go to the bathroom." I called Ben to come get me reminding him to bring my small suitcase.

The constant click of having staples fall into a metal pan gave me chills. I started to count them. Toni gave up counting them after one hundred and twenty five. The next hurdle was removing the catheter. The nurses had to resort to cutting all my pubic hair.

My body cooperated. I wasn't allowed to shower but washed up as well as I could. I anxiously awaited Ben's arrival. The excitement of going home made me forget about food until my breakfast tray arrived. Ben appeared at the same time.

I immediately went into the bathroom to change into my clothes. I combed my hair and put on lipstick. I never before brought lipstick for any of my hospitalizations and had absolutely no idea why I packed a lipstick tube with me this time. It's a pretty good idea. It makes you feel as though you've entered the land of the living again. My roommate even commented about it.

CHAPTER 8

I MADE IT

During my stay at Tremore, alarms went off very frequently and the door to our room was shut. A non-employee said it was a signal someone died. Dr. Mogani told me it wasn't true or the alarms would be going off every minute. A famous person did die in the hospital while I was there. When I took a walk one day I wasn't allowed to go beyond a certain point in the hallway. Only family, staff and reporters were allowed near the area.

I was given my discharge papers with numerous instructions. I had to see Dr. Mogani the following week. My biggest surprise came when Dr. Mogani told me I could eat everything including brownies. I had been mentally been preparing myself for never eating like a human being again.

I took the muffin off my breakfast tray and was determined to eat it. The muffin would be the first appealing solid food I ate in almost two weeks.

I said good-bye to my roommate and wished her well knowing she would never leave the hospital alive. She wished me a good recovery and an enjoyable life.

I was taken out by wheelchair while Ben went to get the car. I was deposited in the lobby and sat on a bench waiting for Ben. This was NYC. There was no parking except in a lot. I went outside to wait for him. I must have been crazy. People were smoking and I had to keep moving. I refrained from telling them what smoking did to the patients inside the hospital. I was getting very tired and thought about going back into the lobby when Ben approached. He helped me get into the car and we took off.

By the time we arrived home I was thoroughly exhausted. Ben helped me up to the bedroom. "Why don't you stay on the couch before you climb the rest of the stairs to get to the bedroom?" Unfortunately there was no bathroom on the main level of the house.

After undressing and using the bathroom I went to bed, remembering to position myself on the opposite side of where I normally slept. To this day I can't comfortably sleep on my left side. I can feel the stub of my rib and the hollowness of the area around it.

CHAPTER 9

KEEP LAUGHING

My grandson's first birthday party was a few weeks after my surgery. No one thought I would make the party. Not only should no one give up on my capabilities, I must remember not to give up on myself!

We picked up my mother in the Bronx and drove to Long Island for Donny's first birthday party. I was alive and wasn't going to miss it. I put together pieces of clothing in my closet to make an outfit. It hid my newly expanded area on the left side of my mid-section. I looked presentable enough and it was more important to be at the party.

I really needed to speak to people who had my condition. My mother mentioned the name of one cancer group and I checked it out. Unfortunately only breast cancer support groups were available.

I called my Aunt Lillian. At least she went through a cancer surgery. She was amazed by her own age. "I don't know how I reached ninety-two. I am the oldest sibling out of eight and yet the only one still alive."

She continued on, "I was the first to have a major cancer in the family." She had breast cancer when she was forty-five. Back then protocol was to remove all the lymph glands under your arm and perform a complete hysterectomy. "My lymphedema from the surgeries is my biggest problem."

"You're a Bott and the Bott's laugh. Laugh and enjoy at least one thing every day. Stay in touch with me." I did. Aunt Lillian and my Uncle Hank could no longer afford to live in New York after all her surgeries. They moved to Florida. The bills for Aunt Lillian's surgeries practically wiped them out. Florida living was much less expensive at the time than the New York Metropolitan area.

One appointment with Dr. Mogani was immediately after 9/11. The air in Manhattan still felt dusty. Ben wanted to go to lower Manhattan to see the devastation and pay our respects. I asked Dr. Mogani. "Go home immediately after leaving here," was his advice.

About six months later Ben again suggested we visit the Twin Towers site after another visit to Tremore. Dr. Mogani said absolutely not. "You are not to go near the area. It's still polluted no matter what the EPA says." Many people who helped clean-up the site have signs of or are dying from cancer.

After a year of CAT scans every three months I graduated to every six months and eventually to one scan a year. Over fourteen years out I go once a year for chest x-rays and an ultra sound.

After five years Dr. Mogani released me to my doctors at home. I expressed my nervousness at not seeing him. "If it makes you feel better you can see me next year." I was not given a prescription for a chest x-ray, CAT scan or blood work.

Dr. Mogani saw me the following year and asked if I had a chest x-ray or CAT scan. "*No.*" His facial expression gave away his displeasure. He has never mentioned releasing me again. The only change I've made is going to a Tremore satellite for my chest x-ray and ultra sound not too far from home. It's a very modern facility and we eliminate the traffic, tolls, and parking fees. The results are sent to Dr. Mogani automatically and they are passed on to all of my other doctors including my oncologist.

Dr. Mogani's office was moved again and he's been across from the main hospital for several years now. My appointment is a yearly visit on a Friday in August when everyone seems to be leaving the city for the weekend. Traffic is always at a stand-still on the way home. Now my attitude is very different. I'm glad to be alive to see Dr. Mogani once a year despite the hassle of commuting.

Dr. Mogani now accepts the blood work from my other doctors. Originally my blood work had to be done at Tremore. I've had more cancer since starting with Dr. Mogani and almost all of the veins in my arms are unusable. Blood tests from all my doctors are done at one time. Lymphedema has put a real crimp in finding viable veins for blood work and I.V.'s. I am very, very limited in where blood can be drawn and it is not required on a constant basis. A port has its own problems subject to numerous infections.

CHAPTER 10

FALSE ALARM

About a month after my nephrectomy I went for my mammography. After the films were taken I sat in the waiting area. The wait was too long and I had a feeling something wasn't right. Perhaps if I hadn't gone through the auto accident and hadn't been released from Tremore a few weeks before I wouldn't have felt that way.

Having your breasts squeezed for a mammography is bad enough but once you've been diagnosed with cancer your anxiety level rises with every test and exam. Many people won't admit to it at first and play a macho game. "I have nothing to worry about. My cancer was years ago." When really pressed for an opinion they will admit it was in the back of their minds. You can breathe a sigh of relief afterwards but you forever remain with cancer of the brain. *No not brain cancer!*

I was called in to have my left breast squeezed even more by smaller plates and my fear was rising. Ben dropped me off and was wandering somewhere outside the building. I had no cell phone to alert him to my new situation. I silently prayed he would realize how long I was gone and would come in to keep me company. My prayers were answered as he walked into the office waiting room.

I was advised not to leave by the tech. The same person returned and asked me to follow her. "You need an ultrasound of your breast." Mentally I was in pretty bad shape. I was still recovering from my nephrectomy, my wounds from the accident weren't healed and now I worried about my left breast. I continued to sit in the waiting room while my films were read.

The radiologist called me into his office. "You have so much scar tissue from your auto accident it's showing up as something other than what it really is. I needed to be sure and that was why I ordered the ultrasound."

Somehow I was going to have to get through this fear of cancer on my own. No support group was available. Hearing from Ben and others, "Every time you have a pain doesn't mean its cancer," didn't help. Not every cancer starts with pain.

Driving home Ben asked, "Why aren't you happy and why are you crying? It's good news." My explanation of having a hard time accepting any good news was difficult for him to comprehend. I was expecting another shoe to drop again. A sigh of relief may have been called for but the emotional repercussions of my last few months were devastating to my spirit.

For years I attended a pain aqua therapy program at a local Y. Aqua therapy worked for me. I felt better in the water. There was an extra major benefit of going. We became a support group for one another.

The original program required a prescription from your doctor and a report of your orthopedic problems. A physical therapist was in charge. The class performed all the exercises as a group in the water but we were individually watched and monitored. Many of us had been there for years and our support group was orthopedic in nature.

When Dr. Mogani gave me the okay to go back in the water I immediately returned to the class again. My first day back was after the incident with my breast. I was uncomfortable with my big bulge sticking out from my bathing suit. It was a constant reminder of what I had gone through. One of the women noticed I wasn't my cheery self and made it her business to speak to me. Whatever she said began to perk me up. It had to do with getting on with my life and dealing with the punches as they come instead of dwelling on what could occur in the future.

A few months later I had to move my mother to an assisted living near us. Problems developed emotionally, physically and financially in taking care of my Mom and a heavy burden was severely placed on my own body, marriage and well-being. All of these issues have been noted to be related to cancer development.

CHAPTER 11

DR. RUSSELL

I learned to swim on my back for my spinal problems from the start of my participation in aqua therapy. My hands lead my arms moving up the side of my body and move outward when I reached my shoulders. My legs remained straight with my feet doing the kicking. After my return to aqua therapy I was unable to lift up my right leg, the leg saved from surgery. My leg just hung down from my knee and swimming became impossible. Out of pure frustration I decided to try something unusual. I mentally concentrated on by-passing my knee and instead worked at connecting my mind to my feet and toes. I pretended there was a string pulling my foot up. I was absolutely floored after repeated tries when my leg actually rose to the top of the water.

A few years after my nephrectomy, I had an incident when urine started to flow out of my body at home. I didn't feel it. This was the same type of occurrence as the time I had a CAT scan after the auto accident. I was afraid to go back into the water.

The next day I saw my internist. "You have to immediately consult with a neurosurgeon and you might as well go to the best." His aide found the phone number for Dr. Russell. He apparently repaired a famous football player who was badly injured on the field and whose prognosis was not good.

I made the call and reached the doctor's residence. His maid gave me the office number. I was given a list of material and information to be sent to Dr. Russell. No appointment would be made until he received everything. A referral from a neurologist was required.

Dr. Snider saw me the next day. "Dr. Russell is famous and an appointment will take months. You can't wait." When one starts letting out urine without feeling it, it has to do with the spine. "It will only get worse and there is no way to reverse the damage." He signed the referral. "I'll send Dr. Russell all the information but see Dr. Fried A.S.A.P."

"You need to be seen by another neurosurgeon immediately rather than wait months for Dr. Russell but I will send your records to him today," said Dr. Fried.

I called one of the women from aqua therapy to speak to her about my newest issue. We had become very friendly. "I have the name of the best neurosurgeon in the U.S. and I was operated on by him." Her son in-law was a neurologist working with him. His name was Dr. Russell.

I don't recall if I had a chance to make an appointment with someone else but a few days after all my reports were sent I received a phone call from Dr. Russell's office. Dr. Russell was sending me for a myleogram and he had spoken to the radiologist.

My appointment was on a Thursday. Ben and I went to NYC for the myleogram. Upon completion of the test my head had to remain steady almost in a prone position. I had undergone many myleograms and I was very familiar with the procedure.

Fluid is removed from your spine and a dye is put in with a needle that feels like a pipe. X-rays are taken of your spine in a variety of positions. I was lying back on a recliner after the procedure was done and the radiologist approached me.

"Have you ever met Dr. Russell?"

"*No.*"

"You will now."

The sun began to set and the radiologist asked Ben to stop by Dr. Russell's office to drop off my films. Ben left to get the car and I was taken out in a wheelchair. I put the passenger seat all the way back to keep my head in a prone position.

Ben stopped at Dr. Russell's office and double parked. I was lying back in the seat hoping a traffic cop or police officer didn't approach. There was no way I could move the car. Ben came down within a few minutes and we left for home.

We were driving through a desolated area and I felt very sick. Ben stopped the car and I had to move to regurgitate. My symptoms were similar to a stomach virus.

Later in the evening Dr. Russell called. He wanted to operate the next day. I was sick and didn't think it was smart for me to go into surgery with a virus. He was going away over the weekend and would be away for the week. After dealing with cancer my fear of germs and their avoidance was a high priority for me. I refused the surgery in spite of being told how difficult it was to get an appointment with Dr. Russell. We mutually agreed to have him perform the surgery after his vacation.

On Sunday evening I received another call from Dr. Russell. "I am going to operate on Tuesday. I was prepared to do your surgery on Monday but now the hospital requires you to be cleared by an internist. The hospital no longer considers the operation an emergency. If your surgery was done on Friday this would not have been an issue. Now you need the internist's approval."

My appointment was scheduled at Lennar for 8:00AM the next morning. I was to have admittance tests and see the internist. One test showed a mitral valve problem. I had absolutely no idea how this would affect my surgery but the internist cleared me. I also had no idea the internist made different plans for my recovery than Dr. Russell.

I still had not met Dr. Russell. On Monday evening a man called me. "Dr. Russell requires me to be in surgery with him. I'm not covered by any insurance." His specialty had something to do with monitoring pain.

Just as I was being rolled into the operating room Dr. Russell came over to introduce himself to me. It was nice to finally meet the doctor who was going to give me a new scar. The man who called the night before introduced himself and told me about his job. He repeated his statement from the previous evening. "Dr. Russell insists I be in surgery with him but I'm not covered under any insurance plan. You will get a separate bill for my services." I think back and wonder, *how I was supposed to deal with bills, drugged up, in the O.R. with anxiety about the surgery?* Those thoughts were put out of my head because the anesthesiologist came in next and knocked me out.

I don't even remember waking up in the recovery room. I recall lying in a bed tightly squeezed into a small corner of a room by a door. A roommate had the whole other area which was considerably larger than my tiny corner.

Ben hired a private duty nurse and she sat outside. There was no room for a chair in my small and narrow space. Apparently the internist decided to put me in a cardiology wing after surgery instead of the orthopedic unit. No rooms were available and I ended up in a corner of a private room.

I was wearing a heart monitor. My private duty nurse made sure I was taken care of on an orthopedic level and monitored my pain medication. I was strapped into the bed to keep me in place though it is almost impossible to move after a spinal laminectomy. I say this after having had four prior surgeries for my spine and never having been strapped in previously. Perhaps the internist ordered the straps.

Ben went for a walk. There was no place for him to sit. The phone rang and the nurse put it to my ear. It was my mother. She was eighty-eight and a half years old at the time. "I just came back from a CAT scan of my spine and I'm in a lot of pain." I couldn't help her. I just came out of surgery and was still groggy. She seemed upset because I couldn't do anything for her.

Ben returned and the nurse told him, "Rosalie received a call from her mother." I related what Mom said. Ben stated, "I'm going home but first I want to make sure it is okay to leave. I'll be back tomorrow."

A few minutes later my private duty nurse remarked, "I'm going out for some food in the hospital cafeteria and will be back in less than a half hour." The floor nurse came into the room and removed my pain pump. I told her not to. The nurse insisted I had enough pain medication and refused to listen to me.

"The pain pump is necessary for recovery in my spinal surgery."

"I'm a cardiology nurse and I know best." I lost the argument.

My pain was unbearable. My private duty nurse came back and saw my disconnected pain pump. "A nurse came in and removed it," I said. She reconnected me. "I'm going to find that nurse and give her hell."

Ben called. "I left a message for your brother and let him know you just came out of surgery. He will have to take care of your mother."

My own nurse began to have me roll over the first night. I knew from all my other laminectomies the first time you turn is the worst. I gritted my teeth and made the move. I was unable to get up from the bed. There was no room to stand.

The next day I was begging the doctor to move me to another room. He was Dr. Russell's partner, "Your move has to be cleared with the internist. Your bed in the orthopedic wing was given to someone else and you have to wait for another opening." The following day I moved to the orthopedic wing and my private duty nurse was released.

My grandson called. Donny asked my son in-law, "Why is grandma in the hospital?" His father answered. "Grandma had surgery and surgery is when a doctor cuts you to make you better."

"Grandma it must hurt very badly." Knowing how much Donny cared about me was my incentive to recover and get on with my life. Sometimes the smallest thing can be the greatest motivator.

Ben's brother was dying of brain cancer. His niece was due to get married in several months. The couple moved the wedding date to the weekend after my surgery. I convinced Ben to go to the wedding if I could remain in the hospital over the weekend. Dr. Russell did not want me to be home alone and approved my stay until Monday when Ben could pick me up.

I saw Dr. Russell one more time.

"What prompted you to do my surgery if you were scheduled for vacation?"

"I was challenged by your situation and wanted to do the surgery more than I wanted to go away."

My body tends to keep all the doctors on their toes!

Ben left on Friday for the wedding and called me when he arrived in Massachusetts. He was feeling guilty about leaving me alone. "That's not the case. You should be with your brother. I have doctors and nurses to keep me company."

CHAPTER 12

ACUPUNCTURE

Aside from aqua therapy over the years my neurologist gave me acupuncture for pain. Acupuncture till this day is not covered by any insurance I know of and definitely not by Medicare. It's too bad because it does work to a great degree. Many people use acupuncture to help with the pain from cancer. It will not fix a broken bone but can relieve pain down to a more manageable level.

My first encounter with acupuncture was in the hospital before my first spinal laminectomy. I had blacked out from pain and was paralyzed in my legs. My ex-husband called my neurologist and then drove me to the hospital. My neurologist's partner Dr. Snider came to see me since this was his area of expertise.

Dr. Snider put me in traction a method I believe is no longer used.

"What if the traction doesn't work?"

"We'll try acupuncture."

I whispered in his ear because of my embarrassment in asking my next question. "Do I have to go to Chinatown?"

He answered very seriously, "I'm a licensed acupuncturist and will be taking care of it." I relaxed a bit.

Traction did not work and my next experimental treatment was acupuncture. Dr. Snider notified me of the day and time he would begin with the procedure. Every nurse and doctor on the floor of the hospital must have heard about my acupuncture treatment too.

I turned on my stomach and Dr. Snider stuck needles in my spine, back and legs. I heard a lot of whispering and slowly claustrophobia began to overcome me. My eyes were closed initially not knowing what to expect. I opened them to see white coated men and women squeezed into the tiny area around my bed. The claustrophobia issue was resolved.

Later on nurses and a doctor or two visited me. They watched in amazement as Dr. Snider put the needles in me. I was not informed others would be watching my treatment. The staff was curious about the way I felt. Considering the fact I was not thrilled my bare rear end was exposed to all of them, I actually felt better. A younger generation can probably relate to the scenario if their naked bottom was displayed on You Tube.

As a footnote to this experience acupuncture was similar to a pain killer or drug in my condition. The more treatments I had, the more I needed them. Surgery was the only option I had left. A neurosurgeon was called in and I went through my first myleogram. I inquired if cancer was involved. "I won't know until I open you up," was the surgeon's answer.

Acupuncture still works for me in certain areas of my body. I go very infrequently and only when I feel desperate about my pain. It's expensive but I will pay for it as long as it works. I resort to the method when all else fails. If I had money to throw around or insurance at least picked up some of the cost, I would probably go as soon as my pain starts. Many cancer patients I have met also resort to acupuncture if their pain begins to get out of control. Acupuncture is a very valid method of treatment as far as I'm concerned.

CHAPTER 13

LUMPECTOMY

I continued to have major problems with my back and called Dr. Russell. My appointment was on a Monday in the beginning of April 2003. Dr. Russell sent me to his neurologist and had me go through the same procedures as previously.

The same radiologist performed the myleogram as before. "I had an almost impossible task getting the needle up into your spine. It's so badly blocked," he proclaimed.

Dr. Russell gave his opinion. "Your spine is one of the worst I've ever seen. I'm going to operate on your lumbar and part of your thoracic area. I probably need to place a rod in your back but won't know until I open you up. Leave it to me. Your recovery will be very painful and your movements will be very restricted for six months."

"Will that be the end of the surgeries?" I inquired.

"*Probably not!* Most likely you will be subjected to another one on your cervical area in about six years."

Ben and I discussed the situation and we made a joint decision for me to have the surgery. A date was set and a cardiology appointment was arranged with someone Dr. Russell knew close to our home. The hospital would call me for donating my own blood.

I went home feeling extremely depressed. *How was I going to take care of my mother?* She was in a nursing home by then and I had so many responsibilities regarding her care. The next day I decided to take the proverbial bull by the horn and called my pain doctor. He saw me the next day. I told him my fears about the pain. "I'll insert a pain device under your skin to help you get through the six months."

We discussed all my other medical issues and how I was having difficulty and weighted down by not knowing what to do first. My pain doctor removed a pen from his pocket and began to draw on the paper covering the examining table. "It's like football game," as he drew his diagram. I admitted my inability to relate to football and the doctor made a triangle putting the things I could let go of at the bottom. A mammography went to the top. My annual one was due in two months. He advised me to have the mammography before my spinal surgery. He gave me some hope about organizing my life and perhaps some relief of pain after the laminectomy.

I made the right call in contacting him. At least I knew where to start with everything on my plate. Somehow the nursing home and my mother would have to get through without my presence at the facility every day.

On Wednesday of that week two days after I saw Dr. Russell and one day after my pain doctor visit, I went for a mammography in Ledges. I went by myself. A problem never entered my mind.

I surmised I was in trouble when the radiologist kept sending me back for more and more pictures of my left breast, the one injured in the auto accident. I underwent an ultrasound. Four hours after entering the hospital the radiologist spoke to me. "There is a lump in your breast. Your films and report will be sent to your gynecologist in another hour. Your situation is urgent and you are to get in touch with your doctor immediately. You need a breast surgeon." I drove home in a shocked state.

Ben wasn't home when I arrived back at our house. I called the gynecologists' office and was told, "Your message will be placed on his desk. The doctor is in the hospital."

Ben showed up a few minutes after I hung up the phone. I related the bad news. "I would have gone with you if I knew." It was just supposed to be a routine mammography. *How much more could I handle? What would I do about the back surgery?* We had to wait for my gynecologist to call me.

By five o'clock the doctor still hadn't returned my call. The radiologist said it was urgent for me to speak to him. I called his office again. "He hasn't come back to the office. I'll leave another message on his desk."

The next morning I was panicking. I called my doctor's office again and he still was not in. "Your films and report were received and they are on the doctor's desk," I was told. A half hour later I called the doctor's office again. I was making a pain of myself. The word URGENT stuck in my mind.

"Your doctor still has not called or returned to the office."

"Does anyone know names of breast surgeons?"

Fifteen minutes passed by and someone on the staff came up with a list of names and phone numbers of surgeons. Panic was causing me to act immediately. I realize now that is my persona. I always work that way on anything and everything I do. Just get it done and over with!

I was reviewing the names of the doctors, their backgrounds and hospital affiliations. The phone rang as I was about to make my first call. My gynecologist apologized for not calling. "I was dealing with an emergency in the hospital and never came back to the office. I went back to the hospital in the morning to check on my patient."

After his explanation he asked me for the names of the surgeons the girls gave me. "I'm ruling out the first and don't recognize the second. The third one is my second choice if you can't reach my top pick." He gave me Dr. Bucker's name and phone number. "I don't think an appointment will be available immediately but try him first. You absolutely have to see a surgeon as quickly as possible and there is no point in seeing me. You can by-pass that step."

It was close to noon and I wondered if Dr. Bucker's staff was on a lunch break. I made the call anyway and lucked out. "Dr. Bucker has no appointments today. He was scheduled for a seminar in New York." The major speaker cancelled at the last moment and Dr. Bucker decided not to attend. He agreed to see me in two hours giving me time to pick up my films and report from Ledges.

Ben encouraged me to have lunch after we left the hospital. "It'll take your mind off the wait." We headed south to Chicken Express. I really wasn't hungry. "You have to eat something." I ordered a drink but had no appetite.

When we arrived in Dr. Bucker's office, platters of food brought in by a pharmaceutical representative sat on a table in the waiting room. Obviously the rep didn't know Dr. Bucker wasn't supposed to be there either. Dr.

Bucker offered us some food. I had the same reaction as in Chicken Express. *No thank you!*

Dr. Bucker read the report and looked at the films from Ledges. He examined me and did another ultrasound. He withdrew fluid from different areas of my breast for biopsies. I alerted him about my scheduled spinal laminectomy. "Your spinal laminectomy will still be viable if you only need a lumpectomy. Anything further is up for discussion."

We went into Dr. Bucker's office and Ben joined us. Dr. Bucker reviewed everything very carefully, answering all our questions. "The lump has to be removed because even if it isn't malignant now, it has the potential to become cancerous."

"You are not a good candidate for any reconstruction," and he explained why. "Your back is the major obstacle since tissue cannot be used from there. Your stomach area is also off limits because of the nephrectomy." My body was so distorted from surgeries at this point reconstruction was becoming a minor issue for me. I would deal with whatever I looked like after the surgery. Fear was my first emotion. I wanted to survive. Depression would even have to wait.

Dr. Bucker suggested we do one procedure at a time and go from there. "Do not cancel the spinal laminectomy yet." Somewhere in the back of my head I heard a voice saying *get a second opinion*. I verbalized my second opinion out loud and would let him know my decision.

We all rose from our chairs and took a few steps to the door when I changed my mind. I wanted the poison out of my body A.S.A.P. My gynecologist already gave Dr. Bucker the highest marks. I turned to Dr. Bucker and said, "I like you and want you to do my surgery. How soon can you do it?"

"I can perform the surgery next Tuesday but you have to be in the hospital on Monday for your nuclear and pre-admission testing. I'll make all the arrangements before you leave my office."

The receptionist put a call into my internist. "Your doctor will see you after you leave our office."

Dr. Bucker's instructions continued, "You will have to go back into the hospital earlier on Tuesday morning if the nuclear test fails to pin point the main lymphatic gland. Don't worry. I'll still be able to do the surgery that day." Later on I found out why he could pull all of this off so fast. He was head of the department and called many of their shots. His patient, me, was getting top-billing.

My internist cleared me that same afternoon. Dr. Bucker faxed over the paper work for him to sign. I was only going to be admitted for one day surgery.

Everything went as planned on Monday but getting through the weekend was very difficult. Anxiety became my best buddy!

I showed up at the hospital on Tuesday morning and headed for the day unit. I was checked in and an I.V. was inserted. Dr. Bucker came in to see me. "Your nuclear test was fine. I'll see you in a little while."

The anesthesiologist paid me a visit and went over my history. A female minister came to see me. She took my hand. I was crying.

"Why is so much happening to me?" She tried to comfort me and left me her card if I needed to speak to someone.

"I know Dr. Bucker and you are in good hands." I thanked her and was wheeled into a waiting area.

Dr. Bucker entered the area and marked me with what he called a birdie. "I'll see you in the operating room."

While I waited to be taken into the operating room I heard a baby crying very loudly. I stopped thinking of myself and wondered what was happening to the baby.

I recalled Mindy in the hospital right before her first birthday as I witnessed her tiny legs tied down to the side of a crib. I.V.'s had been inserted in both of her small thighs. The look she gave me when I stood in front of her will never be forgotten by me. *Mommy, how can you do this to me?* She was totally dehydrated from a bug. Until the bug could be identified and she was put on an appropriate antibiotic, Mindy had to remain that way. The look on my baby's face destroyed me at that point.

What was happening to the baby who just wouldn't let up with the screaming and crying?

A nurse finally came to push me into the operating room. We passed an area with many people milling about. I heard the baby and mentioned my concern to the nurse. She smiled. "Don't worry it's a happy occasion. The baby is having a *bris (a circumcision)*. He's been crying and no one has even touched him yet." I was so relieved.

The next thing I recall is waking up. Dr. Bucker was standing over me with a light touch of his hand on my shoulder. "I took extra biopsies and removed the lump. The biopsy results will be in by the end of the week or at the very latest the beginning of next week. I'm leaving you instructions on taking care of your wound and if you have any concerns call me immediately."

Ben and I left the hospital. I was resting in the den when my voice disappeared. My initial thought was the laryngitis had to do with the scratchiness you get from having a tube down your throat with anesthesia. My voice returned by the next morning.

My nerves felt as though they were crashing into a wall. Anyone who waits for results of any medical test can understand the major anxiety that comes with the territory but with cancer the anxiety level goes up several notches especially when you have dealt with it before.

CHAPTER 14

LEFT MASTECTOMY

At 7:00AM on Friday the phone rang and I picked it up without hesitation. Dr. Bucker was on the phone. "I have good and bad news for you. The good news is you will live. The bad news is the biopsies show you are in stage zero in SITU. The lump was negative for cancer."

"Can you meet me in the hospital waiting room with your husband? I want to discuss your options."

I woke Ben up and told him what just transpired. We drove up to the hospital barely saying a word to each other. Ben put his hand on mine for reassurance.

We went to the waiting room as per Dr. Bucker's instructions. When he appeared women were going up to him and thanking him. It took a while to follow Dr. Bucker to a large meeting room with all the women trailing after him. Ben was sitting next to me on my left side. Dr. Bucker was sitting at a right angle to me.

Dr. Bucker said, "The situation warrants a mastectomy and I'll explain why." I was flabbergasted. I turned and looked to Ben. Dr. Bucker took my hand. "In all the surgeries I've done in so many years no husband ever left his wife because of a missing breast. It is your decision not Ben's or mine."

I wanted the cancer out of my body. "Can you do it next Tuesday?" I knew Tuesday was operating day and once I made up my mind it was easy to say the soonest day possible.

"It depends on the availability of the surgeon doing the reconstruction."

"Reconstruction is not an option for me."

"I'll make the arrangements as soon as we leave the conference room. You have to return on Monday for another nuclear test." A repeat of other pre-surgery necessities was not needed.

Dr. Bucker put his arm around me. "You'll be okay." He shook hands with Ben. "I'm going out to make the arrangements for your mastectomy." He called me about an hour later giving me the time to report for the procedure on Monday. He repeated the usual directions for my surgery regarding no drinking or eating after midnight and to avoid taking my medications. "I'll make sure they are given to you right after your surgery."

I cancelled all my appointments for what would have been my sixth laminectomy.

Nuclear testing went as planned on Monday. I said good-bye to my left breast before we left for the hospital on Tuesday. I went through the exact same procedure as I did the week before. As Yogi Berra would say, "It's deja'vu all over again!"

Dr. Bucker came into the holding room and gave me another birdie. I was wheeled into the operating room and the next thing I remember was Ben standing over me. I was in the recovery room, my mouth was feeling dry and thirsty. A nurse brought me some ice to suck on.

Ben was told to leave for a while and get something to eat. Afterwards he could wait in my room. He followed directions but I never left the recovery the room.

I had no phone or buzzer. I had to rely on my voice to get the attention of the nurse only my voice was gone. My nurse looked up at me and I beckoned her. I asked for more ice. She said, "Speak up" but nothing louder came out of my mouth. "You were speaking louder a short while ago." I was fully awake by now and totally aware of my surroundings.

Ben was gone and I had no intermediary. The nurse was fighting with me. This is exactly how to behave when a patient is in the recovery room after surgery! *Fight with a patient who can't speak.* It boggles my mind how these people choose to stay in their professions. In a whispered voice I mentioned the same thing occurred the week before after my lumpectomy. "I'm getting the anesthesiologist."

Unfortunately the anesthesiologist was involved in another surgery. I continued to lie on a gurney with no voice, no way to communicate, thirsty, with Ben sitting in my room waiting for me. I had no access to my watch or a clock. The nurse disappeared never to be seen again. Shifts changed but no one came over to me.

After what really were several hours I managed to flag someone down with my hand. She was with another patient. "Can you please get me a nurse?"

"Can I be transferred to my room?" I asked.

"*NO!*"

"I'll get my voice back just as I did the week before."

"You're in the hospital now and the problem has to be treated. I don't care what happened the week before."

Approximately five hours passed. The anesthesiologist finally came to see me. He told me the time. I still didn't have a voice. I repeated what happened the week before. "I don't understand why you have laryngitis."

"You were fine when the surgery was finished."

"Can I be transferred to my room?" I asked.

"An ENT has to examine you before you can be transferred to your room."

"Can't the ENT see me in my room instead of the recovery area?"

"No, just in case I have to take you back into the O.R." he said.

"I'm calling an ENT. Do you have one?" My ENT was part of a group. The only doctor who could see me would come when his last patient left.

Ben came back to the recovery room hours after he left. "I've been waiting in your room and was never was told you couldn't leave the recovery area until an ENT examined you. I played detective and searched for you. I took a chance that you would still be where I last saw you." He looked all beat. "Go home," I suggested. It was a very long day for Ben too. My surgeries were taking a toll on him.

ENT's still won't listen to me about laryngitis. I'm sure, in fact positive now the problem stems from my chemical allergies. The ENT showed up about 9:00PM. I spent a whole day in the recovery room. The doctor did several tests on me and found nothing wrong. I was given the okay to be transferred to my room.

At 11:30PM I arrived in my room and moved to my bed. I put my watch on. Ben left it for me with in a drawer of a night table next to my bed. I was hungry. A floor nurse at my end of the hallway said she would get me a sandwich and a drink. My voice started to return. *All that nonsense for nothing!* I called Ben. "The hospital will not put through incoming calls after 10:00PM but I can call out." We both needed sleep. "I'll speak to you in the morning."

I began to relax enough to realize I had surgery. All day it had been about my voice. My shoulder was hurting a bit and the nurse brought me some medication. An aide walked in with a sandwich and juice. I had my own room and had no reason to question it.

After brushing my teeth I turned the lights off and promptly fell asleep. A half hour later I awoke to a big commotion. A nurse was yelling at me. "Get out of bed. You have to move." I thought she was crazy. She was trying to wake me and was shouting. My nurse came into the room. "What is going on?" She began to argue with the loony nurse.

A patient was in a double room and didn't like her roommate. She insisted on being switched to a private room. I was the only person who had a private room and was on Medicare. The nurse decided I was fair game. She did not consult with my nurse, read my chart or know my medical history. I could have had an infectious disease and had to be kept isolated from other patients. If this out of control nurse let her patient get to her, she too chose the wrong profession.

My first instinct was to think she was confusing Medicare with Medicaid where you don't pay at all. It didn't matter. No one should be treated that way. She didn't speak English very well. She took it upon herself to have me thrown out of my room during the night to satisfy a spoiled bitch.

I have had plenty of horrendous roommates but at least waited until daylight to try and be moved. Since when do you walk into another patient's room during the middle of the night when they are not your responsibility and order them to move? Who was she to decide if I should have been woken up? Who gave her the right to tell me to leave my room?

I called Ben waking him up. "Continue to refuse to move and let them know you'll pay the difference." I directed my next words to both nurses. "I'll pay the difference between a private room and a shared one. Leave me alone so I can get back to sleep." The offensive nurse had no choice but to walk away.

My nurse said, "I'm glad you spoke up." She had no idea if Ben hadn't said to me "Refuse to move," I would've gotten out of the bed no matter how I felt and left the room. I have made some improvement in that area. I was not born with the natural instinct to stand your ground. It's been a real learning experience for me.

The next morning a supervisor came into my room and demanded to know what went on. "You are not entitled to a private room."

"This room was given to me. I didn't ask for it. Further who acts the way that nurse did?" She softened a bit and said she would look into it. A few minutes later Dr. Bucker came to see me. He checked my incisions under the bandages as well as the drains.

"Are you in a lot of pain?"

"I haven't even had much of a chance to think about it because of the problem with my voice and then dealing with the problem during the night." I told him what the whole day had been like for me.

"What? Does she think this is a hotel? I'm going to take care of it." Dr. Bucker apologized to me.

"I'm glad you refused to move."

Dr. Bucker said, "I'm releasing you but you must come to my office tomorrow." In retrospect he probably thought I would do better at home than what was going on in the hospital.

He showed me how to empty my drains. "A nurse will come in and go over the procedure again. She will give you a sheet to keep a record of the amount of fluid from each of the two drains as they are emptied."

"I'm requesting a visiting nurse to check on you at home a few times a week. You will be sore and stiff. I'm leaving you a prescription for pain if you need it."

"A TENS machine will probably be enough," I replied.

Dr. Bucker wasn't familiar with a TENS machine. "As long as it isn't invasive, it's fine with me."

"Your husband will be supportive. Remember to see me tomorrow in my office. Call me if you have any questions or need me." He kissed me good-bye and left the room.

Compared to my laminectomies and nephrectomy, a mastectomy was a piece of cake. I didn't think I would need any pain medication and Tylenol was probably enough.

A short while after Dr. Bucker left the supervisor returned to give me a phone gift card for $5.00 as an apology. I never used it.

My phone rang and it was the business office of the hospital.

"You are not entitled to a private room under Medicare," said the nasty, obnoxious woman who called.

"I was assigned to the room and didn't request it. Further you don't kick someone out of a room in the middle of the night. I agreed to pay for the private room rather than be switched at that hour."

"I'll let it pass for the night but from now on you have to pay the private rate."

"What is the difference between a shared and private room?" I asked.

"$15.00 but I'll let it pass for last night." Fortunately I was in a position to pay the amount.

"I'm being discharged." She hung up on me.

CHAPTER 15

RECUPERATION AND AN INTRODUCTION TO LYMPHEDEMA

A woman entered my room and introduced herself as part of Ledges' rehabilitation staff. She told me about lymphedema and demonstrated some exercises. She left brochures and her business card and told me to call her. It was too much to absorb all at once.

I surprised Ben with a call telling him about my discharge. Dr. Bucker originally said depending how things went I might be in the hospital two or three days. "Please bring one of your shirts. I don't think any of mine will fit over my bandages."

We were only ten minutes away from Ledges and Ben entered my room before I was given my discharge papers and instructions. I wasn't allowed to change into street clothes until my formal discharge. Another long wait ensued and I wanted to leave before something else happened.

A nurse came into the room and reviewed emptying my drains, measuring the contents and writing the results on a chart. She helped me change out of my gown and into Ben's shirt. It was the first time I was aware of a lack of motion. It wasn't horrible but then again everything is relative compared to what you've been through before.

A friend went shopping with me Saturday prior to the mastectomy. Dr. Bucker's nurse advised me to buy very large tops that opened in the front. I was still recuperating from the lumpectomy a few days before but had to prepare for my mastectomy.

My friend and I ran around a department store picking up any piece of clothing with an opening in the front and two sizes larger than mine. I was soon exhausted and gave up. A few more items were needed but searching for them was beyond my physical capabilities. I drove my friend and couldn't leave her in the store to shop for me. I asked Toni to purchase some night type shirts and *old lady* type cotton robes that opened in the front.

Even the new large size blouses didn't fit over my bandages. Ben gave me a couple of his shirts. I laughed at the upside of not marrying a skinny man.

I emptied my drains for the first time the afternoon of my discharge. By the second or third time I got the hang of the procedure for draining and measuring fluid. It was disgusting but like anything else you get used to it.

The nurse originally asked Ben to watch in order to help me. He walked out. He couldn't stand the sight. And this was a man who was pre-med in college for almost two years. At least he was smart enough to recognize what he is not capable of doing.

We went to Dr. Bucker's office the day after my discharge. Passover was starting the next evening. "Can I attend a Seder?" He seemed surprised by the question since my surgery was only two days before. Most women would still be in the hospital if their insurance allowed it.

"If you feel capable of going I'm not going to try and stop you. Just stay away from anyone coughing, sneezing, blowing their nose or showing any sign of an infection."

"Call me the next morning and tell me how you feel. Even if you change your mind and do not go to the Seder call me."

We usually attend two Seders but my goal was only for one at Mindy's the first night. A Seder includes a festive meal with a recounting tale of Moses leading the Jewish people in the exodus out of Egypt. The evening is quite long. Mindy and Toni kept telling me to stay home even if I was out of the hospital. I would bother everyone.

I needed to join the land of the living again and get on with my life. I was doing the same thing as previously when I went to Donny's first birthday party after my nephrectomy.

We attended the Seder the next night and sat at the end of the table. Ben was across from me. I didn't say a word the whole evening and responded when I had to. I was just happy to be there and be alive.

After the meal was over the Seder continued. Ben thought I had enough. Actually he had enough but I was getting tired and we had an hour ride home.

Both my daughters loudly exclaimed to each other, "Mom didn't complain at all. Can you believe it?" I was glad I attended proving to myself *"Life"* would continue.

As promised I called Dr. Bucker the next day and told him I had gone to the Seder and was fine.

I received a call from the nursing service to say someone would be at my home that afternoon. When she arrived she took my vital signs checked my bandages and drains. She emptied out the drains herself for her report.

My cousin from Connecticut called. "We're coming to visit and we will bring you a Passover meal." I was not allowed to help at all and was not used to being waited on. I added the day to another enjoyable part of my life.

Once the drains were removed Dr. Bucker continued to draw fluid from my breast. It hurt but again it was nothing compared to other things I had been through. I didn't "kvetch" a good Yiddish word for complaining.

One of my first calls after my surgery was to Gilda's Club. I read an article on Gilda's opening in my county the year before. I had a place for support for both my cancers unlike the situation I encountered after my nephrectomy.

Ledges had a six week breast cancer support program. Your name was automatically given to the nurse who ran the group if your surgery was performed in their hospital. I was contacted.

On one of my visits to Dr. Bucker I mentioned the Ledges support group. "You're doing so well you could probably start your own support group."

I didn't quite get what he meant at the time, now I do.

With Dr. Bucker's permission Ben and I took a trip to Cape May about two and a half weeks after my surgery. The weather was a bit gloomy for early May and rained at least two days of the four day trip. We had to find something to do. We joined the Cape May Preservation Society entitling us to several free trips on their touring trolley rides, free admission to the Cape May Light house and a tour of the Emil Physik Estate.

Ben bought me a small Victorian teapot decorated with variations of red colored roses at the Emil Physik Estate. The teapot is spotted with gold and makes a very colorful statement on a shelf in our house. It is a great reminder of my positive return to life.

We rode the trolley to the lighthouse never thinking I was capable of climbing up all the steps. I reached the top taking the steps slowly. The view was marred by all the rain clouds but it didn't matter. I accomplished an amazing feat so soon after my surgery.

On one of our days away we took a walk on the boards in Wildwood. The weather was reasonably nice and I couldn't help but notice some very interesting people walking by. I wanted to incorporate some of them in a picture I planned on painting and tried to keep their images in the forefront of my mind.

I was unable to avert my eyes from one particular woman. She was very, very full breasted wearing the smallest size bikini top she could possibly squeeze into. She quite obviously wanted everyone to stare at her and Ben was no exception. Her boyfriend had his arm draped around her shoulder and looked like he had just scored the big one. The interesting part to me was a tattoo of a proclamation going across her breasts. The top words were extremely large as in a special headline of a newspaper and the article below continued across her breasts down the rest of the space until finished. All I could think about is what would occur if she had a mastectomy. She would lose half her treaty and the writing would no longer make sense. I told Ben my thoughts and of course he laughed. It was a good indication of where my mind was and it was not in the gutter with all the men staring at her.

I returned home empowered from our getaway trip and could do anything I did before. I wasn't going to let a missing breast get me down.

CHAPTER 16

GILDA'S

The week prior to my lumpectomy I took my wedding band to the jeweler to have it enlarged. I picked my ring up after our return from Cape May.

I decided to pay a visit to the building where the Ledges support group was going to meet. The nurse conducting the program was in the hospital's cancer library. I was given reading material and noticed her staring at my left hand.

She finally spoke up. "You know your finger is swollen. Your ring may be too tight."

"*Too tight!* I just picked it up from the jeweler and had it enlarged."

"Have your hand checked out by a lymphedema therapist."

The nurse gave me the name of the woman who saw me in the hospital. The support group was starting in two weeks. I said good-by leaving with another thing to worry about and deal with.

I made an appointment with the lymphedema therapist. I also went to Gilda's Club for a class in the Alexander technique.

I was walking with a cane when I entered the room. The instructor asked me what the problem was. "I was set for another spinal laminectomy and ended up dealing with breast cancer."

The instructor was a warm and competent lady. "I'm going to save you from another back surgery." Indeed she did. Within a few weeks I no longer needed a cane. I learned how to get up and down from a sitting position without holding onto the chair. The exercises and learning how to keep my spine straight worked better than anything else I tried after five spinal laminectomies.

Two women alternated every week in teaching the Alexander technique to us. They watched over me like a mother hen. Most of the other women in the class were there for social participation. They came to Gilda's Club when they were caregivers and continued to constitute the bulk of the class. The few of us who actually had cancer were in the minority.

After the initial class I signed up as a member of Gilda's. It was the best thing I did for myself. I was assigned to a cancer support group but also participated in numerous programs. In fact the schedule was so hectic I frequently had to choose between which activity I liked best.

I made friends with many people. We congregated in the large kitchen talking, laughing and eating. Even if you brought your own lunch, food always seemed to be around. It was a great place to unload, get away from the stress at home, get information, and participate in activities.

Ben and I frequently took care of Donny when my daughter went back to work. I brought him to Gilda's and he would play in the children's room, paint and watch the fish in the big tank. He was only five and a half at the time. Donny never forgot Gilda's Club and how much fun he had. Even after we moved he asked me to take him back there. Gilda's seemed to be a secret we shared but as soon as his brothers found out they wanted to go. I would have gladly accommodated them except for the distance.

Cancer does not have to be depressing unless you make it so. Frightening absolutely! Unfortunately I too have been the recipient of many people saying how depressing anything to do with cancer can be. I do not agree. Just like anyone else we can make the most of the time we have. Even participating in activities while we are in pain can lead to forgetting the distress we are in. We have to focus on *laughing*.

Gilda's abounded with programs on make-up and dressing. I was only about five weeks out from my mastectomy when Gilda's had a very special day. Fifteen cancer survivors only were invited to a very expensive beauty parlor in the Cliffs. We were treated to a cut, wash and set. Some of the women also had their hair dyed. A cosmetician from a company specializing in covering scars gave us new looks with make-up when we arrived back at Gilda's.

I changed to a newly bought blouse fitting over my new figure. I really looked different. All participants became part of a show in the early evening and modeled our new look. Many big shots attended from the county as well as representatives from large corporations. Food was catered in by a donor. It was another indication of how we can move on and yet cope with disfigurement.

One other time we were invited to have our hair cut and styled and our nails done at a large beauty parlor in one of the fancier malls in the area. The place was quite large and had many beauticians. There were two Asian women who were designated to cut our hair, neither of whom spoke English.

None of us had an Asian hair type which is very different from what is called European hair. We had somewhat curly hair varying in color from blond to dark brown. The Asian women didn't know how to work with our hair at all. They were used to working with straight jet black hair with a totally different texture.

The stylists did everything possible to try and straighten our hair without really succeeding. No one would let them use hair dye to turn our hair black as they held up bottles of the dye to show us the color. We didn't want to insult them but we were starting to get concerned at what we would look like.

We laughed when we saw each other. We looked ridiculous but certainly had fun playing along with the situation. This beauty parlor could have offered us free haircuts for life but none of us would ever step in there again.

Our experience wasn't quite over. Our nails had to be polished and we were told to choose a color. One of the women called out "Cancer pink!" and we all followed suit.

We headed back to Gilda's when we were finished and walked in together with our arms crossed bowing to everyone we saw. Our hair would eventually grow back but the laughs and experience we had would stay with us forever.

Ben made a comment to me similar to the following when I arrived home. "What happened to you? I thought you were going to the beauty parlor. What did you do? Take a short trip to Asia!" When I told him about our experience he was hysterical laughing.

I participated in many of Gilda's frequent programs on make-up and one of my favorites was done by a beautician from Bobbi Brown. She gave all the participants lip liners matching our skin tones. Considering it was so many years ago I still keep the container as a color reference.

Along with the American Cancer Society who did a "Look Good, Feel Better" program every month at Gilda's, other make-up companies showed up as well. If you wanted to know how to live with your new appearance Gilda's was definitely the place to go.

Tickets were provided to us on a regular basis for concerts, shows and movies. One of my favorites was an invitation by the late Gene Shalit, a cancer survivor himself at the time, to a preview studio in Manhattan where no more than twenty of us watched "*Calendar Girl*" prior to it being released in theaters. Ben joined us since he was in a caregiver support group.

It was interesting as to how differently Ben and I related to the movie. He saw it as just a movie while I reacted as a cancer patient. He thought it was cute while I cried and thought it was terrific. The public agreed with Ben. Gene Shalit believed cancer patients would relate to the film and he was correct. All of us were given signed copies of his autobiographical book on his cancer experiences.

I looked forward to one of my favorite programs at Gilda's each year, a month of laughter. The huge living room at Gilda's was transformed into a live theater with all the cameras and sound system provided by a professional studio. Seats were set up theater style for the audience. It was aptly named Comedy Club month.

The same night each week a different set of amateur comedians came to compete for a chance for a month long contract at a comedy club in Manhattan. One of the columnists from the "*Record*" was the emcee. His mother was a breast cancer survivor and this was his way of giving back. He was a riot. His best story which he repeated each year; was about a visit to his doctor's office. He described his long wait for the doctor and his very short exam. His tussle with paper gowns that wouldn't stay shut had us all in stitches. He was better than many of the comedians who performed.

There was always a professional comedic break after a few amateurs did their *schtick*. A full time out took place for everyone to enjoy a catered dinner sponsored by various corporations. The entertainers had to be fed and so were we.

The winners of the first three nights returned on the forth night for the final competition. The winner received the contract for his *gig* but all of us witnessing the shows were the real winners.

Gilda's was the go to place if you were feeling depressed at home. You could close yourself in a room with the large fish tank and calm your nerves enough to face what was coming next.

Not only did we laugh a lot when we participated in the activities but we actually learned something. Flower arranging was one of my favorites. Origami was another fun class. Crafts and painting were taught several times a week.

Knitting and crocheting were an on-going group. One of the participants was unable to catch on to knitting. The instructor didn't have enough time to give her the added attention she needed but she was determined to learn and asked me to teach her.

I was so excited for her when she started to knit scarves. She was constantly going to doctors and always faced a long wait. Several months later she admitted to knitting sixty-five scarves. Every one of them represented time she spent waiting for doctors and tests. I suggested she perhaps try to knit something else.

"No I have no interest in knitting anything else."

"What are you going to do with all the scarves? You don't even wear any you knit."

"I will give them out as Christmas gifts. The rest will be donated to an organization that can use them."

I was still curious as to why she only wanted to make scarves.

"I bang the knitting needles together as fast as I can and that's how I get through my anxiety."

I never mentioned scarves again. *Hey, whatever works!* I draw on paper toweling while I wait for a doctor. Same idea, different medium!

I keep myself sane while awaiting a doctor's arrival in an examining room by drawing images of interesting subject matter photographed in my mind. Sometimes I forget a minute detail but nevertheless retain enough to put the picture down on paper. I always carry a pen and paper towels are readily available. The paper towels provide an interesting texture for my drawings. I'm not sure how well the paper will hold up. I sign and give the pictures to the staff in the doctor's office who admire them. They say they are framing them. I've heard of napkin drawings being framed but never paper toweling.

One night a group of us decided to go out to dinner. We participated in a class in the afternoon and were staying for the evening program at Gilda's. Our group piled into three cars and drove to the restaurant. Little did we realize we were giving up precious parking spots!

When we arrived back at Gilda's I was in one of the cars fortunate enough to find a parking space immediately. Four of us conservatively dressed waited outside of the building for the others. A car with four middle aged men hanging out of the open windows slowed down as they reached us. They stopped and tried to pick us up. We were all hysterical laughing. Someone shouted back. "It's going to be a fast relationship!"

The fact that we were all married had nothing to do with it. We were all missing parts of our body and one of the women had been told to prepare for the inevitable. These men were not youngsters themselves but didn't have a clue as to our situation. Either they didn't know what Gilda's was or they didn't compute why we were standing in front of the building. There was only one other building next to Gilda's with a mammography office as a tenant. The floor above Gilda's was a women's right center. One woman suggested the men were probably newly divorced and desperate.

CHAPTER 17

TEACHING

During my first year of membership in Gilda's a class was scheduled around Valentine's Day on making a candy floral arrangement. Since everything at Gilda's was free to members many classes had long waiting lists. When the people I became friends with saw a class we were interested in we wasted no time in registering. This class was no exception.

The instructor for this particular project was herself a cancer survivor and a member of Gilda's Club from opening day. "I was walking on the boardwalk at the Jersey shore when I spotted beautiful candy bouquets. The price was very high. I thought to myself I can make them for one twentieth of the cost," she stated. The candy bouquets became her challenge to herself. There was only one very big problem; she didn't try to make one before teaching the class.

Everyone struggled to get a candy to stay in each flower they made. The instructor didn't have a clue as to how to make a flower. Everyone was fending for themselves. It was easily noticeable to me that incorrect material was provided to support the flowers and candies. Participants became frustrated and left the room. Others walked in. The class was so enticing people on the very long waitlist showed up hoping to get into the class. They entered as others left and they too eventually gave up. Usually we laughed even if a project was difficult for us but not this one.

A well-intended situation on the volunteer's part *went awry*.

I took some materials home with me. I was determined to figure out how to make the bouquet. I succeeded and felt confident enough to teach others. I felt badly for the woman who was teaching the class. Knowing and having confidence in what you are doing is extremely important.

The next day I went back to Gilda's and joined others in the kitchen. People had dumped their unfinished projects from the night before onto the center of the table. "I know what was wrong with the project." It took very little encouragement for me to show everyone.

One of the women went for the director apprising her of what I was doing. She came to look. The people at the table begged her to let me teach a class. There was a problem. You were not allowed to be a volunteer during your first year after treatment. The rules at Gilda's were made precisely for the patient to recover emotionally as well as physically before taking on something else. Pressure was on the director to break the rules because I was capable at that point of teaching. The director finally gave in but took me aside, "Just this once."

My name and class were put on the calendar for the following month with a blurb in Gilda's monthly paper noting my background. My class was based on making self roses out of paper, ribbon and fabric. After completing the fabric roses many of the women sewed them onto their hats for decoration. The class was very successful. One of the people from the office stayed the whole time to make sure I didn't run into any problems.

One thing led to another. I constantly heard, "Teach another class." I had no problem with it and in fact really enjoyed being able to teach again. This was my chance to feel like a professional and it was great for my demeanor. I relied on those in my class to help me clean-up. I was unable to perform this task.

A few days later the director called me aside. "I'll make an exception for you under Gilda's policy. The staff has noticed how teaching is helping you with your own recovery." The exception came with one caveat. "You have to continue in the one year support group and join the ongoing support group for cancer survivors." I looked forward to being in another group and meeting more people so this was a non-issue for me.

I taught many art classes and geared them to people who insisted they had no talent. It was for fun and to get their minds off their problems. We did a lot of laughing and surprisingly some good art work came out of it.

I enjoyed my new support group and made more friends. Laughing at ourselves was good for all of us. Some of the classes I participated in were totally new to me and again were an outlet for laughter.

I learned to belly dance. My fascination with this form of exercise and entertainment gave me the incentive to crochet a costume with gold yarn. I attached fake coins to the crocheted chains I made so they would jingle as I danced. When we moved my coin decorated chains went into the trash never thinking I would be able to use them again.

There were so many activities going on at one time if you included schmoozing with others you could spend the whole day at Gilda's from nine in the morning until eight at night. It would be easy to compare it to going to the neighborhood bar but without the liquor. Unbelievably there was no charge.

CHAPTER 18

MY BROTHER

One of the most important aspects in your treatment and recovery from cancer is support. After our spouses we logically turn to the rest of our immediate family. The disappointment in my brother's behavior is one that must be addressed due to his lack of involvement in any of my recoveries and the avoidance of sharing the burden in taking care of our parents during my illnesses.

One class I really started getting into at Gilda's was drumming. We began by drumming out the syllables of our names. The instructor led us into a full concert by the end of an hour. One particular evening the class started with the instructor asking us to drum out our feelings. When my turn came I quite literally banged away so hard and fast I surprised everyone.

"What was that about?" Friends of mine asked.

"I'm beating up my brother." The laughter from others reverberated throughout the enormous living room.

When I was drumming many of my frustrations with my brother were released. I even considered purchasing a drum to keep beating him up on a daily basis. It was a healthy way to get my frustrations out without hurting anyone.

My friends and people in my support group knew what a difficult time I was having with him. I was the one who was ill. Not only didn't he give me any support or help but undermined me because he wanted our mother's money. The toll on my health was quite apparent to everyone at Gilda's.

One afternoon I joined about one hundred other women for a lecture by a doctor on genetics at Gilda's. We were of all religions and races. The doctor discussed the groups of people both men and women who tended to be genetically positive for the BRACA 1 and 2 genes. "Research discovered the genes were primarily in Jewish people."

A woman screamed out, "I'm not Jewish and I'm positive." In less than a split second the majority of the women listening to the lecture called out in unison "Jesus was Jewish." She never opened her mouth again.

After the outburst the doctor continued. "Apparently as a group Jewish people are more willing to take part in testing and that may be a reason for the higher percentage of positive results. Scandinavians have started to participate in testing and the results might eventually be highly positive for them also."

Several months after my surgery I had my blood drawn for genetic testing. Since the test was not routinely done at the time I had to prove the test was necessary. It was not covered by Medicare in either case and was quite expensive. I have two daughters and believed the test was a necessity for them as well as me.

I needed information from both sides of my family. Everyone on my father's side cooperated as best they could. There was a lot of cancer in the family and all of us could only confirm breast cancer in our Aunt Lillian and perhaps ovarian in another. No one was sure about the other types of cancers in the rest of the applicable relatives.

On my mother's side of the family cooperation was almost impossible. A first cousin had cancer but I didn't know what type. My brother was very close to my mother's side of the family while I didn't even have addresses or phone numbers.

I contacted my brother explaining how extremely important the information was. Repeated phone messages and emails were not acknowledged. Dr. Bucker needed to make a determination if I should have the test.

Over a month went by and Dr. Bucker decided to use the information he had and wrote a prescription for the test. I heard Tremore did the testing for free and called the hospital. Apparently testing was done in groups and no one knew when the next group would be scheduled. There was also a very long wait list.

My test was done at Ledges. I was determined to have my right breast removed if the tests came back positive. Ben was upset. "How can you make a decision before you have the results?" There is only one lab in the U.S.A. that does the analysis of these genes and the results take weeks. I thought of Dr. Bucker's comment about making the choices for my own body. I was determined to go through with another mastectomy if there was a positive result to the test. Once the decision was made I was not turning away from it. If my right breast had a chance of developing cancer, it was coming off.

I registered for a cooking class at Gilda's one morning and was getting ready to leave the house. I didn't want to be late. The telephone rang. Caller ID showed Ledges. My geneticist was calling to give me my test results. "They're negative." I questioned the results because I again had a hard time believing something medically good could happen to me. "You heard correctly. Your test results really are negative."

I started to cry. Tears were again my reaction to the news. Ben couldn't understand it. He thought I should be jumping up and down. My mind set had been negative and good news was hard to accept.

I looked at my watch. I was going to be late for the class. Lateness or no shows were frowned upon if a class had a long waiting list and this class did. I drove to Gilda's with tears streaming down my face. When I arrived the receptionist was not very happy with me.

I told her about the call and she hugged me. "Great news. Best excuse I heard this morning."

She walked me into the kitchen where the class was already in progress. The class was disrupted as we entered. The receptionist said, "Rosalie just had some very good news. Tell them." I did and even the instructor from the supermarket said she didn't mind being interrupted with my very positive news.

In spite of my brother's lack of help I succeeded in having my tests done with a great ending.

CHAPTER 19

LYMPHEDEMA I

I went to my appointment with the lymphedema rehabilitation department made promptly upon the nurse's suggestion at Ledges.

The same lymphedema specialist who saw me after my mastectomy did a work up on me. She definitively diagnosed me with lymphedema of my left hand. I could no longer wear my wedding band on my left finger. I transferred it to my right hand and my engagement ring has been in my safe deposit box since then.

The therapist cut some netted tubing off of a huge roll. "Wear it over your breast area. Your bandages will remain in place without the tightness around your chest from the surgical bra. You will be seeing someone else for treatments. I don't participate in Medicare." I couldn't quite get that since she was working in the physical therapy department of a hospital but what was the point of arguing? My next appointment was made for the end of the week. "Refer to the exercise sheets I gave you in the hospital and do them on a constant basis."

I returned to the physical therapy department a few days later and met my therapist. She was very young and didn't know what she was doing. My initial thoughts were anyone would know more than I did. I will never work with that theory again. I wonder if she was even a licensed physical therapist never mind her ability to work with lymphedema patients.

My left hand had become very large in a few days. There were no wrinkles on the top or palm of my hand or my fingers. My wrist started to swell. My therapist brought out bandages. "You have to wear them." She was trying to show me how to put them on but was struggling herself. "Just wrap them up anyway at all to cover your hand and go up your arm." She gave me the metal clips that come with the bandages to keep them together. "Do not to stick yourself."

I still use these bandages but tape holds them together. I didn't know about tape at the time and had to find some way to keep the bandages on. I sewed on hook and eyes to the top of the last bandage. It worked to a certain degree. The narrow gauze bandages on my hand continually came off.

After a couple of weeks I showed the therapist a lump on my arm. She brought in the non-Medicare therapist. As she pressed down on the lump she said to my therapist, "You have to keep working on them till they pop, just like plastic bubble packing. I love to do this." Meanwhile my face was contorted with pain. She looked me right in the eye, "This might hurt but you will feel so much better afterwards." She's the one who felt better. I turned black and blue.

I went to my support group at Gilda's after the above session. One of the female participants was a nurse. Her first year after her breast surgery was almost up and she was leaving our group.

She kept looking at me and must have drummed up enough nerve to ask me, "Who wrapped your bandages?" "*My therapist.*" I related what happened during the session and I was still hurting. Her next few comments were carefully worded and in no uncertain terms she remarked, "What was done to your arm is unacceptable. You are not wrapped correctly. Go back to your surgeon."

I saw Dr. Bucker and showed him my hand and arm. "How did you get to these people?"

"I thought you sent the therapist into my room."

"I did not. This is going on at the hospital without my knowledge. I should have been informed. I'm head of the department." He was not happy.

"I'm going to make sure this doesn't happen to any other breast cancer patient at Ledges."

I told him the nurse at the hospital running the support group picked up on the lymphedema and recommended Ledges for treatment. He recommended another hospital instead.

"I have confidence in the therapist who works there."

Dr. Bucker advertised the Ledges support group in his office since many of his patients had a hard time dealing with breast surgery. He also recommended Gilda's Club and was amazed I was already involved with no one pushing me to join.

I cancelled further appointments with my Ledges therapist but had to wait until the following week for my first appointment with the new therapist. Meanwhile I started to go to the support group at Ledges. It was a very small group of perhaps six people. Two others had registered but didn't show.

The first thing the nurse did was tell us a story about her aunt which bears repeating. "My aunt was told by her doctor she was getting older and might die. She went home and sat in her favorite chair waiting for her death. Someone brought her meals and she only got up to go to the bathroom and shower. She didn't want her relatives to find her dead and dirty. She did this every day for fifteen years. That's how long it took her to die."

Whether the story was true is irrelevant. The nurse was trying to get her point across to get out and enjoy yourself while you are still breathing.

The session always ended with guided imagery. We also did this at Gilda's. I initially was introduced to guided imagery when I went for pain treatments at another hospital. It took a while for me to catch on but then I could easily relax if someone spoke with a very soft voice.

CHAPTER 20

LYMPHEDEMA EDUCATION

My mother was in a Wood Lake nursing home and a much longer ride for me then where her assisted living had been. The clothes Mom needed for a change of seasons were stored in our house.

I drove up to the nursing home wrapped in my bandages. I put as many clothes as I could carry on my right arm. The director of the nursing home saw me and sent one of the staff to retrieve the rest of the items. "He'll help you bring down the clothes your Mom doesn't need."

The director wanted to speak to me. He was unaware I had lymphedema from my mastectomy even though he knew about my surgery. He was an observer during an operation involving lymphedema. He was a font of information telling me about the lymph glands directly under the first layer of epidermis and why it is so important to protect the affected area.

"I have two people I want you to see." One was his girlfriend who worked in Perrytown. The other was a doctor who specialized in lymphedema. She was the only one licensed on the East coast to have an experimental lymphedema machine. He continued on. "The machine works differently from others on the market and is superior to them."

The director gave me contact names and phone numbers. "I'm putting a call through to my girlfriend and the doctor."

My mother used a wheelchair and I was unable to push it. I wanted her off the bed and moved into the dayroom to give me space to empty the drawers and closet for an exchange of clothing. At my request someone came and took her from the room. She was angry about leaving but I agreed to spend time with her once I finished.

Ben and I were moving soon but I refrained from telling Mom. Our house was not working for me anymore. Our house search included relocation for my mother. I could not take care of her from afar.

After folding and straightening up I located the man who helped bring the clothes to the room. I pointed out the exchanged clothes and gave him the keys to my car.

It was a very depressing scene for me, not as much the nursing home as my mother's demeanor. My lymphedema was getting worse and more of a problem than the mastectomy itself. My patience was wearing thin. If you're legitimately trying to deal with your own very valid problems it is harder to deal with someone else's and worse if it's your own mother.

I was unable to converse with my mother because she was always down and refused to participate in any activities. One of her nurses came into the day room. "Look at Rosalie. She just had a mastectomy and she's moving." Mom had been such an active woman and now only dwelled on the things she still wanted to do but couldn't. She looked at me as though I had the key to her now awful existence. I didn't know what more I could do for her.

"Would you like to go out onto the large deck? The weather is so beautiful."

"*No.*"

"Would you like to move closer to the other residents and speak with them?"

"*No.*" I kissed her good-bye.

"I'll call you later. I was unsure if I was capable of handling the situation anymore."

The assistant director saw me as I came out of the elevator. She knew I was having a difficult time. "I want you to speak to our psychologist."

I was ushered into the psychologist's office. "Caregivers have so much guilt they will often get sick and die before the person they are taking care of." She used the example of my two cancers. "You have to heal first before you take care of your mother. The nursing home staff will take care of Mom.

Take a break for at least a week. We'll call if there is an emergency." She left the door open for me to speak to her if necessary.

As I was walking out of the building the director saw me. He spoke to his girlfriend and the doctor. His girlfriend would do mapping. I thanked him and left.

CHAPTER 21

MAPPING

My car keys were returned and I wanted to leave the nursing home as fast as possible. The psychologist's words started to click in. Ben helped out with my mother but the bulk of the burden was on me. I had enough to worry about myself and Ben certainly wasn't getting the attention he deserved as my husband. This had been going on since we were married. The toll was getting to me. I also wanted to have time to participate in my grandson's lives.

I made my appointments with the girlfriend and the doctor, getting directions to both of their offices. I checked with Ben and it was no problem for him to take me for the visits. I really needed him to accompany me.

I went to the girlfriend first. Her office was above an old store with very steep stairs. The waiting room was reminiscent of Greenwich Village in the 1950's. Beaded curtains hung from the doorway. Ben's impression was the same as mine. An older woman came down the stairs and she looked *normal*. She was well dressed and presentable. I surmised if she could go to this woman it would be safe for me.

A few minutes later the girlfriend came part way down the stairs and ushered us upstairs. The immediate impression of the large room we entered confirmed our feeling. The room had a decidedly Greenwich Village appearance. I was waiting for her to offer us LSD and marijuana. Apparently Ben wasn't comfortable either.

"Are you going to stay?"

"*Yes.*"

Ben directed his next question to the girlfriend. "How long will my wife be here?" "I'll be back," he said.

The girlfriend took some information and gave me directions. "Undress down to your underpants." There was a tremendous wall to wall floor length window directly opposite the table facing the buildings across the street. She noticed me looking at the window prior to undressing and gave me a sheet.

Where I was going to get my mapping? There didn't seem to be any other room. There was a large king mattress lying on the floor abutting a wall near the window and an examining table in front but the coverings were dirty. "Lie down on the table." Now I had to say something.

"The sheets are dirty." She changed them. I kept looking up to see if anyone was looking in from the building across the street.

"I don't remember what was I supposed to do for you?"

"Mapping."

She began to feel all around my body. *Was I was dealing with a pervert?* The girlfriend worked silently and I had absolutely no idea of what she was doing. I hadn't started yet with the new therapist and the two I saw at Ledges never did anything close to this. Perhaps I could have a good laugh when this was over while telling myself *I can handle it.*

Finally she spoke. "You have a blockage from the scar from your kidney. I have to unblock it. Once it is unblocked I will show you how to map."

She showed me how to massage in order to move the lymph fluid. My time was up. "That will be seventy dollars." I was handed a receipt to submit to my insurance company for reimbursement.

As I was getting dressed Ben returned and he answered in the negative when asked, "Would you like a massage?" I declined another appointment. "It's a bit too far to drive."

Once we left the building Ben admitted, "I was afraid to stay there but worried about you." I related the details of my mapping and interaction with the girlfriend. "I'm glad you're still alive," he said.

Ben found a small charming pizza restaurant in town.

"Can you take me back there for lunch?" He was inquisitive. "Were you offered drugs or marijuana?"

"No but the sheets were dirty."

"Did you see the mattress on the floor?"

"How could you miss it?" I responded and we had a well-deserved laugh together.

We walked hand in hand to the pizza restaurant. This was going to be a date as far as I was concerned. I wasn't going to concentrate on anything but the two of us that afternoon. I know Ben picked up on it.

This was the first time I saw Perrytown as an adult. It was picture perfect with the look of a well maintained older town surrounded by graceful well aged trees. A souvenir postcard was most likely available in one or two of the stores. Nothing was going to dissuade me from enjoying this adventure. I was determined to make the most of the day and the weather couldn't have cooperated more.

I had been up to Perrytown many times as a child when we took the ferry from Manhattan. I remembered the town way up on top of a mountain. It was the last stop on the ride up the Hudson River. We hiked up a hill when the ferry docked at the Perrytown pier and were rewarded with ice cream when we reached Main Street.

CHAPTER 22

MY LYMPHEDEMA MACHINE

The following week I was scheduled for an appointment with the doctor having access to the special lymphedema machine. Ben spoke the words I was afraid to utter. "I hope her office is more palatable then the office we just left." Since I was really just learning about lymphedema all of this was unchartered territory for me. I didn't know what to expect from anyone.

Until my appointment with the next doctor I kept massaging myself the way the girlfriend taught me. It was becoming an annoying tic to everyone I came in contact with. Ben commented about it and my mother let me know in no uncertain terms, "You look ridiculous and stop it." I got a rise out of her so maybe it was a good thing.

Ben drove me to the lymphedema doctor. Her office was in an old very straight laced building. The building itself was a step up from the girlfriend's but the bathroom was down the hallway and lacked paper and soap. The doctor gave me a thorough exam and showed me exercises to get my hand moving again. All the swelling prevented me from bending my fingers. The lymphedema machine was covered by Medicare but her visit was not. "I want to see you again before I order the machine."

I should clarify the girlfriend, the lymphedema doctor, the first session of the support group at Ledges, Gilda's Club, the "tic" massages, our Cape May trip, my on-going problems with my mother etc. all took place simultaneously and within the first four weeks after my mastectomy.

On my second visit the lymphedema doctor ordered my machine. She kept coming up with various exercises to make my hand more mobile. I liked her in spite of the toilet paper and soap issue. I told her about the bathroom. She offered me alcohol pads. "I'm thinking of relocating to another office. My complaints to the landlord go unheeded."

Very shortly after my second visit I received a call. "Your machine is in." I made an appointment but had to wait until the doctor came back from India. I had another few weeks of annoying everyone with my "tic" massage.

At the appointment to pick up my lymphedema machine Ben went into the examining room with me. After an exam the machine was brought in. I was outfitted with a cumbersome sleeve attached to a large flexible plastic tube which was then connected to the machine itself.

My doctor set the machine for a full cycle of fifteen minutes. "I'm leaving the room but will return to see how you are doing when the machine goes off." The feeling was unusual but not uncomfortable as the massage went up and down my hand, arm, and left shoulder. When the fifteen minutes were up the sleeve deflated and the machine went off. The packaging was on the table and Ben saw the attached bill. It was on the carrying case -*$8,000.00!!* We were both stunned.

The doctor and representative from the company returned and asked how I felt. The sleeve was removed and the doctor examined my hand and arm. She made some adjustments to the setting. "Can you try it for another fifteen minutes?" This time she asked me to watch how everything was connected and turned on. I would be doing this myself from now on.

The doctor and rep returned when the machine went off and I was completely disconnected this time. This particular machine has five compartments and the difference between this one and others on the market at the time had to do with clamping. My machine gently clamps down on the area previously worked on to prevent the lymph fluid from flowing back to the just massaged area.

I was told to call A.S.A.P. if there was any problem. I was given an appointment in four weeks. My instructions were to use the machine as much as one hour each time three times a day. "Your 'tic' massages won't be necessary after a while as your hand swelling goes down," the doctor said.

The machine was very noisy. I set it up in the downstairs den and used it while I watched TV. After a few times of using the machine I fell asleep. *The noise be damned!* The only downside was the time I had to invest in using it. The recliner was the only comfortable place for me to do my treatment without hurting my back. There was no pain. I continued to do the exercises as well.

Ben couldn't adjust to the noise and moved to another room with a smaller TV when my machine was in use.

Many years later I received a Medicare statement showing payment for the above machine. I called the company. Someone in their office forgot to send the bill to Medicare when I received the machine and they wanted their money. The listed date for receiving my machine was the present date. I called Medicare.

"You are allowed to receive a new machine six years and one day after the first one," I was informed. It was past four years. I would be denied any other machine until another six years and one day passed.

"My machine was given to me over four years ago."

"Medicare will take over from here."

Eventually I was called by the company and asked to leave their date in as my claim. I refused for the above reason. The person on the phone said, "You can trust us. If you need a new machine then we'll give you one." I didn't trust them.

I started to see my new massage therapist and was taught the proper way to wrap. Her massages were similar to the girl friend and she was covered by Medicare.

I went to week two and three of the support group at Ledges. The groups at Gilda's were better but I made a commitment and continued going. At the third session I met the geneticist I used.

The machine, wrapping and exercises finally started to show some results. I was thrilled when I saw a wrinkle in the palm of my hand. My happiness over my wrinkle wouldn't have been as great if it appeared it on my face.

The nurse running the support group at Ledges mentioned my machine to the non-Medicare woman in charge of lymphedema at the hospital. The nurse called me at home. "What is your machine set at?" I gave her the information. The next day I received another call. "A machine should never be set at more than seven or eight. It can damage your skin."

Now concerned I put a call into my doctor. Her answer was not one the therapist would be happy with.

"Apprise the lymphedema staff at Ledges your machine works differently from any of the older models. The settings are not comparable. Your unit is in a brand new category and the settings are entirely different." The call ended with her stating, "I don't think the therapist knows what she's talking about."

I returned the call to the nurse repeating verbatim my doctor's comments. The nurse said, "I stand by the therapist from Ledges. She's been doing this for many years." I related my reasons for distrusting her and told the nurse, "Dr. Bucker sent me to a lymphedema therapist in another hospital. He's not happy with the lymphedema staff at Ledges." The lymphedema therapist from Ledges was to speak at the next support group meeting. I did not go.

I attended the following week's support group. "Where were you last week?" I told them of my unfortunate experience with the therapist who spoke. "I definitely had no interest in hearing or seeing her nor do I trust her." The nurse began to ask why I missed the prior week and caught herself. By the time I came to this meeting I learned you dump any therapist who worked the way the one from Ledges did.

I went to the last session of the support group and was glad it was over. It started out well but left me with a bad taste in my mouth. Lesson learned. Go where you feel comfortable.

CHAPTER 23

WRAPPING

I was having a terrible time with the lymphedema bandages. They were always coming loose and unraveling even though I graduated to tape. It was frustrating. I was finding out lymphedema is harder to deal with on a daily basis than a mastectomy.

I was greatly annoyed at people who unabashedly approached me asking what was wrong. It was none of their business. One woman attacked me from behind in a supermarket one day. "What happened?" I answered truthfully because I wasn't sure of what to say.

The response of *"You should have seen the other guy,"* is useless as far as I'm concerned. I don't have the nerve to go up to someone and ask what happened to them. Once they answered what could I do about it? It's just rude. These people are being *Yentas.* A good Yiddish expression for nosy bodies!

The unveiling of Ben's brother's stone was taking place in May. I was wearing my compression bandages. The bandages were continually coming off and I was continually rewrapping. Rolling up the bandages to start over is an additional pain in the butt. This was not going to be an easy ride to the Boston area for me.

By the time we arrived at my sister in-law's home I was almost completely unwrapped. I was having a difficult time trying to get myself together and everyone was in a rush to go to the cemetery. Ben's nephew was going with a gynecologist. My sister in-law asked her to help. She didn't know the first thing about bandages or lymphedema.

After the cemetery we went back to the house. Approximately thirty-five chairs were set up in the living room in a very large circle. Some areas of the circle had two rows. I didn't know any of the people except the family.

Initially when I stepped into the kitchen a woman came right up to my face and asked what happened to me. I responded truthfully but inwardly felt it was none of her business.

Everyone made their way into the living room and I deliberately took a seat behind someone else. Ben sat next to me. Conversation was going on at a moderate level when out of nowhere a booming voice directed at me came from across the room. You couldn't miss the loud voice even if you forgot your necessary hearing aids.

"What happened to you?" Everyone looked at me waiting for an answer. If I had it in me to kill which I know for a fact I don't (bugs are the exception), I would have gotten up and belted her. Instead my face turned red and I couldn't say a word. My sister in-law answered. "She has lymphedema from a mastectomy."

People turned away from me. They didn't know what to say. Perhaps some of them realized this woman crossed the line. The men looked embarrassed. Ben whispered in my ear she was a psychologist and once had a private practice with my sister in-law. I pity her clients.

Ben and I rose to leave. It was enough. Others started leaving. This psychologist did a great job of making an unpleasant day even worse. I think she tried to come over to me but I purposely went in another direction. Others came over to me to say they were sorry and wished me well. I didn't even want to hear it.

We silently drove back home with me in the dumps. After a few hours I finally spoke. "I can't believe she's a psychologist. She's an idiot." Ben agreed. I had a very hard time getting to sleep that night.

A few weeks after I started with my new lymphedema therapist I made up my mind to have a good day. I planned on trying to return a gift I received for my birthday almost a year before not really expecting any success. The tags were still on the item. The gift was chosen by the wife of Ben's friend. She was over thirty years younger than all of us. She didn't realize a woman in her late twenties doesn't have the same figure or taste as one who just turned sixty. I put the gift in the trunk of my car. I was going to treat myself to lunch and then visit my mother. First I had to go for my lymphedema therapy.

I drove to the hospital but couldn't find a parking spot until I reached the roof top deck. The spot was a bit of a walk from the elevators. Without exaggeration I was stopped by at least three people. *"What happened to you?"* We're in a hospital. Were they going to ask all the people wearing bandages what happened to them?

I was waiting for the elevator and others came over to ask the same question. It didn't let up. When the elevator reached my floor and the doors opened a man exited stopping to ask what happened. I thought about putting a sign on me: It's none of your Damn business! Perhaps a tee shirt saying, "Don't even ask?" would've worked. But that's all in hindsight!

I transferred to the elevator in another building after a short walk around the lobby. I was stopped again as I made my way. Other people in the second elevator asked the same question. A man next to me had crutches. No one bothered him.

When I exited the elevator I had a long walk to the physical therapy office. Two more people stopped me. I needed a sign. I entered the waiting room, checked in for my appointment and took a seat. I'm in a physical therapy waiting room minding my own business. *Why did people come over to me asking the same question over and over again?*

By the time my therapist called me in smoke was coming out of my ears. We discussed the problem and it was a big problem for me. "You have an approachable looking face and many people don't." I retorted "People shouldn't even try to approach me anymore today; I might scream at them." I wasn't looking forward to visiting my mother. Exactly what I didn't need, more depression!

As I was making my way back people continued to stop and question me. I owed them no explanation nor did I want to speak to them. I was now rude by refusing to respond. When I reached the main lobby I went to the ladies room to wash my face with cold water.

As luck would have it someone I knew from the travel industry was in the bathroom.

"What happened?" I answered truthfully.

"I'm retired but now am doing volunteer work at the hospital."

We went out to the lobby and sat on one of the couches. Our conversation reverted to happier times.

Time was up. I said my good-bye and made my way around the corner to the other elevator. No one approached me. Perhaps things changed for the better. But it was not to be and I was asked again on my way back to the car about my bandages. Normally I would have rolled down my window for some air. Instead I put on the air conditioning and screamed.

I pulled out of the parking space stopping at the gate to give the guard my pass and left the hospital grounds. I drove to Route 17 North and as I approached the exit to turn off to the nursing home changed my mind continuing on to a dollar store two towns away. I shopped there previously and was running out of crossword puzzle books. I desperately needed to do something pleasant for myself.

I was basically trying to avoid seeing my mother. I loved her and was her caregiver. I just couldn't deal with her depression on top of the day I was having.

Besides the psychologist at the nursing home telling me I wasn't taking care of myself I heard the same thing when my mother was in the assisted living facility. I was called into the nurse's office. "You are not paying attention to yourself." On this particular day I was trying to listen to the advice and was determined to take care of me. So far I wasn't having too much success.

I drove up to the shopping center where the large dollar store had been. The store either moved or closed up permanently.

I headed back south and turned off for the nursing home but still couldn't make myself go in. I turned around and drove to the mall two blocks away from there. I spied the store where the gift came from and removed it from the trunk of my car. Fortunately no one approached me as I walked to the counter. As I waited my turn on line I scanned the displayed items and racks of clothing. I wouldn't be able to find anything as an exchange.

The young lady looked at my gift. I could tell by the expression on her face perhaps someone had *re-gifted* it to me or just didn't know me. The first was possible but the second wasn't. I took a gift certificate in exchange for my return. It was never used. Even Mindy and Toni would not be able to wear the store's clothing. Toni is slim and perhaps she might have considered wearing this line of clothing in junior high under peer pressure. In retrospect I should have donated the gift card.

Since I was batting a zero for the day I decided to go into The Beauty Store. I can't take any of the strong odors but once had some of their mild hand lotions that worked well for me. I chose to treat myself to one.

Upon entering the store I heard a big mouth woman's voice espousing nothing worth listening to. I ignored her and kept looking. A young girl approached me. What I was asking for was discontinued but I could look in the sample bin. "Here's a product you might be able to tolerate." The lotion I wanted was not in the bin. I picked up the item recommended by the salesgirl.

I went to the counter to pay for it. The counter itself was intimidating. It was raised and a customer had to stretch up to put their purchase on it. The salesperson could look down on you as if to say, "I'm in charge!" But at that moment no one was there.

I heard the big mouth's voice as she neared the counter. Some items were in her hand as she made her way to the register. The lady purchasing them stood next to me. The saleswoman noticed my bandages, stopped what she was doing and addressed me. "Did your husband beat you up?" This was absolutely not funny on several levels. I came into the store to try and get away from rude people. I had been beaten up throughout my marriage to my first husband with my broken bones showing up on x-rays. The scars from the breaks and emotional pain I endured during that period of time were not going away physically or mentally.

"That's not funny."

"It's very funny. Get a sense of humor. My husband just had his leg in a cast and we would say things like that to him and he would laugh."

Unlike a broken body part in a cast that would eventually heal, lymphedema is for life. The stupid saleswoman then directed a comment to the customer she was waiting on.

"Tell her what a party poop she is."

Fortunately the woman didn't say a thing to me but she didn't defend me either. She just stood there making believe she was above all of this.

My heart wanted to say I wish this on you. Coupled with not having the nerve my upbringing wouldn't allow it. I should have walked out. Instead I paid for my purchase seething inside.

The young salesgirl came to the counter. I spoke to her. "Lymphedema is a side effect of my mastectomy and that is why I'm wearing bandages." My hope was she would let the big mouth know after I left the store. Perhaps she would learn to keep her mouth shut and spare someone else her abuse and what passed for humor in her mind.

I walked back to my car and put my purchase in the trunk. I was valiantly trying to hold back tears but still couldn't make myself go to see my mother. I went to Fresh Bread to have a sandwich. The store was crowded and I waited a bit until someone took my order. "Take a seat and your number will be called when your order is ready."

I wanted to hide and eat my lunch in peace. Unfortunately the back area which is normally empty didn't have one open table. I can't sit in booths. Booths are not geared for people who have had numerous back surgeries.

Someone was getting up at a table for two positioned against a wall. I grabbed it and cleaned it with napkins. No employee was wiping tables down anyway. My number was called and I picked up my food. I purposely sat on the side next to the wall to hide my left arm.

Out of nowhere a couple I knew from town spotted me. Their son went with Mindy to their senior prom in high school and I had him as a student. They were lovely people but I wasn't interested in speaking to anyone. I wondered how they ended up in this particular Fresh Bread.

"Join us when you're finished." They pointed to the place where they were sitting. I had to pass their table to leave the restaurant and therefore couldn't avoid them. They tried not to be intrusive but it was quite obvious they were interested and for the second time that day I felt obligated to tell someone. They were very sympathetic and fortunately didn't press me any further.

We exchanged information about our children and they were surprised I was in the area. "My mother is in a nursing home up the road." I do not recall why they were there. Probably because I was having such a difficult day and using all excuses I could muster up to delay my visit to my mother.

"Do you go up often?"

"Almost every day," I answered. Sometimes I went to the home twice a day if necessary.

"You can do it." The comment was made by the husband to give me strength but personally it reminded me I had a responsibility. *What I couldn't comprehend within myself was why I was taking care of Mom in my condition?* My mother always had an excuse for my brother not helping and he had no health problems at that time.

I drove up to the nursing home still fighting with myself about going in. The director saw me and waved hello. I parked my car and entered the building. I signed in quickly. Cats were roaming around and I'm highly allergic to them. My mother was in the lunchroom and having a very difficult time swallowing her food. She choked on it frequently and a nurse had to be called from upstairs to help.

The nurses wanted me to sign a release for her to eat in the all-purpose room upstairs. "A nurse can be accessed immediately if your Mom needs help." Mom fought me terribly about not giving away her rights. I felt guilty about her being in a nursing home but realized at that moment she really needed to be there. I couldn't physically take care of her. There was no money to hire private help. Guilt continued to drive me but the burden of taking care of my mother was a detriment to my own recovery.

The guilt weighed on my shoulders like an apartment building. Normally I waited until Mom was taken upstairs from the dining room and I accompanied her. I really was feeling down and had no patience. I sat with my mother for a very short period of time and left.

I said good-bye to the staff. As I walked through the door I was accosted by an unfamiliar female staff member. "What happened to you?" She worked in a nursing home with half the woman missing a breast and several patients at any given time being treated for lymphedema and she still had to ask me.

She was standing next to the director who shot me a look. His facial expression said, *"Where did she come from?"* For the first time I answered with a question. "Would you ask a man who had his penis wrapped up what happened to him?" I couldn't believe the words came out of my mouth. What an ending for such *a miserable day.* They both looked at me but I knew the director understood.

I drove home quite upset. Ben was home and I told him what happened.

"Did you tell your mother?"

"You must be kidding. She's only into herself right now and I understand it."

I was unable to get the day out of my head but worst of all I couldn't get the woman from The Beauty Store out of my mind. I made a call to the store's customer service. The number was located on the bottom of my receipt. A lady sounding relatively young answered the phone. I related my experience in the Wood Lake store.

I was directed to read the salesperson's name on the receipt as well as her code. She was the store manager. "We do not tolerate this kind of behavior in any of our stores. She'll be spoken to immediately by the area representative." I expected nothing and only wanted to let off some steam. She asked for my name, address and phone number and apologized profusely. I received a written letter of apology several weeks later with an enclosed gift certificate. I used it in one of their other stores.

CHAPTER 24

LYMPHEDEMA SUPPORT GROUPS AND CONSEQUENCES

I met a few people with lymphedema at Gilda's but many more who were afraid of getting it. I participated in a breast cancer support group at Gilda's and brought up lymphedema. One of the women was adamant. "Lymphedema has nothing to do with breast cancer surgery." If she wanted to be in denial it was her problem. Lymphedema is a high probability once lymph nodes are removed during surgery. Radiation adds to the distinct possibility of lymphedema in your lifetime. This is one group I did not participate in for very long. It was more beneficial to speak to the other women who had lymphedema but were not participants of this group.

I mentioned how badly my Aunt Lillian suffered with lymphedema in her hand and arm. All of us were actively trying to manage the problem. One day I brought in a picture of my aunt and myself together.

"Who is standing next to her?"

"*Me!*"

"But you're short!" I come from a very short family and at my tallest years ago measured 5'4".

When I received a brochure from Tremore about a lymphedema support group at the hospital I really wanted to attend. I knew this wouldn't be a permanent solution for me in terms of support since the drive to NYC, parking and going by myself wasn't feasible. I wanted to hear from others if they were having the same unpleasant experiences I was and find out the way they handled their situation.

Ben agreed to take me. I called for my reservation and inquired if Ben could stay. He would be very welcomed I was told. Input from someone living with lymphedema would be helpful to everyone. We would be a total of eight people.

Ben and I were the first to arrive. We left plenty of time to get to the hospital since it was the evening rush hour and we didn't want to be late. Shortly afterwards others started to enter the room and Ben was joined by a few other men.

The staff running the group arrived and began to set up the room. They were extremely shocked by the large number of people who showed up. The circle of chairs set up for a dozen easily grew to about forty. Ben was the only male who stayed in the circle with us. The other men retreated to the back of the room.

One staff member addressed us first and then introduced the head of the hospital's lymphedema therapy department. She discussed the usual issues of having to be very careful with the affected areas, using suntan lotion on a constant basis, avoiding heavy lifting, wrapping, etc. People started to ask questions and the pump was brought up. The thinking at that time was the pump didn't work. One therapist said, "Those who have pumps eventually end up storing them in a closet."

I stated, "My experimental pump seems to be working." I described the compartments and how they were gently closed off as each section of my hand and arm were massaged. I was not wearing bandages any more except when I flew on a plane. The therapist was adamant about not using a pump and said none of them worked. I was now getting the idea that therapists in general do not abide by using any of the machines.

I heard many sob stories. Most prevalent of all was their surgeons didn't tell them about lymphedema. Almost no one knew that lymphedema could develop at any point in their lives once lymph nodes are removed during a lumpectomy or mastectomy.

A woman in her thirties, a dentist, was livid. "My whole career and dental practice is ruined. I'm unable to put my hand around the instruments or hold up my arm." She was furious at her surgeon for not telling her this would be a side effect of her surgery. The only thing I couldn't understand was what option she would have had if she didn't undergo surgery?

Lymphedema for me was a big life changing experience more than the mastectomy. Once your breast is off, it's off. You can find ways to dress yourself accordingly, be fitted for a prosthetic or have reconstruction. Lymphedema causes you to change the way you function. During the evening I heard from others how their lives were affected in major ways and the dentist was only one of them.

I contributed to the conversation again. "Food preparation is very slow for me. The time to cut fruits and vegetables doubles because I have to be so careful using a knife. I am afraid of cutting myself. The extra time it takes to stand on my feet or sit in one position makes my back pain worse. One problem sets off another." "Clothing that fits over my lymphedema areas is impossible to find," said another woman.

Most of all I heard a lot of anger from the women. The biggest problem seemed in getting proper care and I saw several women who were wrapped incorrectly. The women were upset and they were screaming. The dentist started a barrage of yelling. The evening seemed to end with everyone attending feeling sorry for themselves, angry at their doctors for lack of information, improper care and not knowing how to cope with their condition. The meeting confirmed one thing for me. Everyone with lymphedema was struggling with their lives in one way or another. There is supposed to be comfort in numbers and I think my attendance at this meeting made it pretty clear I was not alone.

The bottom line is we are not just surviving breast cancer. We have to survive everyday living with lymphedema or the fear of getting it if we haven't done so already. It does crimp our way of life. Every major cancer organization and anyone else dealing with cancer survivorship should be publicizing lymphedema in a major way. It should not just be a passing statement from a doctor or a one line comment in a brochure. Lymphedema should be addressed as a major side effect by doctors who do surgery. All doctors and nurses should become familiar in recognizing lymphedema and the associated problems that may arise in treating lymphedema patients with their own specialty. Recognize lymphedema as a major illness and promote it that way.

Protection for my lymphedema areas is extremely important. Having blood drawn, an I.V. and blood pressure taken, lifting, repetition of a movement, all are issues to be dealt with. People just love to show their friendship or make a point by giving me a punch in the arm. Often I've had to duck if I have enough time to see it coming. I feel as though I'm in a boxing ring.

Two of my doctors said to avoid having a pedicure and manicure. Even pushing back cuticles can be a problem if done by a manicurist. I just avoid it all. It's not worth my while to look for more trouble. I do put clear nail polish on my nails for very special occasions.

I gave away all my leather gloves. They no longer fit over my lymphatic hand. The inexpensive dollar store stretch gloves work just fine. Clothing styles change and shopping was easier when loose was the rage. The styles now are the opposite. I'll have to live with *out of style*.

The swelling in my left ring finger is down but not enough to wear my wedding band. I gave up my engagement ring and wear my wedding band on my right hand. I switched my watch from my left wrist to the right one. My left wrist can still accommodate my watch and in the beginning I continued to place it there out of habit. I realized my error and called Dr. Bucker for his advice.

Dr. Bucker informed me if I ever totally do not feel any pain from my surgery I am no longer alive. Knowledge of what is acceptable pain makes a day much less fearful and worrisome. He was not speaking of excruciating pain but of those small pangs one feels every once in a while. He stated, "If medical procedures are necessary (e.g. when I thought my finger was broken and there was a question if it had to be operated on), then your lymphedema will have to be taken care of afterwards."

My life will never be pain free. My back continues to hurt with excruciating pain and at times it can be debilitating. I seem to go from one illness to another. I must take additional precautions for my health no matter who thinks my actions are ridiculous.

I am taking this opportunity to beg medical and nursing schools to devote a few hours with all your students regardless of their specialty and teach them to familiarize themselves in recognizing lymphedema and all the side effects and precautions that need to be taken. Teach your students the way to take blood pressure on a leg or thigh. Make them aware a blood pressure reading is usually higher the further it is taken from the heart. Warn them about needles in a lymphatic area. Prominently use your opportunity to recognize lymphedema as a medical condition instead of ignoring it. Make the students cognizant of the fact scar tissue prevents the lymphatic system from working correctly.

Lymphedema patients need your help.

CHAPTER 25

I ADMIT TO BEING A PAIN

I am a cleanliness freak. My immune system is compromised. My lymphatic system doesn't work properly. I must avoid getting infections because they are getting more and more difficult to treat.

Everyone considers me a pain in the neck because I tell them to wash their hands after they go to the bathroom and wash well before they eat or go near food. I can't seem to stop myself from telling people how important washing ones hands are and only washing one hand is not adequate. You have to wash long enough to remove the germs.

Ben is the one I bother the most about cleanliness since we live together. My hearing is still extremely sharp and I let him know if he hasn't washed long enough. I can easily ascertain how long the water is running when he washes. I'm so afraid of germs I've become paranoid.

As previously mentioned I am unable to sit in a booth. I need a chair that is comfortable for me. I need to sit across from someone to speak to them since I can't twist my neck. Yes I am a pain in the neck quite literally. Sometimes I will force myself to do something that will be regrettable by the next day just to make everyone else comfortable. I must stay away from people who are wearing perfume or any strong odors because of my chemical allergies. I want to socialize and my closest friends know I have many ailments and usually will bounce with it. I am most comfortable with other cancer and lymphedema patients. They need no explanation as to my weird habits.

One thing that has gotten worse in time is my asthma. I can't take strong odors of any kind. I've had to educate doctors who treat me with letters from my allergist/pulmonologist. An offensive smell will make me lose my voice. This is probably what happens to me after surgery. Chemical odors abound in an operating room.

When I was in one hospital for nine days the nurses and orderlies came into my room with strong cologne on. They couldn't come near me. The junk should not be worn in a hospital or doctors' offices. "We wear cologne to cover up the odor of some of our patients." Someone should make the staff aware they are causing harm to patients who have asthma.

There have been several occasions when I was in a restaurant or doctors' office and the female staff inquired about what I have on. At first I thought they were referring to my clothing. *"No, not your clothes! Your perfume! I'd like to purchase the fragrance."* Ben always laughs and answers for me. Non-allergenic soap and water! Some women are so used to a strong perfumed odor they don't recognize fresh when they smell it. I for one would love to see body washes, perfumes, room deodorizers and the like banned. One of my doctors told me they are as much of a carcinogen as cigarette smoke.

Some strides have been made in the area of perfumes and cleaning products. Many of the cleaning products advertise odorless on their containers, ditto for make-up. No one is attacked any more by someone spraying you with perfume as you walk by them in a department store.

CHAPTER 26

LILY

My youngest first cousin Lily, also Aunt Lillian's niece, was diagnosed with breast cancer and needed surgery. She refused citing the fact a mutilated body was abhorrent to her. Nor would she undergo any form of radiation or chemo. Instead she chose to see gurus. I heard conflicting stories about where these gurus were located ranging from India to Peru. She ate all of this disgusting green stuff ground up in a blender.

When we first spoke about her breast cancer her attitude was *whatever will be, will be*. I couldn't comprehend her way of thinking. When I saw her eating her gross concoctions on several occasions, I was happy I made my decision to have surgery. The homeopathic route and gurus are definitely not for me.

Lily died and I regretted the decision she made in the treatment of her breast cancer. She had so much to live for. Giving it all up for the sake of appearance is a very big mistake as far as I'm concerned. I hope never to meet anyone else again who makes such a poor choice in life.

I attended a program at Gilda's Club about an interesting prosthetic. I don't recall the name of the company but it probably can be found on the internet. The company's prosthetic has realistic looking veins and markings.

The company was started by a married couple. The wife refused to accept her mastectomy, declined a regular prosthesis and insisted on matching breasts. She was being fitted for her prosthesis, looked in the mirror and screamed. She absolutely refused to wear something looking so unlike the breast she lost and not a replica of her still existing one. Her loud screams began to disturb other customers.

Her fitter took it upon herself to call the woman's husband into the dressing room. He told her to, "Quiet down. You're upsetting others."

"I want a prosthetic to look like my real breast. I have no intention of wearing any of the prosthetics available."

"You'll get used to it."

"I'll never get used to it. You're a dentist. You make molds. Make me a prosthetic that looks like my other breast."

And that is how this particular breast prosthetic was developed. A mold is made of the breast you have left and veins and colors are copied onto the manmade breast. Therefore anyone of any color can end up with twin matching breasts. Brochures were handed out to show us all the various colors of breasts. The cost was astronomical and not covered by any insurance. Unless you are extremely vain I don't even know what the point is. Perhaps this prosthetic would have saved someone like my cousin.

The prosthetic goes into your bra. You don't even see it. I can't imagine getting into a habit of checking into my bra every hour or so to see what my breast looks like. Women will check their make-up and hair frequently but I'm not aware of women who check their breasts periodically. Perhaps Margarite's Secret knows something I don't know.

CHAPTER 27

ERYSIPELAS

The following episode took place just prior to my first lumpectomy and mastectomy but is relevant to my story. Erysipelas is exactly why those with lymphedema must be so protective of themselves.

One cold winter day I went for an electrolysis appointment. The tech received a call from her daughter. She sneezed into her elbow when she hung up, did not wash her hands and began to work on me again. "My daughter is home with strep." Pores were open on my face from the electrolysis needle. It was too late for me to say anything.

Within a few days of my electrolysis visit I started to feel really crummy. A thermometer reading showed I had a fever. As the hours wore on I weakened terribly and couldn't leave my bed. The next day was Sunday and my only option was to go to an emergency room of a hospital.

Ben called my doctor and a covering doctor returned the call. "The doctor is calling in a prescription to the pharmacy for you." I fell into a deep sleep unaware Ben left the house to pick up the medication.

I awoke briefly to use the bathroom. I could barely stand up but managed to get in and out with my head spinning. I was very afraid of falling but somehow made it back to bed without an incident. My temperature was well over one hundred and three.

Ben returned with the medicine waking me up to take it. He brought me some water and I could just about get the capsule down. I immediately fell back to sleep.

I woke up again after a short while with my clothes soaked in perspiration. With a very weak voice I called out to Ben.

"I'm so sick."

"Just give the medication a chance to work."

With his assistance I again went to the bathroom and then retreated to my bed. Barely able to see the thermometer I took my temperature again. The mercury went to the end. Even when my daughters were young and ill their fever never went so high. With an ever weakening voice I called out to Ben.

"Please take me to the hospital."

"Give the medication a chance to work." I was too sick to understand his reasoning.

"I'm calling an ambulance."

Ben helped me get dressed, managed to get me down the steps and out of the house. I practically fell into the car and we took off for the hospital. My perspiration subsided a bit. It was a bitterly cold January day but I was unable to close my jacket because of the heat emanating from my body.

After a long wait in the emergency room I was taken into a small room to have my vital signs checked. My fever diminished slightly and the attendant's guess was the cold helped bring it down. A resident sent me for a CAT scan and afterwards put me on an I.V. He gave me a double dose of Tylenol.

The doctor entered the room with news my test results were negative. My temperature subsided. "Did I need a doctor's note for work?" "Was I a type 'A' personality?" "Rest and a double dose of Tylenol will cure you." My I.V. was disconnected and I was discharged.

Very early the next day my fever spiked again and my face began to blow up. My doctor's office wasn't opened yet and we returned to the hospital. My face turned red and expanded into a balloon shape by the time my vitals were taken. There was no mirror and I was curious why my glasses no longer fit my face.

I was transferred to a private room in the emergency area. A cancer ENT doctor specialist was needed for a diagnosis. A nurse put a tourniquet around my arm to take my blood pressure and left the room. She never returned. I spotted her in a winter coat as she said to others, "I'm leaving.

My shift is over." I called softly to get her attention. Someone else heard me and I pointed to the nurse. My arm was numb. My nurse came over and removed the tourniquet. "Someone else can take your blood pressure."

Eventually the ENT doctor showed up. He was a handsome man who introduced himself as Dr. Connor. I have seen Dr. Connor a minimum of twenty five times since then, probably more, and he continues to say I'm Dr. Connor. The difference now is he is slightly older, heavier and grayer.

After Dr. Connor examined me he had an idea about my condition but needed to contact the Center for Disease Control before making a definitive diagnosis. Another two doctors looked at me and my internist was contacted. I definitely had to be admitted.

Ben met the original resident. "I apologize for my missed diagnosis and for sending your wife home." Everyone in the emergency room was now aware of Dr. Connor's unusual patient.

Dr. Connor returned and was quite positive I had erysipelas but wanted his diagnosis confirmed by a disease specialist. One would see me the following day. All the doctors in the emergency room were standing around trying to figure out how to spell erysipelas. The disease was supposedly eradicated. I now know if you have lymphedema you are quite susceptible to erysipelas. No one thought to call a breast surgeon or oncologist though I wonder if they would be able to diagnosis erysipelas on a face.

After a few hours I was transferred to a private room and orders were given for my isolation. I was given additional antibiotics. There was no pain with my condition, only extreme fatigue, perspiration, a high fever and a blown up head.

A window in my room overlooked a courtyard and I vowed to get up enough strength to look out. I had to stay in bed with my head and upper back elevated. It was an extremely uncomfortable and painful position for a person who underwent numerous spinal surgeries.

The next morning a nurse let me get off the bed to use the bathroom. This was the first time I saw myself in the mirror in more than twenty four hours. All I could think of was the children's book _Goodnight Moon_. That's what I saw myself as, a full faced moon.

As I left the bathroom a doctor entered and from across the way. "Yes. It is erysipelas brought on by strep."

"Have you been near anyone who had strep?"

I told her about electrolysis. She confirmed the time of my electrolysis appointment to the time my first symptoms appeared. The difference between strep and viral erysipelas has to do with the location of patches on one's face. My antibiotics were switched to two stronger ones. I had to put up with the side effects in order to recover. I was cognizant of how cautious the doctor was while speaking to me.

"Can you use your hands to show me the size of your head prior to the blow-up?" I realized afterwards I could have given her my glasses.

"I'll be here every day to monitor the size of your head." The lack of head pain never caused me to worry about the seriousness of erysipelas.

My internist Dr. Capp came to see me. First he laughed over the fact all the educated doctors in the hospital including himself didn't know how to spell erysipelas. During his exam he laughed again.

"All of these years and I never saw all your scars till now. You look like a road map!" Since then he does a good job of helping me laugh at myself.

On the third day the disease doctor entered the room smiling.

"Your head looks smaller. The antibiotics are working. You will soon feel and see your skin peeling. Your condition is now peeling skin disease. As the fluid leaves your body your skin will continue to peel and you will be on your way to recovery." I still had to remain in isolation.

"I'll give you something mild for the diarrhea." I was having a slight reaction from the antibiotics. "I'll try to drum up something for your very irritated hemorrhoids."

Dr. Capp entered my room. "Now I can tell you we were all afraid you might not make it." I had absolutely no idea my condition had been that dire. The original E.R. doctor will probably never make his incorrect diagnosis on anyone else again.

I was going crazy in the room. My glasses didn't fit and I needed them to watch T.V. Ben visited me and brought the paper but I couldn't read. My eyelids were too swollen. He needed to sit far away from me.

Day four I was allowed to sit up in a chair to eat. I positioned the table and a chair to look out the window. I imagined myself as having a picnic outside in the lovely garden beneath my room window. I kept my eyes on the trees. It was much too cold and early for foliage but that didn't stop my mind for visualizing I was there.

The next day a clown came into the room. She was surprised to see me sitting by the window acting as though I was in a fine restaurant overlooking a beautiful garden. I was entertaining her she said instead of her entertaining me. Everyone she visited was down in the dumps. "I'm making the best of a bad situation," I said. The clown left me some thingy to keep me laughing.

The next day I was told the swelling of my head was reduced enough to let me walk in the hallway. I was going to make the most of this. My glasses still didn't fit on my head. Pieces of skin were falling off my face larger than dandruff. I didn't care because I was being let out of my cage. I put on the robe Ben brought me and left my room. People were staring at me. I still didn't care. I must have been frightening to look at. I tired easily and headed back to my room. I decided to try another walk later in the day.

By the next day my walks became longer, my head continued to shrink and my skin continued to peel. Red splotches appeared where the flakes were falling off but I estimated in another day or two I might be able to get my glasses on.

I felt better, had enough of the hospital, was bored and wanted to go home. My doctors refused to release me. Perhaps they were concerned I would regress but they didn't express this to me.

On one of my walks through the hospital hallway someone called out to me "You are looking so much better." Then a few others joined in. Only some of these people were on staff. I never realized I had become everyone's entertainment. This incident proves to me I won't sit around for long bemoaning my situation. I'm cognizant of the fact I need some time to recover from any negative incident that occurs but my recovery is faster if I work on a solution to the problem.

CHAPTER 28

I'M A STAR

I called Ben advising him I might be going home. We discussed any questions we might have for the doctors making a list as we spoke. One of the top ten was making love. Surprise but seniors still do this.

Dr. Capp visited remarking how great I looked. I went through our list of questions. I was embarrassed to ask a sex question but knew it would come up eventually. *"Seriously!* You have to recuperate a bit first."

My departure was reminiscent of those you see on news programs showing someone leaving a hospital after miraculously making it through what doctors often refer to as a *death sentence.* It was odd I never felt that way. The staff and patients who had been watching me waved and said good-by.

The peeling on my face and scalp finally stopped. I was left with red blotches on my cheeks and forehead. The blotches eventually faded from my cheeks and lightened up a bit on my forehead. No one looking at me would notice but I still see a permanent red area on my forehead. It's actually attractive now giving my face a bit of color. *When you are handed lemons make lemonade.*

Ben went into the examining room with me for my follow up appointment with Dr. Capp. He entered the room and put his arm around my shoulders saying how terrific I looked. I still was not allowed to wear make-up. I looked at him as though he was crazy. He kept me on one antibiotic and took me off the second one.

It was time to tell me just how serious my illness was. Fluid brought on by the strep made my head swell. I could have died from the fluid going to my brain and it was the initial reason I had to practically sit up in bed all the time. The fluid had to drain downward to leave my body.

After hearing how terrific I looked, the lovemaking question came up again. "Look what she looks like. Wait until she improves." I just heard how great I looked and now it was all being taken back. *Looking great is certainly a relative comment.*

I never comprehended just how sick I was or how badly I looked. I saw this moon face staring back at me from the hospital mirror never bothering to look again until the doctor said my head began to shrink.

Chapter 29

HOUSE SEARCH

Our house was getting too difficult for me to handle. The stairs were a real problem and I was kicking laundry bags down to the basement. Getting the folded laundry up the stairs even with Ben's help was difficult.

Snow shoveling was impossible with my back and the lymphedema. Ben complained for days afterwards if he did the shoveling because his back hurt as well. We relied on a landscaper who sometimes took off for Florida in the midst of a snowstorm. It was a hit or miss situation. If we had a hospital or doctor appointment and snow was on the ground we were forced to shovel ourselves.

Landscaping and taking care of the lawn was another major issue. Ben hated and refused to take care of it. I didn't mind taking care of flowers but was unable to do mowing, cut the bushes or do the bending to pull up the weeds.

Ben moved into my house and it was about time we found a new place to share together. Too many past memories of life in the house were very painful to me no matter how we redecorated.

Unfortunately many of my friends moved or were dying. Most of my friends who were left were widowed. We lacked a social life with other couples. Our immediate neighbors moved and their replacements had no interest in becoming Americanized.

Mindy and the children wanted us to move closer to them. I started to look at the pros of staying where we were and made a list of the cons. A nursing facility for my mother had to be found no matter where we moved. I would definitely miss my doctors and familiar hospitals. Finding a replacement for Gilda's Club was high on my priority list and I didn't know if I would succeed in finding one.

I discussed buying a one level property with Ben and we went to visit an adult community in Central NJ. It was easy to find the type of house we were looking for but Ben was turned off by all *the old people* sitting in front of the real estate office with nothing to do. The move was put on hold.

A few weeks later my friend and neighbor came over to tell me she was moving. She was going to the community Ben and I looked at.

Several months later Ben was signed up to attend a conference in Mindy's town. The conference was on a Sunday and I suggested we take a room in a hotel for Saturday night. We could use Saturday for house hunting and Sunday I could spend the day with Mindy and the boys while he was at the conference. Ben agreed.

I located a realtor and set up an appointment. We gave the realtor the parameters we needed for a house. A ranch with everything on the same floor including a laundry room, two bedrooms and two baths, with lawn and snow removal included. We saw several homes with the realtor but nothing worth a move. We wanted easy access to good hospitals.

We passed a place in the midst of construction. The realtor stopped and we assessed the situation looking at building plans and models. It was a condo and Ben reminded me we had enough of apartment living while growing up in the Bronx for me and Brooklyn for him. Condos would be a last resort.

Ben left for his conference on Sunday morning and I went down for breakfast in the dining room of the hotel. Several women were hanging out after breakfast speaking about the adult communities where they purchased homes. A third place was in the works but it was a ride far south to see the models. The girl at the desk gave me all three names, addresses and phone numbers to call.

Ben and I discussed my newly found information on the drive home. Shortly thereafter we had a day when we had no doctor or hospital appointments and the weather was beautiful. I made the suggestion to take a ride to look at the communities.

The homes in "Active Adult Communities" met all our requirements and then some. Swimming pools, gyms, clubhouses, activities and socialization were added bonuses. Neither of us realized nor did we have information on the cons.

We made a decision to move no further south than an hour from we lived yet close enough to Mindy. We wanted an easy ride up the highway to Bergen County until we made all our transitions of doctors to Central NJ. There were several hospitals near these communities and that was an extremely important consideration for us. Ben added especially for me but he was the first one to use one of the hospitals after we moved.

There also was a very close facility that had an available Medicaid room for my mother. This seemed to be the ideal area for our move.

One beautiful day we took the long ride to look at models for the third community. We purchased our present house that day but now had an excruciating long wait to have the house built. My house sold in Bergen County and the closing was set for the approximate the time we were to move into our new home as per our contract. Only the builder hadn't even broken ground. Our belongings went into storage and we moved into a hotel for seven months.

My mother died the week before our move to the hotel. Plans for her move became irrelevant.

CHAPTER 30

FRIENDSHIP

A longtime friend of mine from college had been testing our friendship for a number of years. She liked to talk and lecture, lying wasn't beneath her either. Many people were surprised to find out we were friends.

After several years of seemingly avoiding me, I received a phone call from her a few weeks after my first mastectomy. I was in the shower and Ben came to get me. He knew I was very upset about our declining relationship. I answered the phone still dripping wet but with a towel around me.

My friend went on about everyone's problems including most of whom I didn't know. I was getting chilled and she didn't give me a chance to tell her about my mastectomy. I interrupted saying I was wet, cold and not feeling well. She never asked why. I hung up.

A few days later she called back to wish me a Happy Passover.

"I can't really speak right now. I have to leave for an appointment with a doctor."

"Who makes an appointment with a doctor during Passover?"

She's got to be kidding I thought. How out of touch was she with reality?

I called our Synagogue to tell them of my mother's death and my friend's husband was there. He called my friend in Tennessee who was visiting their daughter. On Tuesday evening during Shiva, our mourning period, she called. During the conversation I mentioned the need to go on my lymphedema machine. She wanted to know what it was. I said it had to with my last cancer surgery and my lymph nodes being removed. "What do you mean cancer surgery? You only had one, your kidney." Spoken in a tone of voice letting you know kidney cancer was not much of anything.

"No, I also had a lumpectomy and then a mastectomy."

She was now screaming at me. "How dare you not tell me?"

"I tried to tell you and you wouldn't listen. I said I wasn't feeling well.

"You're always sick. That meant nothing."

She yelled and berated me so loudly, Ben heard her and he was downstairs in the den. I was in the kitchen.

I kept saying this is not the time for this "I'm sitting Shiva."

Ben insisted I hang up on her. I finally did but was shaking.

Our computer was not disconnected for our move but technically I wasn't supposed to be on it. I didn't care. I needed a way to release my anger. I was typing and time quickly passed by. Ben came to remind me about my lymphedema machine. I needed a few more minutes to relieve the rest of my anger but shut down the computer instead. Treating my lymphedema was my first priority.

I finished my massage after midnight and went up to the bedroom. I sat down on the bed swung my legs over and put my head down on my pillow. My eyes were still open when I felt a breath going across my face as when someone is speaking. My mother said she was all right. *I don't believe in this sort of thing so how could it have happened?* I jumped out of bed and told Ben what occurred.

It really happened as I tried to convince Ben. He said "As long as I believe it and it comforted me; it was important." There was no question in my mind. Mom's breath went from left to right as she was passing me to say she was all right. I probably wouldn't believe it if someone told me that story. I would think it was a bunch of hogwash.

I decided Mom took that particular moment to tell me she was all right for a reason. She was no longer a burden to me anymore leaving me free to deal with other issues that were a cause of consternation in my life. I actually felt at peace for my mother and it made me happy.

CHAPTER 31

CLUBS AND CANCER AWARENESS DAY

I love having the laundry room on the first floor of our home and having a separate room for my art work. The view behind our house is majestic at times from the way the icicles form on the bare branches in the woods in the winter to the pastel colors in the spring and bright oranges, yellows and reds as the trees change color in the fall. There is always something to paint if I look outside.

Our new community has a clubhouse and upon its completion the community manager requested that the owners start clubs. I started two, a cancer support group and a "Busy Needles" club for knitting, crocheting and any other type of needle work. I kept the "Busy Needles" club alive for several years. Other clubs formed and we were constantly asked to move from the craft room or take other times on the calendar slowing participation in the group. I had many other things to concentrate on and called it quits.

The Cancer Support Group started with a good number of people. Cancer becomes more prevalent in the older population and I had many people to work with. Unfortunately I was the one who had to keep coming up with ideas to keep the group going. I say unfortunately because we could have passed information onto one another and given each other so much help. Our support group slowly started to disintegrate. People really couldn't get the hang or the purpose of being together for the same reason. On the other hand until this day people will call me privately and ask for any information I may have. They still think of me as the "Cancer" lady.

The one thing I successfully did basically by myself was a Cancer Awareness Day. I planned it on a grand scale and the residents in my community never caught on to what I was trying to accomplish or how I wanted it run until the day was over.

The community director insisted I involve one of the big clubs. Their members had absolutely no comprehension of the meaning of the day but did not want it to be depressing. They couldn't understand why our club didn't charge dues and needed support from other clubs in the community. "Our club is a support group and dues are not collected." My explanation fell on deaf ears. The other club fought me every inch of the way.

I was determined to make this day a success. I just lost another very close friend to cancer and refused to give up with the Cancer Awareness Day. I also had the experience other people in the community did not have. Many of the activities I planned to do for the day and how to go about it were part of my second profession within the travel industry and my past volunteering endeavors. I also had a savvy New York background and helped my mother with sophisticated fund raising functions for Tremore and her cancer group.

My goals were many for this day. The first was to educate people about the various types of cancer. I contacted numerous places to send me written material. I had cartons of information to sort through and set up an information center in our community's ballroom.

I contacted the American Cancer Society and decided to make all donations on their behalf. At my request they gave me a letter showing my intent to raise money for them and gave me their state tax exempt letter. I planned a walk to raise money for Cancer Awareness with all funds going to The American Cancer Society.

Many activities were planned and I succeeded in all of them but needed help to run things. Amazingly enough only one person from our cancer support group actually helped me. One called to say, "This isn't what I signed up for."

"Can you put some folding chairs in front of your house for the walk in case some people have to sit?"

"*No.*" I was hitting a brick wall but I started this function and I was determined to finish it successfully.

The community manager insisted I have meetings on a continual basis with people who could help. I was happy to delegate because many people were needed to make the day work. All they did was fight with me. I will not go into details but the people in the room aside from the other support group member, never experienced cancer themselves nor did they have a close relationship with someone who did. I was asked the most basic question, "What do you do if you have cancer?" That was my original motivation for trying to do this day. It was called "Cancer Awareness." Seemingly they couldn't even compute the meaning of the name.

I was drowned out. One person said her daughter was a fund raiser. She lived in Florida. *Did this person learn her daughter's job through osmosis?* I easily could have responded so was my daughter and she did it internationally. I was not running this on my daughter's successful credentials.

This same person volunteered to make the directional plan for the walk itself setting a maximum number of miles. I suggested marking off streets where people could return to the clubhouse if they were unable to complete the walk. I was handed a layout with no turnoffs. Using a calm tone of voice I explained why alternative routes were useful. "Some people are in wheelchairs, others use canes and even more are physically incapable of walking the whole distance." Angrily she ripped her plan. "Everyone in the complex is healthy enough to dance and play in major sports. The whole thing is going to be a flop with ten people showing up and I'm not going to be a part of it."

I had a reaction to all the negativity which took on the appearance of a stroke. I will not go into details about all of this but I'm living with this condition for six years now. When the feeling comes on I take a small dose of an anti-anxiety pill, give the medication a few moments to kick in and I'm back to normal, i.e. normal for me.

I spent nine days in the hospital, hair shaved off, hooked onto monitors, only to be told my problem was related to breast cancer. This diagnosis came after a PET scan on a Friday. My assigned doctor's nurse practitioner had no involvement with the oncology department of the hospital. She was unable to schedule a mammography for me for several weeks and I was an inpatient. I attribute the delay more to the doctor than the hospital itself. Since when don't you have emergency tests when you are lying in a hospital bed? I avoid this doctor now as if he had a plague.

Ben immediately called Dr. Bucker. I was told to check out of the hospital. "Breast cancer cannot be detected by a PET scan." Dr. Bucker was setting me up for an exam and mammography of my right breast on Monday. I left the hospital and followed through with my appointments. No breast cancer was discovered at the time but emotionally I was having difficulty with another scare.

I went back to handling the Cancer Awareness project. The community manager panicked asking people to do things who had no idea of what the day required. I took control again and out of necessity delegated tasks to people with no experience. When they did the job half-assed I learned to just let it go and did as much as possible by myself.

No committee member was successful in getting items for a raffle. I managed to get seventy-five gifts to raffle off including shows in various theaters, baseball games, restaurants, wall art, jewelry, etc. and asked for donations from people in the community. I was anything but shy, learning my lessons well from my mother and some of my supervisors at work. This day was very important to me and probably would be my last big hurrah in the community. I made a decision to never risk my health again.

Two supermarkets gave me gift certificates and I used them to buy fresh fruit and protein bars. A major big store gave me water and sent someone over to help. I went to a trade show and walked out with additional gifts to raffle off. Every merchant received a tax exempt letter and I followed up with thank you letters to each donor. Donated balloons were blown up to line the walk route.

One woman put on a bubble show and entertained the children who were encouraged to come. Someone else invited her friend to do caricatures. We had a drawing room for the children and the bocce club gave the children lessons. I wanted the day to be fun for children and encouraged their involvement. A prize was offered to the child who collected the most pennies. The entertainment was a poet and a one man band. I was glad someone heeded my call for help in this area.

Empty books were available for people to write in; one as a memorial to someone who died from cancer, one for a cancer patient or survivor to tell their story. The representative from the big store left a donation jar on the desk where the books were placed.

The community manager arranged for the local volunteer ambulance to come while we had the walk, *a just in case precaution*. Members of a newly formed bicycle club agreed to ride the route with water bottles *another just in case scenario*.

I made arrangements with our deli to have a percentage of their profits from that day donated to the American Cancer Society.

The mayor was invited and said he would be happy to come but just remind him of the date. "I'll speak to the crowd." I left a message on his machine, emailed him a week before and again the day before. He never showed. When I saw him again out campaigning two weeks later, I reminded him he didn't show up. "I forgot." He didn't get my vote in that election even though he received it previously. I too am one of his constituents and a cancer awareness day was one he should have attended.

One other entertainer didn't show up. She was a lady who was supposed to do face painting. The golf club was to have activities for the children but they seemingly forgot.

I was in the hospital when publicity for the event went out. The day was open to the public and people had to be notified of the when and where. Out of necessity I delegated the job to someone who volunteered because of my own medical situation. She tried very hard to do something she was unfamiliar with and her success was very limited. The community manager was in advertising previously. Multi-tasking wasn't his strong point and he just found out he was not going to be rehired. Advertising was one area he should have handled but instead it went by the way side. Central Jersey's largest paper never advertised the event but the local TV station did. Some outsiders came mostly invited by other residents but we had over three hundred people. About forty percent of the people entered the ballroom where all the give-ways, literature, entertainment and tables were. Thankfully many volunteers showed up to help and I was very grateful for their participation.

The big day arrived and the weather report was for a record breaking heat wave. By eight in the morning the temperature was well over ninety degrees. The walk was to take place at noon and was scheduled to have those who went to church join us.

By eleven in the morning the temperature was over one hundred. People asked me to have a symbolic walk in the clubhouse. There was much concern for the health of the walkers. I acquiesced and changed the walking venue to inside the ballroom. The community manager cancelled the volunteer ambulance. Not too many of us took the symbolic walk.

The biggest interest was in the raffle. I wrote down numbers from one to seventy-five and the name of the gift next to it on a large board. I put the matching numbers on the gifts. It was easy for the volunteers to give the winners their prizes.

Everyone who participated in the raffle was thrilled but I was asked to give some of the gifts up for another cause. The gifts were donated to be used for a dedicated purpose to raise money for the American Cancer Society. Now a club was asking me to donate the gifts for something else. Additionally my resentment was giving up gifts I worked so hard to get under the American Cancer Society's tax exempt number to a group who fought me at every turn. It wasn't even a legal request.

A tiring day was finished but we made over three thousand dollars. The manager singled me out for my accomplishment. Ben and I brought the money and checks collected over to the American Cancer Society on Monday.

We had another few meetings of our Cancer Support Group and I arranged for a brunch at a local restaurant. A bug of some sort was going around the community and the get together had to be cancelled at the last moment. I never had another meeting again.

CHAPTER 32

JAW LUMP

I felt a lump inside my lower jaw and had a hard time swallowing. The first thing that came to mind is cancer. I had an appointment with Dr. Wurtz, my dentist at the time who said I should be seen immediately by my internist, an oncologist or a surgeon.

I didn't have an oncologist then. Instead I called Dr. Bucker who saw me the same day. "An ENT has to see you immediately." I asked about Dr. Connor, the first doctor to diagnosis me with erysipelas. He specializes in cancer and rare diseases. "I know him. He's the perfect choice."

Dr. Connor sent me for a CT scan and the test was negative. Every test he sent me for was negative. He felt the problem would go away. He was right. The lump just disappeared on its own.

A year later the lump reemerged. Dr. Wurtz, studied with a Dr. Otz who apparently had an unusual way of treating patients. Dr. Wurtz now seemed to have a sideline of not only doing dentistry but treating patients with Dr. Otz's methods. A major recommendation from a dentist or physician explaining why ordinary tests have not helped with a diagnosis is a prerequisite for seeing Dr. Otz.

Dr. Otz comes to NYC only once every few months. An appointment is made by your doctor or dentist. Dr. Wurtz said, "Stay in the city for the Friday night prior to Dr. Otz's arrival on Saturday but you must be at his hotel by 7:00AM that morning. Your appointment does not go by time." Apparently you just line up and hope Dr. Otz gets to see you. I was unaware of the line-up when Dr. Wurtz brought up the appointment with Dr. Otz.

Prior to seeing Dr. Otz, Dr.Wurtz said, "You must start abiding by the rules for wellness." Dr. Wurtz did something with his hands and pointed his fingers at the spot where there was a problem. I think the method has something to do with kinetic energy. Things became even weirder. "You must get a new wardrobe and bring the clothes to me before you wear them. Avoid all dyes."

During this process I discovered even whites are dyed. The whites I brought in for approval were a no-no. Dr. Wurtz did the same thing with his fingers on every piece of clothing. Several of his patients including myself held hands in his waiting room. None of us knew each other. He touched the fabric of each piece of clothing as the other patients continued holding hands. I started with twenty clothing items and only two passed the test. Dr. Wurtz gave me a list of additional personal objects to avoid. Ben and I went home wondering what I had gotten into.

The following week Ben had an appointment with Dr.Wurtz. He gave Ben a few unfamiliar nuts and had him buy a special light. He never told him what the light was for. It went in the trash when we moved. "Tell Rosalie Dr. Otz will be here on Saturday. Book a hotel room in Manhattan."

Hotels were either sold out or ridiculously expensive. Out of desperation I booked a room that was costly but took it for a lack of anything else. I had until Friday at 4:00PM to cancel.

On Thursday night Mrs. Wurtz called to remind me of what I was to take with me.

"Make sure you take the underwear and bra Dr. Wurtz approved." Dr. Wurtz never looked at my underwear.

"Your bra can have no metal or latex." I told her my prosthesis was in my bra and the bra had metal hooks in the back. I still had my right breast and it was quite large.

"I'll be lopsided without the bra." She put me on hold for a minute.

"Dr. Wurtz can't take you if he hasn't checked your underwear. You'll do it the next time Dr. Otz comes to NYC."

I cancelled the hotel reservation after informing Ben my underwear hadn't been checked by Dr. Wurtz. We laughed while breathing a sigh of relief.

When Dr. Wurtz saw me again he informed me I never would have been able to see Dr. Otz. People were lined up from the night before and the line was huge. Perhaps Dr. Otz is related to the religious healers who put their hands on your head or shoulders and tell the paralyzed person before them to walk. Miraculously the person gets up and walks. I don't think this kind of thing works for me.

Meanwhile my lump was still there. Dr. Connor sent me for a cookie test along with a few other tests. The diagnosis was Zenker's Diverticulum and was not malignant. The lump is supposed to be looked at every year. I went for a check-up the year after all the tests but not since then. I hope the lump stays away because I have enough to deal with.

CHAPTER 33

MY EYES

During one of my hospitalizations a freckle was discovered in my eye. Other doctors started to notice it too. The question of cancer came up. "Do not concentrate on that now. You're being monitored," I was told.

The day of an appointment to finalize the details of our house a new problem arose resembling a lightening flash across my eye. My doctor accommodated me immediately. The retina in my eye began to detach and I could have lost my vision.

Double vision became my next hurdle. This problem had been festering for a while. My ophthalmologist instructed me to wrap one of my eye glass lenses with a tissue until my normal vision returned. New Jersey laws permit you to drive with one eye. He retired and his partner sent me to a specialist who dealt with double vision. A temporary prism was attached to the lens of my glasses.

My neurologist in New York wanted me checked out by a specialist in his hospital. "It's imperative to find out if your double vision has any relation to your neurological problems." Fortunately they didn't. I wore my glasses with the temporary prism until my glasses broke. Dr. Mato continues to examine me periodically and so far she has been the only doctor capable of writing my lens prescriptions.

Another flash of light experience occurred in my other eye and I was taken care of by a retinologist in our new area. Both Dr. Mato and Dr. Winter discovered an ocular occlusion in my right eye at the same time. Dr. Winter began to give me shots in my eye to reduce the swelling and save my vision. My eye has reacted well to the shots and they are now spaced further apart from one another.

At first the shots made me very nervous. The first time I was given antibiotic drops to use afterwards and had an allergic reaction. The covering doctor misdiagnosed my condition for pink eye. I refused the antibiotic the next time and have been able to tolerate the shots better each time. I still have my vision.

On one particular visit Ben and I were sitting next to one another in a small area of the waiting room. Two women sat next to us in other chairs. My eyes were dilated. Out of nowhere the office seemed to sway and our bodies moved. The two women felt nothing. A man passed by speaking to no one in particular, "Did you feel the earthquake?" My mind filled up with thoughts of my doctor giving me a shot. *What if there was an aftershock and he missed his target as his body reacted to the earth's movement?* I told Dr. Winter my fear when I was called in for the shot. "There was an earthquake?" he asked. Apparently he didn't feel it either but his assistant did. The earthquake went up the East coast causing extensive damage to the Washington Monument in D.C.

I had been through an earthquake previously and didn't know it. I was in a hotel disco on one of the Caribbean islands. Many different effects were taking place in the large room and bar area. When the floor started to shake I thought it was one of those effects. I was amazed by the technology. The next morning I went down to breakfast with several others from our "FAM" (travel language for familiarization trip). We were greeted by two hostesses. "Did you feel the earthquake?"

CHAPTER 34

SECOND MASTECTOMY/BEN'S LAP BAND

Ben decided he was going to have lap band surgery. He was disgusted with the way he looked and all the weight he had gained. Eating is a very popular activity in a senior community. It's socialization 1.1. His doctors agreed it would probably be in his best interest and might help him reduce some of his medications.

I accompanied Ben to a meeting hosted by a specialist in the various techniques of stomach surgery. The doctor informed those in attendance of the parameters required for the surgery. Mass body weight was one of the biggest factors. I was surrounded by extremely large people in the room. Ben almost looked thin next to some of them. Many women were eyeing me and I am no slouch in the weight area. One person asked me outside the room if the doctor operated on me.

I listened to the lecture but Ben had to decide if, when and what type of surgery he wanted. I stayed out of it. He did the research and could decide which surgery was best for him. Since it was elective but important for his health I would support him in any way possible.

Ben made his decision. "I'm having lap band surgery." He made an appointment with the surgeon. I went into the examining room at his request and listened to the information disseminated by the assistant, pocketing the knowledge in my brain just in case Ben had questions afterwards. A nutritionist followed. Written instructions were reviewed. I had multiple questions since I was preparing Ben's meals. I don't believe Ben absorbed a thing that was said. He was too focused on the surgery itself.

The surgeon came in and went through the procedure showing us the ring to be placed around Ben's upper stomach. The hospital required him to stay overnight. Looking at me he said, "You can probably sleep in his room." That wasn't happening. I would find a hotel close by.

Ben needed a week to prepare for his surgery with a set diet. I had previously planned appointments for my mammogram, breast surgeon, and internist. My appointments were on a Monday and Ben was having his surgery on Thursday.

My wait was extremely long for my mammography and I approached the desk to ask what was going on. "We forgot to call you." They agreed to take me in next when I said I would be late for my next appointment.

My name was called in another twenty or so minutes. I undressed, put on a gown and walked to the machine to have my right boob squeezed and told to go back to my room and wait. The technician needed to take more pictures. I was on alert. After being flattened even tighter this time I was sent back to my room and waited again.

The wait was even longer this time and a red flag went up in my mind. The tech returned telling me the radiologist had to do an ultrasound immediately. "Can my breast surgeon do the ultrasound at my appointment in a few hours?" She left the room to consult with the radiologist. "The radiologist spoke with Dr. Bucker." The tension was starting to get to me and my nerves began to jump. I was late for my appointment with my internist and gave the tech the phone number to his office.

I was the cooperative patient and climbed onto the examining table. The radiologist came into the room and introduced himself. "Please face the wall." I heard someone else enter the room and was introduced to her by the radiologist. I couldn't see her in my position. She held onto my right arm. I had many ultrasounds but no one ever put a comforting hand on me during the test. This was a first. I was sure there was a reason.

The test was over and I was given the bad news. "You have a lump in your right breast that must be removed. I'm going to type up my report and hand deliver it to Dr. Bucker along with the films. You can roll over to your other side." A child's story book depicting an old fashioned kindly looking grandma with the requisite white hair stood in front of me. She gently put her arms around me. I looked up at the radiologist. "Is the bad news the reason she is here?" He shook his head nodding yes and that's when I started to cry.

Ben was called in and I repeated my diagnosis. He must have been in denial. "Let's see what Dr. Bucker has to say." The grandmother was a nurse and said to ask my internist for a sedative. I thanked her, got dressed and left for my appointment with Dr. Capp.

My mind was made up. I was going to have a mastectomy. Another lumpectomy was unacceptable. I had several scares in two years and couldn't handle anymore. I also wanted to avoid the same scenario I had with my left breast, a lumpectomy one week and a mastectomy the next. In certain areas of my life I had become very stubborn. This was my decision and nothing was going to change the way I felt.

When we arrived at Dr. Capp's office instead of a reprimanded for being so late I was immediately taken to an examining room. Dr. Capp came right in and I told him what happened. I gave him my reasons for my decision to have a mastectomy not a lumpectomy. He didn't even try to dissuade me.

It was Monday and Dr. Bucker operated on Tuesdays. I wanted my surgery the next day. Dr. Capp had no problem with it. "Ask Dr. Bucker to fax over the forms when you get to his office. I'll sign them immediately approving you for surgery."

Dr. Capp had no samples of sedatives and sent his aide to different doctors within his group office to find something for me. One of the doctors sent in a pill of his own.

Next I informed Dr. Capp about Ben's surgery on Thursday and how he had begun to prepare for it. I was bluntly told, "Your surgery comes first and if necessary take a limousine to the hospital." He kept reiterating how important my surgery was and it had to take precedent over Ben's. "I'll speak to Ben." He rushed out of the examining while telling me to meet him at the front desk. He too seemed unnerved. This was the third major cancer he was going through with me. Dr. Capp needed a sedative.

When I reached the appointment desk, Ben was walking through the doors. We both met Dr. Capp at the same time. Dr. Capp shook hands with Ben. "I understand you're having lap band surgery on Thursday." He mentioned a name and Ben acknowledged his surgeon. Dr. Capp said it was between the two of us but "Rosalie's surgery is the urgent one and has to be considered first." Ben said he understood.

Dr. Capp said he would see me in the hospital and reminded me to have Dr. Bucker send the surgical clearance form to him immediately. We drove to Dr. Bucker in relative silence.

I could not say no to Ben's surgery even though he asked me. His preparations had started for his surgery and we would have to deal with both our problems.

My mind was already working as to how we were going to handle the situation. I was prepared to have my surgery the next day. Ben could drive me to the hospital early the next morning and could stay at a hotel for the next two nights and drive himself to surgery on Thursday. Another choice would be to drop me off at the hospital, drive home that night and come back on Thursday for his surgery. He would have to leave the car parked in the hospital lot and we would take a limo back home. When one of us was able to drive we could take a limo back to the hospital and retrieve the car. Or we could just take a limo for all the trips back and forth to the hospital. First I had to ask Dr. Bucker.

As soon as I entered Dr. Bucker's office the look on the nurse and receptionist's faces gave them away. "You know." The nurse hugged me and took me back to what I called the surgery and testing room and I never sat down in the waiting room. I undressed while stating I wanted my breast off the next day. The nurse knew me well enough to know I meant it.

When Dr. Bucker came into the room he put his arm around me.

"I want you to do the surgery tomorrow. Dr. Capp is waiting for you to fax the surgery approval form over to him."

"I can't do the surgery tomorrow because of new hospital protocols but I can definitely do it next Tuesday." My plans were for naught and my brain started to conjure up new ones.

Additional testing had to be completed before my surgery. "Do you want me to cut and take the specimens now or return tomorrow and we'll do it in the hospital? The specimens need to be analyzed and cutting is necessary. If you chose my office I'll ask Ben to run the samples up to the hospital."

"Please do it right now."

After Dr. Bucker examined me I was placed in an operating position. "It hurts a bit but I'll give you some numbing shots first."

"Do most women choose to have the cutting done in the office?"

"Only the brave ones!"

"A very loud noise similar to a vacuum will occur several times during the procedure. The sound is worse than what is happening."

I handled the whole thing in my usual manner, I joked. "At the very least I will be even." Fortunately Dr. Bucker is a joker himself and I endured the procedure without tears.

I was bandaged up as though I had a mastectomy and the nurse donated her lunch bag to take my bra and left prosthesis home. Dr. Bucker gave Ben the specimens to take to the hospital and I waited in his office until he returned. "Do you want a pain killer for when the anesthesia wears off?" I declined.

Dr. Bucker's receptionist faxed Dr. Capp the medical approval form while I was given prescriptions for the tests needed at the hospital. My pre-admittance tests would be done the same day Ben went in for his surgery. The lymph test was set for the following Monday. The results of the specimens would be back by Friday at the latest.

Ben returned and I was given more hugs by the nurse and receptionist. "You'll be okay. You are in good hands."

We drove home and my head was drumming up new schemes. Ben asked me if I wanted him to go through with his surgery. I said yes without any thought about how it would affect me and my own recuperation.

My newest idea was to drive Ben to the hospital on Thursday, have my tests, stay at a hotel and take him home the next day. I would drive up to the hospital for my lymph test on Monday. We would stay at a hotel and then I would drive myself back to the hospital for my surgery with Ben as my passenger. We had to wait to see what Ben's doctor said about his driving after surgery to make final plans. I kept the thought of hiring a limo in the back of my head if necessary.

Mindy was going up to Bergen County on the day of my surgery to see her dentist. "I'll take Ben to his surgeon and if his doctor doesn't approve of his driving, I'll take him home. We'll come back the next day to get you." The car would remain in the hospital parking lot. "I'll drive up with Jack over the weekend and bring your car home." On the other hand if Ben's doctor gave him permission to drive he would stay at the hotel overnight and drive me home on Wednesday. Transportation was resolved.

CHAPTER 35

BEN'S SURGERY

Ben required liquids for his recuperation and I bought them while he continued to prepare for his surgery at home.

Another problem came up regarding my surgery. A tooth was pulled a few weeks before and I ended up with dry mouth. Dr. Capp suggested I ask my oral surgeon to write a note stating there was no infection at the tooth extraction site since it was not his area. The note was to avoid any problem with the hospital.

My oral surgeon lacks communication skills and I didn't relish the thought of asking him for the note. I spoke to one of his nurses who told me to come to the office. Ben's surgery was the next day. It was a very long ride to the oral surgeon and I was getting more nervous by the minute. Just as I hung up my friend Betsy called and insisted I not go by myself. I picked her up and we drove to the oral surgeon.

The doctor refused to give me a note. "It's your internist's job." I explained my internist filled out the forms but could not do anything about oral surgery; the approval had to come from him. His nurse begged him to write something. He did but the note did not indicate I was healed and well enough for surgery. The girls in his office wished me well and the nurse hugged me. She gave the doctor a dirty look and under his breath he said something I'm guessing was supposed to be positive.

Betsy saw me and knew something wasn't right. I showed her the note. "I hope the hospital accepts it." She cursed him and couldn't believe how cold hearted he was.

Very early Thursday morning we left the house with me driving to the hospital. Ben prepped himself the night before. We took my car since it was easier and more comfortable for me to drive.

I parked in a handicapped spot closest to the entrance. We left early and I had my choice of places to park. We entered the building and checked in at the desk. Ben went down to the surgical area by himself and I went to the lab. I would meet him as soon as my tests were completed. Several of my blood tests had to be done on an empty stomach and I was anxious to get them completed.

As promised I went to the lower level to be with Ben. My movements were robotic doing what was expected of me with a total lack of real emotion. I would fall apart if any feelings entered my psyche.

One of the nurses was kidding with me about what Ben would look like in a few months, thin. His doctor encouraged him to take before and after pictures. "I'm going to undergo a transformation myself next week but I'm not planning on taking before and after pictures."

Ben's surgeon came to see him and gave me directions where to meet him after the surgery. "You can sleep in Ben's room overnight." I had a hotel reservation but thanked him anyway. I really did not want to stay in the hospital and needed the one night's respite away from there.

Ben's turn arrived. I wished him good luck, kissed him, said good-bye and would see him later. My movements and statements were perfunctory. I was so worried about myself and the guilt was weighing on me as my husband was being taken into surgery.

I went up to the hospital lobby and realized I hadn't taken my medication or eaten. I finally broke down and did not know who to worry about first. Ben was in surgery. He should come first. But I was a nervous wreck waiting for Dr. Bucker to call about my test results.

I called my friend. "Could you sit with me in the hospital?" Linda came even though it was raining. She never drove in bad weather. I was so grateful. She said, "Let's go for something to eat."

Ben said there was a better place than Ledges Garden, *the eatery* in the hospital. There were more choices and it was cheaper. The hospital had grown quite large over the years. Linda and I were having trouble walking and wondered if this other eatery was a figure of Ben's imagination.

At last we saw sign for the cafeteria but we weren't allowed in. We argued but lost and made our way back to Ledges Garden.

Ledges Garden is quite big and extends a far distance in length. We were seated in the middle section next to the wall. The restaurant is run by volunteers. Linda ordered coffee and a muffin. I said lunch was on me. She didn't want anything else. I had absolutely no appetite. Linda pushed me to order something.

I called Dr. Bucker's office. The receptionist said Dr. Bucker was on with the hospital at that moment. I gave her my cell number. My phone rang just as I hung up. It was Dr. Bucker.

"You definitely need surgery. Do you want a lumpectomy?"

"Absolutely not! I refuse to go that route again. I've had too many emergency appointments for my right breast. I'm not capable of handling the tension any more. I don't want a lumpectomy one week and go back for a mastectomy the next week as I did for my left breast. I want my right breast off."

"Women who are in your position often choose the same path but I'm required to ask. Your nuclear test is set for Monday. I'll request a surgical room for Tuesday."

"Will there be a problem?" I inquired.

"No. I'm the head of the department but I have to go through all the formalities. I'll see you Tuesday morning. My office will call you with the time."

While my conversation with Dr. Bucker was taking place our volunteer waitress came over to me. "Get off the phone." This was not going to happen. She became very forceful while admonishing me and tried to grab my phone. Dr. Bucker asked, "What is going on?" He said to ignore her. Linda interrupted the waitress' tirade. "She's on with her surgeon. Let her finish the call."

Linda tried to convince me to try and save my breast.

"No way! I can't go through this anymore."

"Ask Jack for his opinion," said Linda.

"I'm not interested in anyone else's opinion. Dr. Bucker taught me to make my own decision about my body."

We left Ledges Garden and went to the sitting area to await Ben's doctor. Linda stayed another hour but the weather continued to deteriorate. She was afraid of driving in the heavy downpour. I thanked Linda for coming and we would certainly speak right after my surgery. "I'll call to see how Ben is."

Shortly thereafter Ben's surgeon came to speak to me. "Ben's in the recovery room and someone will come to get you when he is brought to his room. I want to see Ben in a week."

"I'm having a mastectomy this coming Tuesday. My daughter will take Ben for his follow-up appointment but the time frame is only five days out from his surgery. Will he be able to drive?"

"I'll know after I examine him." He wished me luck with my surgery and left.

This was turning out to be an exceptionally long day. It was almost 4:30PM and we had left the house about 5:30AM. I was totally worn out. Someone called Ben's name. I raised my hand and was given directions to his room. He wasn't there when I arrived.

A nurse came to tell me I could sleep in Ben's room overnight but I again declined. Ben was brought into his room and was on the gurney when I went over to him. I kissed him and tried to speak to him. He was out of it. He was transferred to his bed and a nurse came over to give him instructions. He wanted a drink. He's a diabetic. Between the diabetes and anesthesia he would be on a real thirst binge all night.

A limited number of staff is on at night to take care of the patients and a spouse is needed. They wanted me to stay and wait on him. It just wasn't happening. A nurse gave me instructions and when I repeated I wasn't staying she inquired why? I guess breast cancer was good enough to get me out of serving my husband that night.

I stayed with Ben until he came around and said I was leaving for the hotel. "The weather is very bad out and I'm unsure of where I'm going." I avoided telling him about myself. He was in no shape to listen in his post-surgical condition.

I ran in the biting rain and wind to my car. Another unanticipated part of my day began. I was familiar with the road showing the hotel's address.

I exited on the northern side of the highway for the same road leading to my mother's nursing home. I didn't recall a hotel along the route but a few years passed and perhaps one was built along the way. I previously checked with my friend who resided in the town. She too was having a difficult time remembering where the hotel was located or if she ever passed it. I kept driving on the correctly named road in the right town. There were no lights and the sky was almost black. The rain came down so hard and fast my windshield wipers couldn't keep up. I saw a light in the distance and aimed for it. It was an old barn turned into an antique store. I took a chance and pulled into the lot. The ground was saturated and I sunk into the mud heading to the door.

The owner was just closing up. I was on the right road going in the wrong direction. Unfortunately the road would not get me to the hotel. I had to head back to the highway, go north two exits, make a U-turn, head back south and get off the first exit. There was no exit sign for the road I needed. The road started up again once you made a right turn off the exit ramp of the highway. I would have to *"worm"* my way around to the front of the hotel.

I checked with the hotel and wasn't told anything about the convoluted roadway. Directions from MapQuest didn't help and the GPS was useless. By the time I arrived at the hotel dinner was being set up in the dining area. I checked in but was too tired to even make it to my room and come back out again. I cleaned up in the lobby's ladies room, put on some lipstick, and combed my wet hair.

I went back to the dining area hoping to emotionally pull myself together. I wasn't too successful. I put a call into my cousin. I desperately needed to speak to someone about my day but ended up leaving a message on her machine.

Food came out and I saw people rushing to it as though they had never eaten before. I decided to get something healthy and settled for a big salad. The salad sat on my table with me staring into it. Two Asian businessmen took a whole apple pie to their table. I thought Asians ate a more healthy diet than Americans. Nothing tempted me except the apple pie. I went to get some. "It's all gone," said the cook. I knew where it went to.

I parked my car at the closest entrance of the building where my room was located. I lifted my small rolling suitcase out of the car and headed for the door. A man tried to pick me up. He started in by offering to help with my suitcase. Then it really got hairy. "Can I take you to your room?" No he did not work there nor was it innocent the way he approached me.

He looked like a businessman who was probably looking for some fun while he was away from home. I was familiar with this when I did a lot of traveling for one of my jobs. He wasn't bad looking and was relatively well dressed. *What would he want with someone like me who looked like hell?* "I saw you in the dining room." He really was desperate.

What he didn't know is I had all I could possibly handle with one man and didn't need another at that moment. Also he would have been in for quite a shock when he saw a one breasted woman soon to be no breasted with scars all over her body. When Ben was feeling better I would tell him what happened. He might as well get a laugh out of it.

I tried everything possible to relax. I took a shower and put on TV. I called my daughter not telling her about my day only about Ben and the confirmed date for my surgery. I kept hoping my cousin would call back. I couldn't expect her to be there just because I needed to speak to someone.

I thought about calling my other cousin but she drives me crazy. You say something and then she has to relay it to her husband. The phone call usually can go on for hours and I'm not exaggerating. She says a phone call is a visit. A visit was not what I needed that night. I put in a wake-up call to the front desk just in case I fell asleep. I didn't have to return to the hospital until noon the next day and would be able to sleep a bit longer.

I must have dozed off at some point during the night. The ring of my phone woke me up. It was my cousin. She wanted to get back to me before she went to work. She had been to the theater the night before and came home very late. We spoke for a few minutes and she gave me some much needed support.

I showered, dressed and headed down to the dining area for breakfast. I kept an eye out for the man from the night before. If I spied him my plan was to walk in the opposite direction.

Before I checked out that morning I made a reservation for an additional two nights at the hotel starting with the night prior to my surgery. I packed my few things, brought my luggage to my car and left. It was much easier getting out of the hotel than getting in.

The sun was shining and it looked like it was going to be a beautiful day. Our vacuum cleaner had to be brought to the store where we purchased it for repairs. There was enough time to drop it off and then head to the hospital. Ben or Mindy would pick it up the day I was discharged.

I drove to the repair shop. The owner was able to fix the vacuum in-house and it could be picked up on the way home from the hospital. He agreed to wait until I returned.

I went to the hospital hoping the doctor discharged Ben. His doctor hadn't arrived. A call came from Dr. Bucker's office. One of the tests I took at Dr. Capp's office was unreadable at the hospital. He said to pick up a copy in his office on the way home and bring it to the hospital Monday morning. Since it was now encroaching on the staffs lunch time I was concerned no one would be there when I arrived. The nurse said she would wait for me.

Ben's surgeon showed up and I listened very carefully to the instructions. I was quite sure Ben was not concentrating. He received his written instructions and I went to get the car as Ben waited for transport. My luck wasn't as good as it had been the day before in terms of parking and my car was quite far from the hospital entrance.

The valets tried to chase me away while I waited for Ben but I refused to move. I saw Ben coming down the ramp inside the hospital through the glass windows. When a valet came over again I pointed to my husband and he walked away. The volunteer helped Ben get into the car and we left for Dr. Bucker's office. Dr. Bucker's nurse was waiting for me and again wished me luck. I drove to the vacuum store and as promised the owner also waited for me.

We drove home. After getting Ben settled I left the house for more items listed on his doctor's discharge paper. I had to get ready for my surgery.

CHAPTER 36

RIGHT MASTECTOMY

On Monday we left the house and I drove to Ledges for my nuclear test. I had to consciously keep a check on my nerves. Upon completion of my test we went to the hotel as planned. I had some dinner but Ben was only allowed liquids. I wasn't allowed any food after midnight.

On Tuesday morning I did my usual thing saying good-bye to my right breast, dressed and went into the dining room with Ben for breakfast. I ate nothing but he asked me to keep him company. He had liquids only.

"Can you put my overnight bag in the car?" he asked. I couldn't comprehend why he was taking it with him when the bag could remain in the hotel. I drove to the hospital turning right instead of left on the way there. I knew where I was and couldn't understand my error. This is what happens when you drive yourself to a hospital for a mastectomy.

Ben was ornery from his liquid diet and started to yell at me for my mistake. Just what I needed going into surgery. I found my way out and made it to the hospital on time.

I handed Ben all my belongings which were kept very light since he was still recuperating from his own surgery. After check in I went to the same area Ben was in a few days before. The nurse who took care of Ben actually remembered me.

My vitals were taken and an I.V. was to be inserted into my arm. I held firm in waiting for the anesthesiologist to insert the I.V. I refused to let a nurse try to find a vein.

Dr. Bucker came over to my gurney.

"Your nuclear test is fine."

"Are you going to mark me with a birdie?" He laughed and was surprised I remembered. It wasn't done anymore; bedsides he knew I only had one breast left.

"I'm going to scrub and I will see you in a few minutes."

The anesthesiologist came over to my gurney. I never saw her before and thought I knew them all. After the usual questions she said, "I'll be waiting for you in the operating room." She was very pleasant. Most anesthesiologists have no personality. I've dealt with so many of them I feel comfortable making that assessment.

Mindy arrived to take Ben to his appointment. They wished me luck and would see me later. They both kissed me good-bye and I was on my own. The orderlies came for me as they were walking out.

The anesthesiologist was terrific and used an oral device to put me out. She must have inserted my I.V. afterwards because I felt nothing.

Ben was in the recovery room when my surgery was over. He was given the okay to drive and cancelled the hotel room for the night. "I'm going home and will come back for you tomorrow. Mindy will be up to see you as soon as her dental appointment is finished." I asked him to call me when he arrived home.

My pain threshold is so high I didn't really feel too badly. Dr. Bucker came to see me and said everything went as anticipated. "Do you need a pain killer?" I declined. He kissed me good-bye. "I'll see you in the morning." I was transferred to my room. My bed was near the window.

On the day of my surgery I noticed my right arm and hand were swollen. I worried about lymphedema. Where the heck was I going to put a watch now? I thought about my grandmother's neck watch. It really was a costume piece but I treasured it because it was hers. Perhaps someone could get it to work again.

My daughter stopped by to see me after her dental appointment. I was really happy to see her and mentioned my right hand and arm were swollen. My concern was where I would wear a watch. "You'll get one to wear around your neck. That's just a minor issue." *Funny how my mind worked!* I didn't think of my now missing right breast as a problem but instead worried about lymphedema. *How does one function with lymphedema in two hands, wrists and arms?*

A roommate was brought in during the night. It must have been her first time in a hospital. I gathered this from her rather loud conversations. She wasn't much younger than me but was completely oblivious as to how lucky she had been in her life. Flowers started to arrive for her as soon as the sun came up. I received many beautiful floral arrangements after my first spinal laminectomy. It never happened again. Perhaps I was jealous. She had a hard time accepting the fact she was in a hospital. She was yakking the whole time on the phone. I really didn't care. I was going home.

I caught myself realizing just how lucky I had been. All my cancers were found. I had many spinal surgeries but I wasn't in a wheelchair. Even with all my other issues I was still a functioning human being. That's lucky! Most of my doctors have credited me for playing a big role in my own recuperation. More than once doctors told me most of their patients would have given up. If I wake up and I'm breathing then I have to function to whatever degree I can.

Dr. Bucker came to see me and I pointed out my swollen arm and hand. After a thorough examination he thought it was coming from the I.V. It would take a while to know definitively.

He checked my bandages, asked me how I felt and if I remembered how to empty the drains. He gave me a refresher course and said the nurse would go over it again. He was giving orders for a visiting nurse to see me at home. I was to call his office and make an appointment for the following week. He kissed me good-bye telling me to call him if I needed anything.

I phoned Ben. "I'm being discharged." He was still sleeping and I woke him up. His ride was a long one back to the hospital and Ben admitted he should have stayed at the hotel. "Call Mindy and ask her to pick me up," I suggested. He wanted to drive himself.

Someone came to speak to me about a visiting nurse service. The lady was going to check on a service in Central NJ. She returned with a full sheet of instructions. "Call the nursing service as soon as you arrive home," she said.

A nurse went over my discharge papers and reviewed emptying the drains, the measuring and recording of the fluids. She gave me the containers for measuring and put all the material in a plastic bag.

Ben arrived but he had to park a distance away from the front of the hospital. Even though I had the heavy mastectomy bra on with many padded bandages I was flat chested and clothes didn't seem to be an issue this time as with my first mastectomy. There was no need for one of Ben's shirts. I was able to wear my own top home. A nurse said, "I'm calling transport." She told Ben to get the car and pull up in front of the hospital entrance.

This time it was not a volunteer taking me down but an aide from the hospital. *Did she ever like to talk to anyone and everyone she met?* When we embarked from the elevator to the first floor two women stopped my transport lady and asked her a question. The women kept asking questions and the aide kept talking. Finally I interrupted. "My husband is waiting for me with the car."

As we were going down the same ramp where I spotted Ben, I saw a big to do in front of my car. Sure enough the valets hassled Ben. One of them directed Ben to pull back using his hand to show him where to go. Ben backed into a pole damaging my car. The valet took off and as far as I know never to be seen again.

The security chief was filling out a form about the accident. People saw the valet take off but no one knew his name. Ben was livid because he couldn't find my insurance card and registration. Mrs. Talkative wanted to get me into the car. The paper work for my car was strewn all over the place. Ben was unaware he was berating me because of the car's missing papers. I knew they were there but in the mess it was impossible to find them. I put a call into our agent but the security guard refused to speak to her. Ben wanted a copy of the report and was ordered to "Pick it up next week," by the security chief.

Ben got behind the wheel and I sat with strewn papers all around my feet and ankles on the drive home. After pulling into the garage my goal was to rest and hide from the tense situation between us. First I put a call into the nursing service. Someone would call within 24 hours to set up a schedule.

CHAPTER 37

OUR RECUPERATION

I took care of my drains. It was like learning to ride a bike. Once you learn you never forgot. Putting it in perspective I never learned to ride a bike but the saying is applicable in this instance. I was hungry. One of my friends made some meals for me and I heated up my dinner in the microwave. I asked nothing from Ben. I wasn't feeling very good about myself. Ben had no qualms about asking me to bring him his liquid drinks because he was feeling miserable. Here I am twenty-four hours away from my mastectomy, not just serving myself but Ben too.

Another friend brought over some food. Thank goodness I had the meals and a working microwave.

I didn't hear from the nursing service and put another call through. I was supposed to hear within an hour. This went on for another 24 hours. I left a message again. This went on every day. No one showed up. Not only was my blood pressure to be taken but my wound was to be checked for infections and my drains were to be monitored. No one called me.

By Friday I decided to call the hospital and reached a human voice. "Your nursing service was approved by Medicare and the hospital is unable to make changes." The lady said she was going to call the nursing service and have them get back to me. A few hours later I received a call and was informed someone was authorized to see me.

"You should have been seen at least twice."

"No one showed up nor have I received any replies to my calls."

"Someone will definitely be there today." Again no one showed or called.

I called the nursing service again the following Monday and left a message. On Tuesday my message to nursing service took on another tone. "I'm seeing my doctor tomorrow and he's not going to be very happy with your lack of nursing care." By 4:30PM that day I received a call from someone who promised to be at the house by 6:00PM.

A nurse arrived who knew nothing about breast cancer. She had absolutely no idea what she was supposed to do. She took my blood pressure and looked under my bandages. She couldn't help with the drains.

Meanwhile Ben was miserable and avoiding me. At first I thought it had to do with the car but soon realized that was not the case. *What was the problem?* Then I assumed he was angry because I lacked breasts. I so very much needed him to put his arms around me and tell me he still loved me. *Anything but happened!* Ben closely passed by me making sure we didn't touch. I could deal with having my breast removed but the feeling of rejection depressed me to no end.

Ben drove me to Dr. Bucker the next day. An insensible feeling went through me. I was happy in Dr. Bucker's office. The women came out to hug and greet me.

"How do you feel?"

"Before this mastectomy I felt like a unicorn." They laughed.

Dr. Bucker examined me and looked at the drains. He aspirated more fluid from the surgical area and changed my bandages. I told him about the nursing service. "Forget about the nurse. If they can't send a knowledgeable nurse by now they probably don't have any. You're doing a good job. I'll see you next week."

We stopped at the hospital for Ben to pick up the security report for my car. It couldn't be found. Ben was given a phone number of a person to call.

My situation with Ben was affecting my recovery to the point I couldn't sleep and wondered if our marriage was over. I was determined to find out. That night I asked Ben to speak me. I stated how I felt since he was completely ignoring me. "I just had a surgery that makes any woman feel terrible and unfeminine. Is that the problem?"

He apologized for making me feel that way. "It has nothing to do with you. It has to do with my surgery and only being able to drink liquids for three weeks." He again apologized for losing his temper. "I am miserable and never expected my recuperation to be like this."

Obviously in terms of my own healing process I made a bad decision in agreeing to have Ben forge ahead with his surgery. It's all water under the bridge now and we both survived. I don't know of anyone else who has driven themself to the hospital for a mastectomy or managed care of their own drains. I know many, many women who have had mastectomies and even single women who had other friends and family help out. I guess we can be stronger than we think we are.

No wonder I have no patience with women who complain about breaking a fingernail. Don't even tell me that is your biggest problem. I have absolutely no sympathy for you no matter how harsh that sounds.

Dr. Bucker received the biopsy report and other information from the lab and called me. He kept repeating, "I'm glad you insisted on a mastectomy. You would have been in real trouble if we waited until your next mammography." I could hear him breathe a sigh of relief. "I'm going to consult with my team and we'll determine if you should be put on medication." This mastectomy wasn't an open and shut case as my first one.

Dr. Bucker continued, "There is no rush to go on the medication." After the first mastectomy I was deemed not a candidate for Tamoxifin and nothing else was on the market at the time. Now there were several other options. I was familiar with the names of now available drugs to help ward off a recurrence of breast cancer.

I continued to see Dr. Bucker at least once a week to be checked and have fluid drained. At one of my visits I asked him about a swollen area in my back. He didn't think it was lymphedema at the time attributing it instead to swelling from all the cutting during surgery. The swelling on my right hand subsided and went down on my right lower arm. I was able to wear a watch on my right hand.

I saved all my paraphernalia from my first mastectomy and was able to use much of it for the second one including the comfortable mesh tube that went around my upper body. It held up my bandages without using band aids or wearing my surgical bra. It was much more comfortable than anything else I had.

I did not need the extra-large shirts and blouses saved from my first mastectomy. I was flat chested and my regular tops fit better than before my surgery. Everyone remarked about how thin I looked. That's what happens when you no longer have C sized breasts. It did not account for the fact my stomach area was now emphasized.

CHAPTER 38

BODY HAIR

Prior to the discovery of my second breast cancer I was having a major problem with hair growth on my face, body and breast area. I mentioned it to every doctor I saw. The answer was always the same, electrolysis. This went on for years but the hair growth was getting worse and worse. My technician said something had to be medically wrong.

My gynecologist asked, "Did you ever have a testosterone level check?" When I answered in the negative she gave me a prescription to have the test taken. The results were also sent to Dr. Capp.

The test results were not in when I heard about my right breast cancer. Testosterone was pushed to the back burner.

A week after my mastectomy I left Dr. Bucker's office and went to see Dr. Capp for a follow up visit. I remembered to ask for the testosterone test results. He was unusually serious. The results came in the day before and he didn't know how to tell me. "I wanted to see your progress since the mastectomy and I was going to use the weekend to think about a way to give you the results of your lab tests." My immediate thought, *"Is there such a thing as testosterone cancer?"* Or more sensibly a by-product of one of the organs that produce it!

My testosterone levels were almost off the chart. Something had to be done about it. "I didn't want to throw you from one bad scenario into another within a week. I wanted to let your body have a chance to heal."

I was going to attack this issue A.S.A.P. I think he was shocked to see me take such an aggressive attitude to reconcile the situation when I just had the mastectomy. I continued to amaze him. An endocrinologist was imperative and I asked for a recommendation. I had two horrible experiences in Central NJ with endocrinologists in two separate offices.

I was refused a visit to both doctors and my appointment was not even acknowledged in both places. Each office sent paper work for me to be filled out prior to my visit. The date and time of my appointments was written on their paper work.

"Where would I have gotten the paper work from if you didn't send it to me?" I asked at both offices.

"It doesn't matter if you have paper work. It was sent in error." I was not allowed to see the doctor in either office.

The best one Dr. Capp knew was Dr. Charles. I knew her. She was the head doctor in the office where Ben went for his diabetes. Ben initially wanted to see her but she was too busy. I asked Dr. Capp if he could call from his office to get me an appointment. "You'll have to wait months to get an appointment with Dr. Charles. I could try with one of the other doctors in the same office." He mentioned the name of Ben's doctor. He was definitely acceptable and Dr. Capp agreed to make the call.

If more surgery was called for and done within thirty days of my mastectomy I wouldn't have to have all the pre-admittance tests again. I was on a mission to complete my newest dilemma before thirty days were up.

Dr. Capp's secretary called for an appointment for me with Dr. Charles expecting a negative response. Luck again was on my side. There was an opening for the following Tuesday only three business days away. Dr. Capp was surprised. "You'll like her. I'll forward all your test results."

Dr. Charles examined me thoroughly. "Testosterone in a female is made in the adrenal glands primarily or in the ovaries. Since you are minus one adrenal gland I'm ruling out the other one as the problem but I'm sending you for a test to make sure. Once the results are in I'll make a recommendation about your ovaries."

I followed Dr. Charles into her office and Ben was called in. Another wrench was thrown into the works. Ben was on a testosterone product prescribed by his doctor. Fortunately Ben's doctor was in the office and Dr. Charles left the room to consult with him. It was decided Ben should go off the testosterone for a week. I was given new directions. "Wash all clothes and linen with gloves on." She handed me numerous pairs of rubber gloves. "You are not to go near Ben until all his clothes are washed." She shook her head in disbelief. "I'll see you in a week."

I wasn't worried about Ben going near me. As stated above he avoided me as though I had a contagious disease. It turned out he could possibly be the one causing my problem. I had to keep my sense of humor.

We went home and Ben dumped all his clothing in the laundry room. He was feeling sorry for himself. My arm and shoulder were still stiff and I had hanging drains. I was feeling sorry for myself too. I put on the rubber gloves and started to do washes. Ben had to help doing the laundry or he would be walking around the house nude.

The following week my appointment with Dr. Charles was prior to my seeing Dr. Bucker. My test results were negative for testosterone of my adrenal gland. On examination testosterone from Ben's medication was ruled out. He could start *using* again.

The only thing left was my ovaries. "Is there cancer involvement?" I asked. "I'm not sure but I can definitively say yes to testosterone." She answered. "You really do not need your ovaries and *if it was me*, I would just have them removed."

She knew of a doctor in New York. I needed a special surgeon dealing with cancer. I wondered how we would continue to juggle all the doctors and hospitals in different cities and states. Dr. Charles asked me to call her the next day and she would have a name for me.

I told Dr. Bucker about my latest problem. "I have a perfect team of doctors for you." The biggest problem was getting an appointment within the time frame I wanted. Dr. Bucker's nurse called their office giving them all my information. My appointment was four or five days before my thirty days were up.

The next day I called the newest surgeons office and was told to have all my paperwork sent to them or the doctor would not see me. I called my other doctors' offices asking my reports be forwarded to Dr. Feinberg giving their staff his fax, telephone number and address. Dr. Charles' office was the first one called requesting my paper work be sent as soon as possible to Dr. Feinberg.

Every few days I called Dr. Feinberg's office to ask if there was a cancellation. Each of the two doctors in the practice only came in the office once a week. The rest of the time they were in surgery.

The week before my appointment I received a phone call from Dr. Feinberg's office. "Your reports and records were not received from Dr. Charles and they are needed the most." I put a call into Dr. Charles' office. The receptionist said, "I'll pass the message to the person handling files." I specified the material was imperative for the surgeon.

A few days later I again received a call from Dr. Feinberg's office. "Dr. Charles' material still has not arrived." Once again a call to Dr. Charles' office ended with the same spiel as the time before. "I'll pass the message to the person handling files." We were going up to Bergen County the next day and I asked Ben to stop at Dr. Charles's office.

I wrote down all of Dr. Feinberg's information on a piece of paper. Ben waited in the car and I went up to Dr. Charles' office. I waited my turn. There was one very miserable person working there. Prior to my starting with my endocrinologist, other people complained about this staff member including Ben. She was at the desk. "Dr. Feinberg's office never received my information." I requested his name, fax and phone number be given to the person in charge and handed her the piece of paper with the information on it.

"We don't need it. We know who Dr. Feinberg is." I insisted the receptionist take my paper.

"Please make sure your information is correct." She did me a big favor by taking it from me. I was quite certain I saw her crumble up my note and toss it into the garbage.

The day before my appointment with Dr. Feinberg I received another call from his office. "Your records still haven't arrived at our office." I immediately called Dr. Charles and was given the same runaround as previously. This time I refused to let them off the hook.

"I'm picking up a copy of my records before I go to Dr. Feinberg tomorrow. Make sure they are ready by twelve noon." My appointment was for 1:00PM. Dr. Charles' staff blamed everyone at Dr. Feinberg's office for not having the records they supposedly sent over. It's good they didn't take that as a deposit to the bank. I was polite but firm and reiterated, "I'm picking up the records and have them ready for me by twelve noon." The person I spoke to agreed to place my records at the front desk.

Ben and I left our house early but traffic was heavy. It was a rainy day and the inclement weather contributed to the problems on the road. We arrived at Dr. Charles office a few minutes later than expected.

I went upstairs to get my records and again had a long wait. I was concerned about being late for my appointment with Dr. Feinberg. The disliked woman at the desk was arguing with each person on line in front of me. Her attitude gave her a sense of power.

My turn came and I asked for my records. She couldn't find them. After another delay I was given an envelope found exactly where it should have been. As I was signing for the envelope she grabbed her umbrella, put on a rain hat and ran out the door before I had a chance to turn around and leave the office.

CHAPTER 39

MORE SURGERY DISCUSSION

Ben was just getting out of the car as I came downstairs. I was going to be late. "What was the holdup?" I explained as he drove to Dr. Feinberg's office. The office was in another town. Ben dropped me off and went to park the car.

I checked in at the front desk and took the elevator to the doctor's office. I signed in and was given a stack of papers to fill out. I offered the large envelope with my records but was told to hold it until I brought up the rest of the completed forms.

My cheat sheet covered many of the questions but one required an answer I was sure was in the records from Dr. Charles. I opened the envelope and saw a covering letter. It was written to a Dr. Feinberg in Teaneck. I now knew the source of the problem regarding my records. They were sent to the incorrect doctor.

Ben arrived and seats were at a premium. No two were together. I handed him the letter and he brought it to his seat to read. He verbalized out loud, "I can't believe the incompetence." Obviously I was correct when I saw Dr. Charles' receptionist throw away the paper with Dr. Feinberg's information.

My paper work was completed and I brought it up to the front desk with my records. I showed the receptionist the cover letter in the envelope made out to the incorrect Dr. Feinberg. A voice from behind the desk bellowed out, "I'm the one who kept calling you." She shook her head in utter disbelief. "The doctor likes to see the records before he examines the patient. He takes them home with him to review and become familiar with the situation. I'll explain the error to Dr. Feinberg so he won't be upset with you."

A seat opened up near where I was sitting and Ben moved over. We came to the same conclusion. Dr. Charles should definitely be told.

I was called into the examining room and the aide did not know how to take my blood pressure on my leg or thigh. She had an excessive amount of a perfumed product on her body. I started to lose my voice, a sign of an onset of an asthmatic attack. "I have to work with someone devoid of perfume." She was very insulted. I heard her tell another lady about the difficult patient in the room.

Another lowly person was insulted. I didn't come to see her. I came to see the doctor who employed her. Furthermore after the experience I had with the control freak in Dr. Charles' office, I really didn't care how she felt. I had to protect myself.

The doctor entered the room. "I was taking some time to read your records before I examined you." I was advised to ask for a mesh to be added at the time of my surgery to prevent urinary leakage. It was much easier to do when having an oophorectomy. I inquired about a full hysterectomy. "Yes to the mesh but no to the hysterectomy. I do no other surgery than what is needed. There can be dangerous consequences for doing more." My mind was thinking the more unnecessary organs removed from body the less I had to worry about cancer.

"The surgery is done through two tiny incisions on both sides of your tummy area. Robotic arms actually perform the removal as I manipulate them." I requested the anesthesiologist who was with me a few weeks before at my second mastectomy.

He gave me the name of the surgeon I was to call for the mesh. They worked together all the time. The two of them would coordinate my surgery date but it would be taking place within the next two weeks. "I'll see you in the hospital. The girls in the front will give you all the information you need."

One woman worked with me and set up the hospital date a week from the following Monday. I was to report to one day surgery at 6:30AM.

My appointment with the urologist for the mesh was set up almost immediately. I had to redo all my blood work. I was unable to meet my goal of having everything taken care of within thirty days. My EKG was still acceptable. I was given the phone number of the anesthesiology department and told to request the person I wanted.

We drove home planning for my next surgery. There was absolutely no way I could possibly, even if I wanted to, kiss my ovaries good-bye.

CHAPTER 40

THE UROLOGIST

We drove to the urologist two days later and realized we were going to same office as the urologist Ben was using. My guy was the specialist in the mesh area. I was told he is a most congenial fellow and indeed he is.

What I'm going to say next is disgusting but then again we all endure revolting tests e.g. colonoscopies. My goal is to not only to tell my experience but for you to be prepared if a sling or mesh is suggested to you. No one will discuss beforehand what you will endure. If anything the testing procedures will be sanitized verbally. Since you are awake and must cooperate you might as well know what to expect.

It was obvious the urologist was wearing a very expensive suit, shirt and tie and yet only put on gloves when he examined me. He assuredly used his hand for examinations and tube placement in the vagina of many women that day. I wondered if he sent his suits to the cleaner's on a continual basis. I thought it would be more appropriate if he removed his jacket, rolled up his sleeves and put on a medical jacket. This may not have anything to do with his surgical abilities but it left a sanitary question in my mind. The pre-surgical testing was a two day affair.

His aide was an R.N. She couldn't take my blood pressure and neither could the doctor. He asked me to find out how to do it. I called my cardiologist and was told to stop in their office for someone to show me. It's a rarity when someone actually knows how to take my blood pressure on my leg or thigh. I was now minus two arms to take my blood pressure because of the double mastectomy and lymphedema. The urologist wanted me to teach him when I returned for the second part of my test.

We left his office and went to the cardiologist. After somewhat of a wait I was called in and was shown by the nurse practitioner how to take my blood pressure both on my leg and thigh. "I'll take your blood pressure and write it on a prescription pad in case the doctor still has difficulty," he said.

I was totally unprepared for my next day's visit to the urologist's office. My wait wasn't too long to be taken into the examining room but I struggled emotionally with the rest of my exam. I showed the R.N. how to take my blood pressure but she wasn't successful. I was handed a short paper gown to change into and I mean short. One of those the doctors use when they are only examining your top quarter of your body and you keep your pants or skirt on. Only I was completely nude except for this ridiculous paper top without anyway to secure it. My scars were evident and one was still very raw.

My shoes and socks were off and I was told to sit in a chair while waiting for the doctor. I didn't like the idea of placing my naked butt on a chair that someone else may have sat on. I spied a paper towel container and removed enough towels to cover the seat of the chair. I removed a sheet from the examining table and covered myself. I didn't care what the directions were. The sheet could easily be removed.

When the doctor came in and shook my hand. Something in me wanted to scream. It was as if he was making a deal with a prostitute. I also didn't know where his hand and lower part of his arm had been. He again was dressed immaculately in an expensive suit, shirt and tie. His square gold cuff links gave me the chills as I thought about the probability of the sharp corners scratching me when he examined me.

I gave the urologist the prescription with my blood pressure written on it. He took out a stethoscope. "Can you show me how to do it?" He moved from my thigh to my ankle. He claimed he heard something on my ankle but not in the back of my knee.

Then all the indignities really started. I climbed onto the table with the sheet covering me. The nurse removed the sheet and hell was about to begin. During my preliminary exams a narrow tube was first inserted into my vaginal area. A larger tube was inserted afterwards. On this day the larger tube was used first.

I soon found out why my socks and shoes were removed and why I only had a short gown on the second day. I stood up on a hospital bed liner with the blue plastic on one side and soft white cotton on the other with my legs spread apart. A pail was between my legs.

The doctor controlled a machine filling my body with water. It must have somehow been connected to the tube that was inserted in me but it was out of my visionary field. The nurse kept adjusting the tube. If I thought giving birth was intrusive and stole my dignity, this test surpassed it. At least you had a child to show for it when you give birth. I would never see the mesh. The test is the female version of waterboarding.

After the erect test was completed I went through the same thing sitting down. This time the test was done on a hospital potty with the pail beneath it. My craziness set in and I refused to sit down until I was reassured by the nurse the seat had been sanitized.

Throughout the process the doctor entertained himself or perhaps he thought he was taking my mind off all the indignities by singing. "America, America" or "Downtown Races, Do Dah" sung with an Asian accent. Perhaps it might have been hysterical if I wasn't in such a horrendous position.

The tests were finally over. "Dress and meet me in my office." I wanted to use the bathroom but there was none available in the room. I had no choice but to get dressed first. If any examining room ever needed its' own bathroom, this was it.

Ben met me in the doctor's office. While we waited I gave him a very brief overview of the tests. "You don't look great." I pretty much looked the way I felt.

The cheery happy go lucky doctor entered his office with all the test results.

"You have two problems." Really! After the indignities I felt as though I could add another.

"One problem is leakage when you sneeze, cough or laugh. The sling will help that. The other is just holding you urine under normal circumstances. The sling won't help that condition. Go to the bathroom very frequently." He suggested a two hour time period whether I felt like going or not.

"I can give you medication." I nixed that idea. I was on too much already and might soon be going on a cancer drug.

"I will be doing your surgery immediately after your oophorectomy. I have already spoken to Dr. Feinberg."

What is interesting to note is neither he nor Dr. Feinberg said anything about my back or described the position I would be placed in. This is the one thing covered when I was in Tremore. This failing became a major issue. I know now I myself must bring it up if a doctor doesn't.

CHAPTER 41

DOUBLE SURGERY

Surgery prep was standard, no medication, food or liquid after midnight. The alarm went off at 4:00AM though I don't think Ben and I had much sleep during the night. We headed out by 5:00AM and arrived at the hospital a half hour early. We were concerned about problems on the road but at that hour traffic moved freely.

I checked in and Ben went to get something to eat. He was on solid food by then. I was brought to my bed in the day room. All of the beds were separated by curtains. My bed was on the end facing the right side of the large room. There had to be at least twelve beds, six on each side. I was the first one to arrive but within a few minutes the beds started to fill up.

The nurses came to check my vitals and review my records. I refused to let them insert an I.V. into my arm. I didn't want them digging around until they found a vein only to tell me they had to try another area. I was previously called a professional patient and knew exactly what was best for ME!

Ben came back to the room about 7:00AM. I was using the clock in the room to keep checking the time. Other patients were taken out and I was still there. By 8:00AM there was a complete turnover of patients. I was bored, hungry and didn't have my medication.

About 9:00AM the urologist came in to see me. He was leaving for his office.

"How do you know when to return to the hospital to do my surgery?"

"I will be called and will come right over."

I envisioned him trying to find a parking spot while I had to spend additional time under anesthesia.

"There is no problem and do not worry." I thought the time warranted the following question.

"Why wasn't I taken into surgery since I had to be in the hospital at 6:30AM and was scheduled for 7:00AM?"

"You have to ask the other doctors."

Change overs with the beds seemed to be happening every hour with a few patients leaving in between yet I was still there. Ben got very impatient and left to get coffee. One of my surgeons arrived about 11:00AM. He said Dr. Feinberg and himself were a team working together on the surgery. I was already aware of that and it was a non-issue for me especially since he was the one Dr. Bucker recommended in the first place.

The anesthesiologist I requested was hung up with another patient and they were waiting for her. In the meantime they completed surgery for someone scheduled after me. He left with the very familiar comment, "I'll see you in the operating room."

By 11:30AM the whole room was empty except for me. Ben returned and we tried to entertain each other. He started to sing. He had been a band leader and music teacher so the songs were coming easily to him. "Let's dance." I left my bed and went into his arms. He sang and we danced to our own music.

Lost in our own world we were brought back to reality when a nurse proclaimed very loudly, "I've been at this job for thirty years but this is the first time I've ever seen this." Her comment brought several other workers and nurses into the room. I just made sure Ben kept his hand on my backside so my gown didn't fly open.

Ben was turning me around and I noticed a woman behind a curtain of another bed. She was typing away on her laptop. If we had seen her initially we probably wouldn't have started dancing. The lady must have been waiting for a patient to come back from the O.R. She looked up for a sec when the nurse made her comment and then went right back to whatever she was doing. Usually you must leave the area and stay in a waiting room. *How do some people manage to by-pass rules?* I'm glad she didn't prevent me from having some fun. The dancing helped get my mind off the long wait. By the time our dance was over there was a large crowd in the room and outside the door. We were given a round of applause.

Shortly after our performance my anesthesiologist entered the room. She apologized for taking so long. She was on a very early surgery and there turned out to be complications. "The record department sent me your incorrect file. I'm waiting for the correct one. Surgery will start as soon as I receive it. Your surgeons are waiting for me."

None of my medications or fluids had been given to me and I only had one kidney. "I'll have you on an I.V. very shortly but a different type of anesthesia is necessary from your previous one. You absolutely need an I.V. in a vein. I'll numb each site and work with you."

Finally and I mean a big finally, I was taken to the O.R. Ben kissed me good-bye and would see me later. I was to return to the same area and bed.

A major problem came up in the O.R. when I was transferred to the cold metal operating table. My back was hurting. I was accommodated with a pillow under my knees. My anesthesiologist was having an impossible time locating a viable vein but as promised she numbed each site. I was going to be black and blue all over my right arm and hand. My left could not be used. The anesthesiologist turned to someone saying in a tone of voice I hadn't heard before, "If you don't raise the table I'm going to be in the same shape as my patient."

You are probably much better off being out cold when they bring you into the operating room so you don't hear or see anything. Unfortunately all my surgeries in the last twenty years in various hospitals no longer use this procedure. Therefore you have the wonderful opportunity to see all of the apparatus including the sharp knives and cold sleek steel equipment peeking out on a table covered by a white sheet. The thought that these instruments are going to be used on you are a good enough reason to make you jump off the table and say, "I'm outta here!" You must remind yourself to be brave as you remember what put you in this position in the first place.

The anesthesiologist wasn't having much luck and I suggested a vein. "If it doesn't work I'll have to insert the I.V. in your foot. I'm trying to avoid it." The foot is a very painful area and if the I.V. stays in after the surgery your walking ability is severely limited. I heard her breathe a sigh of relief and knew I would be out in a few seconds.

CHAPTER 42

ADMITTANCE

I awoke in the dayroom and on my bed. The pain was excruciating. It was a 12 out of 1-10. Ben said it was almost seven o'clock and no one was in the dayroom but me. The staff started to go home. I had to go to the bathroom to be released. "I can't move."

I couldn't get off the bed. Ben tracked down someone on staff telling them I couldn't move.

"She has to move because the room is shutting down."

"Get a supervisor." The woman left the room and came back with someone else.

"Get off the bed and go to the bathroom so we can send you home," she admonished me.

As hard as I tried my body wouldn't cooperate. My pain was way off the scale. Working together they managed to get me up. Ben and the first woman held on to me. The other one left to get a walker. My legs refused to hold me and there was no end to the pain.

With the use of the walker, Ben and the women, I made it to the bathroom. I refused to sit on the seat.

"It's filthy from a whole day of being used by everyone passing through this room."

I agreed to sit if a high pile of toilet paper was placed on the seat. I directed one of the women to paper placement. Not enough here, not enough there and so on. If they weren't in a rush to leave I'm sure the cooperation wouldn't have been as great.

Now it was time to sit me down. I didn't think the pain could get any worse but it did. I was unable to sit. I screamed. "Help me up." They got me back into bed. I couldn't catch my breath and it scared the women. Ben refused to take me home in that condition.

"My wife has to be admitted."

The women were reluctant to call the doctors. Staff at the desk had left for the night. The two women wanted to leave. It was almost 8:00PM. Ben threatened the women.

"I'll report you."

One left the room and returned shortly afterwards. She spoke to one of my first surgeons. He refused to admit me. He claimed I was fine when their portion of my surgery was completed. If my pain was so bad she should call the last surgeon.

Ben insisted one of the women make the call. It was now after 8:00PM and the cleaning crew came into the room to prepare for the next day. They were cleaning around my bed. The door to the room was to be locked after they left. Ben warned them.

"Do not lock my wife in the room." My I.V. was still in place and I never had my medication. *Did anyone have any common sense?*

One of the women agreed to call the other surgeon. Realization must have set in she wasn't going to get paid overtime. She had to get rid of me one way or another. She reached a covering doctor and he agreed to admit me. I didn't leave the dayroom until close to 10:00PM. I still had none of my medications, liquid or food. Ben went with me to my new room and gave me the medication bottle I keep in my bag. He left for home and promised to call when he arrived. "I'll bring back anything you need tomorrow."

I had a very good nurse. She brought me water and encouraged me to take my own meds since there were no orders from any doctor. If I didn't take them the hospital would have to treat me for all my other conditions. The pain wouldn't subside but at least no one was forcing me to get up, go to the bathroom and go home.

My nurse kept coming in to check on me. "You're the only one of my patients who isn't sleeping." No one could possibly sleep with the kind of pain I was in. "I'm not authorized to give you anything. I put a call into several doctors but no one has called back." Ben left her my medical sheet. "You at least warrant some Tylenol."

The Tylenol wasn't strong enough to alleviate all my pain but helped it subside within a few hours. This same nurse managed to dig up some gelatin and drinks for me. The snack was better than nothing. Then the shifts changed and so did my new nurse's attitude.

I fell asleep a few minutes after 5:00AM. A clock was hung up on the wall directly opposite my bed. I kept looking at the time every few minutes. Every second of pain felt like an hour. The clock seemed to be standing still for me.

My sleep was very short lived. The staff started came in to check my vitals and tried to draw blood. There were no orders for my care. No one could give me food, water, or medication. This was now worse than a prison. At least inmates were not deprived of food and water.

I used a bedpan during the night but the nurse had to search for an orthopedic one. I was incapable of raising my body to use a regular bedpan.

About 8:00AM one of my first surgeons came to see me.

"Why did you have to be admitted?" I told him about my excruciating pain. He examined me.

"May I have some pain medication?" I asked.

"The pain isn't from my surgery. Ask the last surgeon. I'll order food and drink for you. Make an appointment with my office for a follow-up visit."

Breakfast was brought to me. I asked my nurse for my medication. She had to find a doctor to order it.

A call came from the urological surgeon. Mister Happy asked me what happened. A message was left by the covering doctor who admitted me.

"I am in excruciating pain."

"No it's not from my surgery."

"The surgery took a little bit longer than expected because I had a difficult time inserting the mesh. I'll see you later."

"I need my medication."

"Have your nurse call me."

The whole experience was bizarre. My nurse was running around like a chicken without its head. She was having a very difficult time trying to keep all of her patients' records in order and was incapable of multitasking. Perhaps the nurse meant well but this scenario was not for her. She would do better as a private duty nurse only dealing with one person at a time and probably make more money.

It was now close to 11:00AM and I still had no medication. My pain level was down to about an eight with Tylenol and never went lower. It was still better than off the scale. My urologist showed up around noon. He examined me and saw I was still in pain. "I want you to leave the hospital and recuperate at home." I requested something for my pain. He ordered a mild pill to get me home but nothing for when I arrived there.

I was trying to understand the situation. I had two surgeries and none of the doctors ordered any type of pain medication. I had numerous minor surgeries and doctors asked if I needed something for the pain. More often than not I said no. Now one of my present surgeries was considered major, removal of my ovaries and I was denied medication.

"Make a follow up visit with me for next week. I'll remind the nurse about your medications." He left the room while making one of his lame jokes.

I called Ben, "I'm being discharged." I asked him to bring me my clothing and medications. I went down the list of what I needed and asked for them to be placed in one small bottle. This was a very wise decision.

After twelve noon my roommate received her lunch. I received nothing. I still had no medication. My nurse came back into the room and went to the computer in front of my bed. I asked her about lunch.

"Oh! You are not having any. The doctor discharged you."

"If that's the case; where are my discharge papers and why is the I.V. still in my arm?"

"I haven't gotten the papers ready yet."

"So therefore I don't eat. Also where is my medication?"

"Okay, I'll try to find you something to eat. I haven't put the order in yet for the medication."

"Can you please do that now since I was supposed to start taking my pills at 8:00AM?"

"I'm working on someone else. You'll just have to wait."

Ben arrived about 12:30 and the first thing I did was take my medication. If the hospital questioned why I medicated myself the response was easy, "No one else gave it to me."

The nurse must have forgotten about the lunch she was going to find me. An aide was already collecting the dirty tray from my roommate. Ben left to get me something from Ledges Garden.

The nurse came back to work on the computer in front of my bed. Other computers were down on the floor so she resorted to this one. I played dumb and asked about my medication.

"I have to wait until the pharmacy sends it up. They're having a problem locating one of your drugs."

"What about my lunch?"

"Okay. I'll see what I can find."

"When am I going to be discharged?"

"When I finish with others, I'll do your paper work."

About half an hour later the nurse handed me a ham sandwich which I wouldn't eat and a cup of gelatin.

Ben came back and handed me a bag of food. Just as I started to eat the nurse brought me my medication. One pill was definitely missing. A mantra of mine needs continual repeating, "You really have to watch out for yourself when you're in the hospital."

The nurse returned with my discharge papers. I signed them and she told me to get dressed. The I.V. had to be removed first which the nurse apparently forgot. She gave me my pain killer and I hoped the medication was strong enough to get me home without a problem. Ben helped me dress. The nurse left the room but returned a few minutes later to speak to Ben. "Bring your car around to the front. I'm calling transport."

As you can tell this was an experience anyone who still has all or even some of their marbles would never forget.

CHAPTER 43

IT WAS MY BACK STUPID!

I was in agony going home and immediately went into my recliner when we arrived. The only thing helping the pain was my TENS unit.

I called the two different surgeons offices and made my follow up appointments. During one of the conversations with a staff member I found out my legs had been spread apart and each one was placed in a harness. The position threw out my back and was the reason for all my pain. None of the surgeons took my back problems into consideration. They only focused on their areas of expertise.

If doctors do read my book I hope you take my suggestion about informing the patient about the position they will be placed in for surgery. Alerting the patient and being cognizant of the ramifications after surgery if they have other medical issues to contend with is extremely important. Necessary adjustments for your patient's overall well-being will help for a speedier and more pain free recovery. This in no way diminishes your ability as a surgeon. If you did the above I wouldn't have had to go through the experience I did. You would have known I needed strong pain medication due to my back problems and a possible overnight stay might have been considered. Medications, food and water would have been ready for me as well.

I have alerted every doctor and dentist since this incident. Doctors tend to gloss over my back but pick up on the cancer. I need them to pick up on all of me!

AND that is what distinguished my Tremore experience from all of the other hospitals I have ever been in. I was warned my back would go out during my surgery because of my body placement. I was given all the pain medication Tremore could provide at the time.

I hope never to need surgery again but the following question will be put forth to any doctor operating on me: "Will the position you put me in affect my back?" If it's a positive answer I will ask how can my pain be minimized. What are you going to do to help me afterwards?

I hope this encounter was an anomaly but I will take the extra precaution of alerting my internist. My internist could take over where the surgeon(s) leave off. I have to look at this horrific experience as a learning one.

My back pain subsided a bit over a week and it was time for my follow-up visit to the urologist. By the time we arrived at his office the pain in my back was returning full force.

I have never encountered any doctor as cheery as this urologist. Maybe it takes his mind off what he is doing. He walked into the room with another expensive suit, shirt and tie on. I took the painful position for my examination. I kept my top on. I assumed he wore gloves. The mesh was in place and I was to come back in six months for another follow up visit. I haven't been back since. I leave it up to my gynecologist to check on the mesh.

I let the urologist know the position I was put into during the surgery threw out my back. Hopefully he will use this knowledge for others in the future. I asked for pain medication to get me home and the urologist cooperated. I was given a shot of pain medication. Thank goodness the shot worked and for the first time since my pain nightmare began I was able to function again.

My follow up visit to Dr. Feinberg went a bit differently from the urologist. He examined my small incisions and went over the biopsies done on my ovaries. Good news! There was no sign of cancer.

"Why did you have to stay overnight?" I described my pain and lack of movement. I still was in some pain but could handle it.

"What number was your pain in the hospital?"

"Off the scale!"

"What pain are you in now?"

"Three or four."

"Why couldn't you get out of bed and go to the bathroom?"

"I couldn't move because of my pain and my legs refused to hold me up."

I related what went on in the dayroom after the surgeries, told him about the dirty toilet and how I insisted the seat be lined. He laughed. "I'm surprised the nurse even listened to you."

"I don't need to see you again," he said.

"Thank you and Good-bye." I left the office happy to hear the biopsies of my ovaries were cancer free.

I saw Dr. Charles one more time for a follow up after the surgery. "Your hair should stop growing. It will take time before the remaining hair falls out." Too bad the hair on my head hasn't grown as well as it did on my body.

Dr. Charles brought up the incident with her staff about sending the records to the wrong doctor. She apologized and dismissed me.

Now I could go back to taking care of my missing breasts and the consequences of treatment.

CHAPTER 44

WEIGHT GAIN

I was ready for a bra and went to my fitter. Medicare allows you to have a whole new set of prosthetics after a second mastectomy even if your two years and one day are not up for the first one. Since this was the case I wanted to go down to a B cup. My fitter dissuaded me and I again had C breasts. My slimmer appearance disappeared. I was also not very comfortable. The enlarged area from where my left kidney was removed prevented any style bra to be comfortable for any length of time.

One morning I decided to weigh the boobs. I used a food scale for Ben when he went back on solids after his surgery and it was perfect for weighing a prosthetic. Size C is *heavy*. And I was given the lightest and newest one on the market. It was a wake-up call as to how much extra weight women carry on our bodies because of our breasts.

My body kept expanding after my second mastectomy. My bras appeared to be getting tighter on a daily basis and my comfort level was getting worse. We went out to dinner with friends and I considered going into a ladies room and taking off my fake boobs. I pictured myself coming back to the dinner table with everyone staring at me and decided to contend with the pain. I was often so desperate to undo my bra driving home I fought with my clothing in the car. I wasn't very successful especially in winter when I wore layers of clothing.

Under Medicare new bras can't be purchased until one year and one day passes. It's not in our budget to buy new bras every few weeks. A department store's coupon and sale do not exist for prosthetic bras. I bought extenders for the bras making the shoulder straps too wide for my upper body. I tried bra strap pads. They didn't work. A new "tic" started. I was continually pushing the straps back onto my shoulders yet the area under my breast continued widening.

Going without a bra was pure relief. Thoughts of my Aunt Millie entered my head. She was naturally flat chested and told me she didn't bother with bras in the summer. No one knew the difference. Then again she was very thin all over.

I resorted to wearing some very inexpensive light weight sport bras bought through a newspaper ad. I filled them with the soft puffs I wore after my mastectomies. After a while even these bras were becoming uncomfortable as my expansion continued.

I was also gaining weight. I asked Dr. Bucker about the situation. He thought about it for a few moments.

"How much weight have you gained since the surgery?"

"Ten pounds."

"You have to diet and lose weight."

"Can the swelling be from lymphedema?" as I pointed out the big lumpy area on my back.

"I don't think lymphedema is the problem."

Dr. Bucker was so up on the situation when lymphedema appeared in my left hand I had a hard time comprehending how he missed this. The wonderful thing about Dr. Bucker is his warmth and caring for his patients and it is never beneath him to have something pointed out to him. This is why all of his patients love him. I didn't know it at the time but lymphedema in a hand is very obvious. Trained therapists are better at diagnosing the condition in other areas.

"Do I have to wrap both arms when flying?"

I asked the question even though I couldn't make myself get on a plane.

"Hold off flying for a while."

Flying became an issue because we were invited to Ben's nephew's wedding in Minnesota. Ben wanted to fly and I didn't. He didn't want to go by himself. I agreed to take a train or drive there and make a vacation of the whole trip.

We never went to the wedding. Unbeknownst to me Ben called his nephew and left a message. "We won't be coming to the wedding. Rosalie had a mastectomy." I refuse to use cancer as an excuse for not doing something. If I am unable to do the *typical* then I will find another way. Ben doesn't think the same way I do. He was only focused on the wedding and could not conceive of it being a part of a vacation.

CHAPTER 45

THE AUTO TRAIN

Emotionally I may have used the wrapping of my arms as an excuse not to fly. Aside from my concern over wrapping, my fear of flying was also a result of 9/11. My tremendous fear of being blown up in a plane is certainly not totally unfounded.

Not only was it a horrendously cold, snowy winter in 2011 but our furnace kept breaking down. This meant we had no hot water. The plumbing was connected to our heating unit. We had problems from the time we took possession of our house and our builder promised to fix it. None of the fixes turned out to be permanent. Our major heating failures left us very cold at the time heat and hot water were needed most.

We spent a small fortune having the boiler fixed only for it to break down over and over again. Our sleep was disrupted for fear the unit would shut off during the night and our pipes would burst from the cold. Ben and I often bumped into each other in the dark to see if the furnace continued working. We waited until our driveway and the roads were shoveled from each storm to drive to the clubhouse for a shower.

After four months of torture and $7,000.00 later, we were told the unit was stable enough for us not to worry for the rest of the season. We had to get away. Ben kept mentioning Florida where so many of our neighbors went during the winter but I refused to fly. Ben wouldn't drive. The only transportation left was a train.

All hotels of the type Ben agreed to stay at were sold out except for one. I booked three weeks and made reservations on the auto train.

"Pay for the trip. I'm ready to go."

Our reservations were in the handicapped car and fortunately a great group of people travelled with us. The seats are awful and not conducive to sleeping. The train is noisy with people continuously slamming the door to leave the car.

The one area never cleaned during the eighteen hour ride is the bathrooms. They were disgusting after a few hours. There are not too many bathrooms and sanitation is definitely an issue. People with lymphedema especially must be constantly cognizant of filth and germs.

The lounge car is filled with smoke fumes. This car is supposed to be a smoke free zone but vents from the smoking car go directly into the lounge car.

If smoking on planes is forbidden by law, the same rule should apply on trains. Smoking is supposedly the number one reason for lung and throat cancers. *"Why should non-smokers be subjected to the fumes?"* Smokers should be required to take a tour of Tremore or another cancer facility and see what the habit has physically done to patients. I don't know which would get top billing as the worst part of the trip, the seats or the bathrooms. The lounge car can be avoided except when passing through to the dining cars. You don't have to stay up there.

There was one upside of this whole adventure for me personally. I didn't have to wrap my left lymphedema hand and arm or have to check my right hand and arm for swelling. Just the thought of wrapping both sides had me cringing.

CHAPTER 46

FLORIDA I

Ben was too tired to drive when we reached Florida. I took the wheel of car. This was a trade-off I agreed to; no lymphedema wrapping for me and if Ben couldn't sleep on the train I would drive. We made a pit stop and discovered we were only about ten miles from our destination.

The amazing thing was our GPS didn't work in Florida. In fact Florida didn't show on our GPS at all. We had the GPS checked out and everyone was surprised to learn *"Florida just doesn't seem to be in the U.S."* I printed out directions from the computer and was very glad I had back-up.

Ben slept during the car ride and my rest had to wait. Our arrival at the hotel and our terrific accommodations made the whole train ride worth it. I really didn't want to go home and needed at least another week. It just was not going to happen that year.

One of my greatest fears of a three week trip was being away from my doctors. When I was younger with only a few major issues three weeks away from home was manageable. I was mentally trying to prepare myself for our departure. The Friday before our scheduled ride home on Tuesday I knew something was wrong. My self-diagnosis was a urine infection. I hoped to hold out until we arrived home. The next day I was feeling worse with every passing hour. I couldn't board a train feeling the way I did.

It was Saturday and a hospital was my only recourse. No hospitals were listed directly in our phone book. I discovered phone numbers were listed by a doctors' medical expertise. This means you should have some idea of who treats your condition. Of course I was *very experienced* in this area and easily found a urologist. The doctor I called was in a hospital. "Come over any time. Medicare is accepted."

The hotel staff printed up directions to the hospital. Ben verbalized exactly what I was thinking. "I was hoping we could get through this vacation without any hospital or doctor visits." It was not to be.

The hospital was quite large and we were directed to a separate entrance of the building. Ben dropped me off and went looking for a parking spot. A handicap license plate is on my car but there wasn't a spot to be found.

The waiting room was packed. I signed in at a desk perched in the middle of the room and was required to write down my self-diagnosis but noticed people before me wrote *not sure* or *feeling bad*.

Seats were all taken. This was going to be a whole day event. Someone rose and I sat down. There were no seats for Ben when he entered and he decided to search for food. It was past our usual lunch time but I had no interest in eating.

Someone's name was called and about five seats opened up. No one should come to an emergency room with so many people. It's just not fair to the other patients who may have to sit. One relative or friend should stay with the patient and the other concerned people should wait outside. At the very least the accompanying people should have the decency to get up and give patients their seat. Patients including those with crutches came in after me and were lined up against a wall. Patients should have first access to seats in each and every medical facility no matter where you live.

I think it is a very bad move to bring very young children to a hospital and just let them run amok. I do understand some people have no choice but for the others, leave them home.

Little by little names were called. The place started to slow down. Another patient told me they closed at three and it was almost two thirty.

My name was called and I went back to the desk. A man asked me some pertinent questions though not overly intrusive. He saw my address.

"I come from Central New Jersey. I'm living in Florida for ten years and had enough."

"How is the quality of the medical care here?"

"It's surprisingly good. You'll be okay." I thanked him and took a seat again.

Ben came back. The cafeteria was closing but someone took pity on him because he had a conglomeration of food in his hands. He was given whatever was left but only purchased what he thought he could eat.

My name was called again and I was taken back to the hospital area. I was given a gurney between two rooms. I was ordered to "Lie on it until the doctor sees you." My room number was listed as three and a half meaning I had the hallway between two rooms. There is a first time for everything and even with my professional patient status this was the first time I ever had a room listed as half in a hallway.

Almost an hour after keeping my place at the half, a charming doctor about thirty-five years of age came over to me. "You diagnosed yourself. How did you arrive at your diagnosis?" He agreed with me. I gave him a urine sample and he immediately sent it up to the lab. Now we had to wait.

Staff passed. "Lie down on the gurney." I refused. My back hurt lying there. I plastered myself against the wall. Ben managed to get me a chair. We put it as close to the wall as possible. I had to stay away from everyone and out of trouble. A tall order for me!!

The doctor caught my eye and gave me a *thumbs up. Did that mean I was right in my diagnosis or was I okay?* The doctor approached.

"You are right. You have a urine infection. I'm staring you on medication in the hospital." He gave me the name and dosage and wrote a prescription. "A nurse will bring you the medicine and water."

You really have to be on top of your game to stay well. I know it sounds like an oxymoron but mistakes are made constantly. Try to get someone to go with you to a hospital or a doctor if you think you may miss something, especially a mistake. Use a recording device. At least you can play back what your instructions are.

A nurse brought me the right medicine but the incorrect dosage. I refused to take it and an argument ensued. The doctor returned. "There is no other dosage in the medicine cabinet," she said. He left and returned a few moments later with the medication I needed.

"Could you please look at a rash?"

"Not to worry."

I was a cancer patient many times over. I worry about every new problem until it's examined by a doctor. I was given a paper with a name and phone of a doctor to follow up with on Monday. The very personable doctor shook my hand and wished me well.

As we were leaving I made a comment to a lady sitting at a desk. "No one took any of my medical insurance information." I was sent to another desk in the lobby area to give them my insurance information and was told I hadn't been seen. Eventually at my insistence the woman made a copy of my insurance cards after arguing with me that my secondary insurance wasn't accepted. I'd been down that road many times and would deal with the secondary insurance when the time came.

We left the hospital and went to a drugstore to fill my prescription. I was thinking ahead and decided to buy plastic covered underwear my mother used to wear for the train. I didn't want to take a chance with the bathroom situation.

The medication started to work a bit within a few hours. We tried to enjoy the rest of the evening and Sunday. Our plans for Monday included picking up oranges at a grove to take home with us. First I called the doctor's office the hospital doctor recommended and left a message. I left several messages after that. No one picked up at the office or called me back.

By one o'clock in the afternoon I checked with my own doctor. Her advice was to keep trying to get the doctor on the phone and see him before I boarded the train the next day. I left another message. We had a favorite park with a beach we enjoyed going to and decided to spend our last afternoon there. I would take my chances on the train.

At five o'clock in the evening I received a call from the receptionist at the recommended doctor's office. "The hospital never should have given you his name. He has a very long waiting list and sees no one the hospital recommends. I'm calling back because you called so many times."

"Sorry, but we can't help you. Get in touch with your doctor at home." My decision was made about the way to handle my situation and a call by that time was useless.

CHAPTER 47

THE TRAIN RIDE HOME

I put on a pair of the disposable underwear before we checked out of the hotel and added a few extras in my carry on. They were surprisingly comfortable.

Accommodations on the return train were the same as our trip down except for two obnoxious men in our car who made life miserable for the rest of us. My medication put me to sleep for a while. The trip was even worse for Ben despite all the contraptions I brought on board to make the ride easier. He couldn't stay in the lounge car for an extended period of time to escape the two men. The smoke was unbearable and he couldn't breathe.

Ben woke me for dinner. Sleepiness was at the top of the list for side effects of my medication. This was actually a good thing for me. I would sleep for much of the train ride home or so I thought. The crazies as we were now calling the obnoxious men in our car kept me awake. No one could sleep and I was having a hard time keeping my eyes open. I took another pill and was one drowsy lady but the fighting both verbal and physical coming from the other end of the car was a constant distraction.

"We should get an attendant."

"We should mind our own business but we are never taking the train again." I would have to fly.

Unlike a plane there are no attendants doing anything in the rail cars. You are on your own. In this day and age a supervisor is necessary to periodically check on all the cars and bathrooms. It is just not a safe or healthy atmosphere as the return trip was proving to be. Eighteen hours is a long time to be spending time with people who have no respect for others. Some supervision is needed. No one is physically checked by going through an x-ray machine or similar the way you are in an airport. Your cars are photographed but that is the extent of it. Someone with evil ideas can certainly have easy access for destruction on a train.

I wasn't able to pull my share on the drive back home from Virginia. I slept.

My doctor saw me a few days later and my urine came back clear. I had another urine infection about six months after that and my doctor thought it might be attributable to my sling. I was given a prescription for the same antibiotic as previously.

"Start to take the medicine as soon as you feel the infection coming on even if it's during the night." I was definitely relegated to be my own physician and my status changed.

CHAPTER 48

ARIMIDEX

I was due for my yearly tests and check-up with Dr. Mogani a few months after my mastectomy. We agreed I should have an oncologist. My gynecologist recommended two people. I was familiar with one of the groups the doctor was affiliated with and turned off by the name of the other doctor. His last name was the same as the doctor who left it to his incapable assistant to make a mammography appointment for me. I was afraid the two doctors were related. I did not come to the conclusion of this unpleasant doctor's ability by myself. Friends were visiting me when this doctor came to see me. They wanted to strangle him. The doctor never went near me and walked out when I asked a question. His behavior was the same every day.

I made my appointment with the first oncologist mentioned. He was located in two offices. One office was almost diagonally across from St. Augustus Hospital but he was only there on Tuesdays. There were no appointments available for weeks. The other office was further away but I was given an appointment almost immediately.

I was very much prepared for my appointment with Dr. Finn. I had test reports with me from all my surgeries and my updated medical list. At the last minute I packed up my yearly medical files going back to my first cancer.

Ben went with me. The waiting room was quite large. I checked in, filled out the necessary forms, and waited and waited. At Ben's insistence I went up to the desk and inquired why I was still sitting in the waiting room when people who came in much later than me had been taken and were leaving. "I'll check."

A few minutes later Dr. Finn came out to me. Someone called my name and I didn't respond. One thing I do know about myself, my hearing is exceptional and if I didn't hear there was another reason. Dr. Finn spoke to me for a few minutes. "Someone will come out to get you." I liked him.

Within a few minutes I found out why I didn't hear my name called. A young woman stood in an alcove between the examining and waiting room whispering someone else's name. The person called didn't hear either and didn't respond. A new method is needed. Perhaps just actually walking into the waiting room and speaking in a louder tone of voice would help.

I must really be a prize to deal with. I have spent so much time in doctors' offices and hospitals I'm totally aware of what needs improvement. I'm still a good student and the encouragement I've been given to let people know the error of their ways is making me quite bold.

Dr. Finn was surprised Ben hadn't come in with me. My explanation was simple.

"We see so many doctors we've learned if we're needed someone comes to get us. Do you need Ben?"

"No. I'm so used to the patient being unaware of what is going on I usually speak to the other party. You appear to be with it."

"Thanks for bringing all your paper work. I'll need some time to go through it."

Dr. Finn was of the same mind regarding medication as Dr. Bucker. It slipped from my mouth when I asked if he meant something like Arimidex. Tamoxifin was out. He went to make copies of everything he wanted in my files and to make a decision about medication.

Dr. Finn was gone awhile and on his return he acknowledged consulting with his partners. Everyone was in agreement. "Your patient should probably take something." Dr. Finn spoke percentages to me if I took the medication. We discussed well-known side effects and how long I would be on the drug. It was extremely costly. The prescription was for a sixty day supply and my reaction would be monitored.

I had an exam and blood was drawn. A follow-up appointment was made for six weeks later.

I met a woman from Cancer Support who said to call her if I wanted to talk or needed information. We met before my filling the Arimidex prescription. She talked numbers, reviewing the advantage I would have by taking the drug. "I believe the percentage is too low to risk all the side effects and that is why both Dr. Finn and Dr. Bucker hesitated about putting you on one."

The women she saw in her groups bitterly complained about the side effects. All the complications had to be addressed by taking other drugs to compensate for the damage from Arimidex. We decided to speak regularly but I left with the knowledge the drug might cause other problems for me.

In between Dr. Finn's visits, I saw Dr. Bucker.

"My team decided you should be on medication."

"I have an oncologist now. Dr. Finn's team concurs with you about the medication."

"I'm happy someone will now be following you."

I started on Arimidex and had no reaction for a while. Then night sweats began. I lowered the temperature in the house and Ben raised it. One doctor told Ben to put on extra sweaters. My knees started to give out and I was in tremendous pain. I saw an orthopedist specializing in knees. He began a series of three shots one each week for the pain. The shots couldn't be given again for six months. An excruciating, debilitating Baker's cyst formed behind my left knee.

I was feeling miserable and began to get the impression Dr. Finn was getting annoyed with my complaining. Some of my complaints could possibly be attributed to side effects from my other medications. The lady from Cancer Support and I spoke. She didn't agree with any oncologists about the hormonal drugs because of her experience with so many patients who were miserable while on them.

After a year of taking Arimidex, Mindy went with me for a visit to Dr. Finn. My grandson's Bar Mitzvah was coming up and we were all excited. I again complained about the medication. Mindy broke in with, "You want to be here for all the boys Bar Mitzvahs so stay on the drug."

That ended my verbal complaints for a while but didn't diminish a continuing deterioration of the function and pain in my body.

Another problem began in my left foot immediately after Donny's Bar Mitzvah. I didn't recall spraining it nor had I fallen. My knees were hurting and my overall demeanor was downhill. I looked up Arimidex on the computer but this time read comments from women complaining about the side effects.

Most of the women stopped the medication and were feeling better. The damage from the drug was irreversible including side effects never discussed with me or mentioned on Arimidex's web site.

My bone density test showed I was starting to have a problem. A shot of medication could be given to me for a year's coverage. Dr. Finn wanted me to have a written note from either one of my two internists. Both internists know each other well. One pointed the problem out to me and the other said I should probably wait for my next bone density test in two years. My fear was my bones would disintegrate even more in the two years if I waited. *If I had the shot and a reaction what would I do?* The medication would remain in my body. I decided to wait.

A very low reading on a Vitamin D test necessitated a very high dose prescription of the vitamin to compensate for my deficiency. After six months I was retested and was up to speed and was able to switch to a lower dosage of an over the counter vitamin D supplement.

The continued lack of deterioration of my body and spirit had to be addressed. I asked Ben and Mindy to accompany me on my next visit to Dr. Finn. He opened up the door to the examining room and was surprised to see all of us packed into the tiny space. He backed out of the room as quickly as he came in, shutting the door behind him. A moment later he reentered the room. He never saw me come in with my army. I reintroduced him to Ben and Mindy and then we discussed Arimidex.

Dr. Finn suggested a compromise. "Stay off Arimidex for one month. If you are feeling better than the drug is responsible." He reassured me. "One month off the drug is not a problem." We dropped the issue and everyone left the room but me. I stayed for my exam.

My retinologist, Dr. Winter, had a tech in his office who was previously on Arimidex. She switched to Aromasin. Our in-depth conversation began when a fan was on in the dead of winter and the office heat was not working very well.

When my month was up I felt slightly better but still not great. Dr. Finn said I could try another drug and I suggested Aromasin since it worked for the tech. He wrote a prescription and I headed to the drugstore. My wait for my prescription was very long. I questioned the pharmacist about the delay. "I don't think you should be on Aromasin" and he cited his reasons. He put a call into Dr. Finn and hadn't heard back.

I called Dr. Finn. "Aromasin is fine." I mentioned another drug, Femara. "I don't want you on it." I handed my phone to the pharmacist and my prescription was quickly filled.

I had no reaction to Aromasin for the first few months and then all hell broke loose. On December 25th of the same year Mindy's family was coming over for a Chanukah party and I had plenty to do. My body refused to work with me. My knees buckled under me and I collapsed on the floor. I couldn't get up and didn't want to wake Ben. Somehow I dragged myself up into a chair. After a few minutes I was stable enough to retrieve a phone to call Dr. Finn. His covering doctor called me back shortly afterwards. "Stop the medication immediately and call Dr. Finn on Monday." I called Dr. Finn's office as directed and left a message. I was never told Dr. Finn was away on vacation and out of the country for a few weeks. I was off the medication for several weeks before seeing or speaking to Dr. Finn again.

CHAPTER 49

MY KNEES

After New Year's I saw my knee orthopedist. He sent me for an MRI. I had to wait weeks for an appointment and was unable to receive my test results until then. My appointment was for the end of January. Ben came into the examining room with me.

The orthopedist never once looked up. He spoke to my knees. "You need replacement surgery." He left the room returning with brochures describing the surgery and recuperative period. "My receptionist made a surgical appointment with the hospital. Stop at her desk on your wait out." Ben and I both had questions. The orthopedist looked up and saw tears in my eyes. All I could think about was another surgery and cancelling our trip to Florida.

We left the examining room purposely passing the designated desk. I was sent back to the desk. I wasn't mentally prepared for additional surgery and said so.

I checked with several people in my community who had knee surgery and everyone was recommending another surgeon. I called my internist. She too recommended the other surgeon. I called for an appointment explaining we were leaving for Florida in two weeks and needed to know if our plans had to be put on hold. I was given an appointment for the following week and brought a copy of my MRI and additional tests.

Ben went in the examining room with me. When the doctor came in to see me I was totally prepared for surgery in my head. So was Ben. We both had given up on our second Florida trip.

Dr. Watts was one of the nicest people I've ever met. "An MRI really isn't the best test for knees and I'm sending you for an x-ray." We were stunned by the doctor's pronouncement after looking at my x-ray.

"Surgery isn't necessary yet though the x-ray shows an abundance of arthritis in your knee. You need to use a cane for now. Do you need a prescription?"

"I do have one at home."

"Florida weather is good for you. Go on your trip. Use weights on your ankles for exercise. I am suggesting an anti-inflammatory but check with your internist first."

I had an appointment with Dr. Capp the next day. He gave me some samples of an anti-inflammatory and a prescription.

I saw Dr. Finn a few days before leaving for Florida. My body as a whole was slightly better by then. I was off Aromasin for close to seven weeks. No other medication was discussed. Dr. Finn said I was now going to the right person for my knees. "I wouldn't let anyone else operate on me."

"Do I have to wrap both arms for lymphedema when I'm flying?"

"It's not my area of expertise. Go see the girls in St. Augustus. They'll know better than me."

"You can leave your car in my lot while you walked to St. Augustus."

My bag was in one hand and my cane in the other. I walked to St. Augustus and arrived at the wrong end of the building. The woman at the desk noticed I was falling apart. *How would I retrieve my car?* She was insisting on calling a wheelchair for me. I decided to rest awhile before taking on a trek to the other wing of the hospital.

I regained enough energy to continue with my walk. Other hospital staff passed me in the hallways. "Do you need a wheelchair?" Thanks but no thanks. Luckily there were no mirrors to observe myself or I might have said yes.

I arrived at the physical therapy department and gave the woman at the desk my prescription explaining I couldn't start therapy immediately. My concern was wrapping for my flights.

I waited while the receptionist inquired if someone could see me. "Kate will meet with you when she finishes with her patient." Kate came to the waiting room and we went into her office. I described my predicament.

"Wrap as usual on your left arm. Can your husband wrap your right arm?"

"I don't think so." I had a quick laugh and made it abundantly clear this was not viable request. I pointed out my back where the large lumpy ball of skin protruded. Directions changed once Kate saw the area.

"Do not wrap your right arm. The lymphedema will get worse." Ben was off the hook.

Kate gave me a sample of a wider bandage for my fingers after realizing the source of my consternation about unraveling. She expressed surprise at the narrowness of the bandage I had been using. I hate flying wrapped up. Kate showed me a new way of wrapping. Wrapping to the end of my finger covering my fingernails was no longer necessary, only to my nail cuticles.

We set up an appointment for two days after I returned from Florida.

I went home to quickly pack remembering to throw old clean underwear into the pile I was going to take with me. Old underwear can be tossed and you have more room for items you acquire on your trip.

I stacked everything I needed on the couch in our sunroom. Ben only goes in there to shut the blinds at night or to take food when we have a party. The sunroom has my name all over it. It's where I paint, do all my art work and sew. The room is my haven. I can get lost in there for hours at a time.

I assembled all my clothing, making a list of what I was taking with me. I have a perfect beach bag Mindy gave me years before. The bag is made of nylon, is pliable, light weight and dries quickly. I couldn't find it and instead grabbed another bag she gave me from a trade show. I had to move quickly making up for the time lost taking care of my knees.

My directions from Dr. Watts included using my cane as I moved about. *Forget it.* The cane was in my way and I was tripping over it. When my packing was complete, I'd use the cane again.

I made a list of items to buy in Florida instead of taking them with me. They weren't worth paying for the extra weight on the plane. I quickly went through coupons hoping they could be used to purchase what I needed. The most difficult part came next: my medication. The majority of them are in very large bottles with pills and capsules for ninety days. Only thirty were required with an extra weeks supply. It was unnecessary to take all the big bottles yet I was afraid they might be confiscated at the airport if placed them all into one big bottle. My solution was to remove the labels off smaller bottles of medication and replace them with labels from the larger sizes. I retained the separation of the medications each with their own label. I did not want the TSA to arrest me for illegally carrying or dispensing drugs because of the enormity of the amount of pills I take.

The bottles looked convincing but they were time consuming and generally a pain to make. Instead of discarding them when we returned I was determined to save them for our future trips.

Next came packing up my make-up bag and I opted for the least amount possible. More could be purchased in Florida. Suntan lotion and bug spray were added to my shopping list. They were too heavy to carry yet an absolute necessity with lymphedema. These two items had to be bought as soon as we landed.

My most debatable question was what to do with both my prosthetics. I decided to take the puffs instead and save the weight. I had to add 5lb weights in my luggage for my knees. I packed bathing suits forgetting my real prosthetics were necessary to go into the water.

Kate told me to not bother with a bra on the plane and to wear very loose clothing. My friend and I went to a free standing department store. The store was nearby and one stop shopping was possible. This was going to be a rushed shopping trip. I needed a loose outfit for the plane and a bag to wear on my waist. If you're carrying a cane in one hand and a bag in another you have no way of lifting anything else.

I possessed an old waist bag yet it was practically new. It remained hidden away after my nephrectomy. It wasn't wide enough to stretch across my permanently swollen waist area. I found a bag with a longer strap to accommodate my figure.

I chose a black loose fitting jacket with a small amount of white trim. It was perfect to go over an old white, short sleeve shirt. A short sleeve top is necessary to allow for my bandages to be place directly on my arm.

Matching drawstring pants were not available in my size. The pants style was perfect for my body. I took the next larger size into the dressing room. The pants were falling off me. My friend and I laughed hysterically and our next stop would have to be to the bathroom. More laughter erupted when I put them in my cart. I decided to double the pants at the waist. Three of my *pulkes* (legs) could fit into one pants leg but I didn't care. Time was running out. With luck I wouldn't meet anyone I knew which meant everyone else would be a stranger and most assuredly I would never see them again. My arms were enough of a concern.

Ben put his clothing on the bed. My job is packing. He always sees more space after I pack and sneaks in extra shoes. Ben's starting to catch on about how much shoes weigh.

Tightly rolled clothing takes up less space and leaves fewer wrinkles. Left to his own devices Ben would end up with three suitcases and the extra airline fees make additional bags too costly. I pack one suitcase for him. He's in charge of his carry-on.

A small flash light is a necessity. I floundered in a darkened laundry room the year before and didn't want a recurrence. Ben took the GPS and phone charger.

I decorated my cane to make it unique. Canes are easily left anywhere. I attached my name adding a few extra letters and my daughter's cell number. She has our itinerary and if called would contact me immediately.

I do the same thing inside my suitcases. On my departure I put my destination with the phone number and address atop of my clothing before zipping the suitcase closed. On the return I use my daughter's cell and her address. Ditto for the luggage tags.

CHAPTER 50

FLORIDA II

I left home with a prescription for antibiotics for urine infections and packed some disposable underwear in case I needed them. I wore my lymphedema bandages, had my cane for my knees and went braless. Wheelchair service to and from the gate was a necessity.

At the airport I was patted down. Security exchanged my cane for one of theirs while mine went through the scanner. I was tested for gun residue on my bandages.

Questions about my bandages began at boarding. A female attendant asked, "What happened to you?" Between the cane and bandages I looked like a recent accident victim. I truthfully answered. "These are compression bandages used for flying due to lymphedema from my mastectomies." She understood the mastectomies but not the lymphedema and wondered how the cane fit in. I heard the *poor dear* and how she would look out for me.

Interestingly enough a man was seated on the opposite side of us who looked in worse shape than me. He came on board with his own wheelchair. Ours eyes met and he gave me a knowing look as to what it is like to travel with disabilities. When we left the plane he made a concerted effort to say good-bye to me. I had tears in my eyes. Things can always be worse and I have to remind myself of that frequently.

The cane was a pain in the neck while we travelled even though it was to help me walk. It's very difficult carrying a handbag no matter how light it is when one hand holds a cane. You feel the need for a third appendage.

I crocheted a small bag to go across my shoulders and around my neck. It wasn't a full solution because the bag had to stay light enough to not pull down on my spine.

My temporary beach bag fell apart and I crocheted a bag. I used no pattern and did my own thing. The pieces for the bag worked up quickly. Many people at our hotel inquired how I worked so fast and knew exactly what to do. Others asked me to teach them how to crochet. I purchased my yarn from a craft store in a mall nearby and was offered a job when I went back to purchase a button to secure the bag and grosgrain to give it body. Neither my cane nor age was a deterrent. At a Yankee game a security guard asked me if I made the bag and then wanted to know if I sold them.

I did do a lot of art work and the visual difference in landscaping from the Northeast was a great incentive for me to paint. I wasn't really happy with the medium I chose to work in but it was light in weight and easy to transport.

CHAPTER 51

DENTAL AND MEDICAL

My Molar

A few days before we were leaving Florida an upper left side molar started to hurt me. I thought it was the surrounding gum. I did my best to chew on my right side of my mouth. I didn't want to start with a dentist in Florida and finish in NJ. There were only a few days left and I was determined to stick out the pain until we arrived home. I had a feeling my first lymphedema appointment at St. Augustus' therapy department might not take place.

A skycap pushed me in a wheelchair with lightning speed through the terminal to a wheelchair lane at security. A man was in front of me dressed similarly to a skycap with his hands on a wheelchair. He turned around to me and laughed. "What does the other guy look like?"

I was furious and had to put up with another insensitive stranger. My first thought was to ignore him. Until this trip I hadn't worn my bandages in public in almost three years. I decided to educate the man and perhaps teach him not to open up his big mouth to someone else. "It's a side effect of cancer treatment." He crossed himself and kept repeating, "You're going to be all right." So he went from being an idiot to a sage.

We prefer the seats on the right side of the plane. Ben takes the aisle seat and I take the middle. He protects my left arm from continually being bumped into and takes the brunt of the swinging handbags and backpacks.

We landed late in Newark and I left a message for my periodontist. I had to wait for the following day to see him. I cancelled my first appointment at St. Augustus for lymphedema therapy. My molar split down the middle. Every time something moved on one side of the broken tooth the gum moved with it. Dr. Rosen examined me. "You have to have your tooth removed right now. I don't know of anyone who could wait as long as you have. Others would have been to a dentist the same day it happened." My pain level is high. When I say something hurts, doctors should believe me.

"I'm saving you a second surgery and additional pain. I'm going to do an implant too." I had a milkshake for dinner.

Opinion

My next appointment was with Dr. Watts. He made a decision. "Surgery isn't necessary and you can give up the cane." My internist saw the MRI of my knees and her opinion was different. "Your knees are in worse shape than most of my patients who had surgery." Dr. Watts said he would write her a letter and see me again in six months.

The next time I saw Dr. Watts he dismissed me. We discussed the fact my improvement must have something to do with going off the Aromasin and with him telling me, "You own your body."

Unfortunately my newest doctor, a nephrologist whom he knew warned me. "Stay off anti-inflammatories. Patients who often chose to take the drugs for pain eventually are placed on dialysis." I have bottles of anti-inflammatories in various doses in my medicine drawer. Most unopened!

CHAPTER 52

LYMPHEDEMA AT ST. AUGUTUS

After my pulled tooth began to heal my lymphedema therapy started full steam ahead three times a week with Mani. At first I had a slight problem understanding her dialect but it didn't take long for the two of us to mesh. I had to *unlearn* some of the things from my old lymphedema therapist since new methods were developed in the intermittent years.

Mani said, "Loosen the waist of your pants around your stomach area. The tightness contributes to lymphedema." I drew the line when she suggested maternity pants for a variety of reasons.

I was determined to save my pants but still do what was necessary for the lymphedema. Tossing out brand new pants just bought in Florida wasn't going to happen. I experimented with an old pair of pants by opening up seams and cutting the elastic. I bought ribbon and attached it to both sides of the opened seam. In the beginning my stitches were impeccable and then slowly deteriorated as I was in a rush to finish them.

Mani had to approve what I did with the first pair. "How did you think of this idea as a solution?" Sewing is slow. No matter how careful I am, I invariably stick myself. I immediately wash the area off and apply liquid bandage afterwards. If there is blood I use an antibiotic ointment and a regular band aid. I am unable to sew with thimbles. I once tried wrapping my fingers with masking tape. That didn't work either.

The removed stitching comes off in tiny pieces. The thread is so light and airy it flutters from the sunroom where I sew throughout the rest of the house. One morning I was at the bathroom sink and Ben rushed in to flush all the *bugs* down the toilet. "We're having an infestation and I have to call Bobby." Bobby is our exterminator. "What are you laughing about?" I showed him the threads from the pants were not alive.

I thought about Aunt Lillian who had to bring all her tops and dresses to a dressmaker. No sleeve fit over her lymphatic arm and additional fabric had to be added in the sleeve area once the seams were taken apart. No wonder so many lymphedema people hate clothing shopping. We have to constantly take into consideration the adjustments needed for our garments.

Mani enjoyed hearing my stories including all the trouble I seemed to get into. Many of our appointments were scheduled around my hairdresser. Mani kept telling me to get a wig!

I had a few weeks when my back pain was quite insufferable. The deep breathing exercises seemed to make the pain worse. As my pain continued to increase Mani encouraged me to see a doctor. I saw my internist first. She wrote a prescription for a new medication, a muscle relaxant. We decided together to wait and have it filled after I consulted with my pain management doctor that same afternoon.

Ben drove me to his office for my appointment. He was sitting in the waiting area along a parallel wall to the examining room. My doctor prescribed another MRI for me.

"I'll make a determination of what to do after I have the results of the MRI and speak to you. In the meantime take this OTC drug." He handed me the name on a prescription. I was quite sure the drug was one I was to avoid.

I showed him the prescription from my internist and was shocked by his response. He was walking through the door raising his voice while repeatedly saying, "Do not take this. It will kill you! It does something to your brain." He was so adamant and loud Ben heard him in the waiting room. He looked like a mad scientist as he continued to repeat his declaration.

I wanted to avoid another MRI for my back. The previous one almost scared me to death. A spot was discovered and this particular doctor thought it was cancer. My oncologist ordered another MRI done at another facility. If it was cancer there really was nothing that could be done for me except pain control. I went for another MRI and the results were negative. All I really wanted was something to help me with my back pain.

I was more frightened after seeing the pain doctor than before. As Ben was driving home I called my internist. I asked one of her office staff to please check with the doctor A.S.A.P. about the two medications. I repeated the pain doctor's doomsday revelations of my impending death if I took the drug she prescribed. I also asked about the other OTC drug.

A call was quickly returned to me and this ridiculous conversation ensued.

"The doctor said you should do as she said."

"Excuse me but that doesn't answer my question."

"That's what the doctor said."

"It doesn't make sense. Did you tell the doctor the pain specialist said the drug she prescribed could kill me? Did you ask about the other drug?"

"Yes. But that's what the doctor said."

My internist has an excellent reputation and came highly recommended. I really like her and know she is extremely careful. Her office décor and front office staff are another matter. I didn't think she would prescribe a drug that would kill me and in fact she was overly cautious about giving out medication. Ben wanted to know what I was going to do.

I wrote a letter to my doctor relating my conversation with her employee and how I still didn't have an answer to my questions. I remarked how this person could really do damage to someone who wasn't on the ball with his or her own health. Ben drove me to her office and I gave the letter to her reliable assistant.

Our phone was ringing as we returned home. It was my internist. "I would never prescribe medication that would kill you or interact with your other drugs. I also gave you a few pills to see if they worked. I don't want you to stay on it for any extended period of time. You can't take the OTC drug. It will interfere with your kidney function. Always leave a message for me to call you back. I apologize for the confusion."

Fortunately my back pain was only a temporary set-back and Mani was able to continue with my lymphedema massages. Mani encouraged me to write a book. "Many of my patients seem to give up and you keep going with a smile on your face. Perhaps you might have a positive influence on them."

CHAPTER 53

BELLY DANCING

A class was starting at St. Augustus for lymphedema and breast cancer patients. There was an introductory session and then six weeks of classes afterwards. Mani encouraged me to go, stressing the importance of my attending. The first class was quite full and I learned a lot from Kate who conducted the beginning segment.

I was not at all impressed with the second part. A woman spoke who couldn't seem to get over herself trying to promote her business. Ben dropped me off. We were at least twenty minutes past the time the class was to end. The class was going on and on with seemingly no end in sight. Ben kept calling me and I decided to leave. Others left before me. I stopped in the ladies room before leaving the building and heard women's voices talking about how the class was a waste of their time. They had no intention of ever going back.

When I saw Mani the next day she asked my opinion of the night before. At first I was hesitant to tell her but apparently patients before me had the same impression. Kate saw me on the way out and asked me what I thought of the introductory class. I didn't hold back. The class had been run before and this was the first time there was ever this type of reaction from so many people.

Mani and Kate continued to badger me to return. "We promise the next session will be different." They wore me down and I went. The class was to take place in the main hospital. The week before it was in another building and parking could be found on the street. Going to the main hospital meant I had to use the valet service.

I left my keys in my car for the valet. The class was much better than the week before but many others couldn't be convinced to return as easily as I had. There must have been anywhere from one third to a half less attending than the prior week.

Certain faces started to make an impression on me. Not only did they have a look of stay away from me I'm not approachable, to I'm not happy and I don't know how to go on with my life or the rare I'm happy or I'm doing this because it's supposed to be good for me. I think it's the artist in me contributing to my sensitivity to facial expressions and body language. My look if someone was capable of reading it, "I'm doing the therapy department a favor by coming back."

Kate and Mani both asked me, "How was last night?" My response was unexpected. "The class was better than the first night but a parking solution has to be found for returning my car."

I left my car with the valet but had no way to retrieve it after the class. No one was at the security stand. I waited awhile since this was a frequent occurrence. The valets often are parking someone else's car. After ten minutes I went back into the lobby and headed for the front desk. I was informed valet service goes off at 7:00PM. It was close to 8:00PM. A security person found my car keys but had no idea where my car was parked. I use the valet service because of my inability to park my car when I arrive or pick it up when I leave.

The security guard at the desk made a call to see who could get my car. I waited another fifteen minutes and asked again. Another call was made. "The only security person able to get your car went for dinner," she remarked.

Ben called wondering why I hadn't come home yet. He offered to come and get me but I still needed my car. At 8:30PM a security person walked through the front door. He had food in his hand. *What was he doing during his dinner hour if he brought his meal back to the hospital?* I asked myself.

I went back to the desk. "The security person will get your car after he puts his food down." The lady was right about that; only the food didn't go down on a table, it went down the security guard's mouth and landed in his stomach. He took his grand old time eating it. I again waited outside by the valet stand. At least the weather wasn't freezing cold as in the dead of winter with snow falling down.

Ben called again. "What is going on?" I told him. "Do you have any idea what time it is?" It was almost nine o'clock.

I spotted the security guard at the parking garage and walked as fast as possible to reach him before he entered.

"Are you going to get my car?"

"I have something else to do first." I was not happy and vowed never to place myself in this position again.

At 9:40PM the security guard brought my car to me. This was a full two hours and ten minutes after the class ended. My cell phone was ringing again as I drove home. I knew it was Ben calling but don't like to answer while I drive. When I pulled into the garage Ben was standing in the doorway wondering what happened to me.

There was no way I could go to the class and have this parking debacle happen each time. Mani promised to check into it. There is no solution. Valet service is shut down at 7:00PM and the keys are brought to the front desk. You are on your own. Someone is supposed to be able to get your car but nothing can be done if they're on their dinner break. Several questions need to be answered. *"Does the hospital pay the salary for someone to take over a two hour dinner break?"* If they can't tell you where your car is, *"How can you possibly retrieve it?"*

Ben and I worked out a plan whereby we would go for dinner, he would drop me off at the hospital and come back to get me. It worked and we continued that way for a few weeks. Then Kate asked for an extension of the class encouraging all of us to continue. Ben wasn't so thrilled with chauffeuring. By now he considers it routine Monday. The only thing I will have to deal with is if his schedule changes.

The class whittled down to less than ten people. I was very cognizant of two ladies with the sourest faces and unfriendly manner not returning. Perhaps if they started to speak to people they would have been happier. Some of us became friendly and were meeting in the hospital lobby before class to chat. Knowing each other gave us more incentive to return each week.

I still had one very major issue with the class and know for a fact I was in very good company. When Kate ran her part the class was terrific. Not so with the other part. Now that I know her better perhaps Marcia's nerves, being unsure of herself, not really having come to terms with her own cancer or emotionally working out her own feelings was the cause of her not coming across well. She also was in a constant promotional mode for the business she was developing. Numerous things about her personality were really abrasive to me at the time. I did not find her amusing and she couldn't move beyond her own breast surgery. We were all tired of her saying how old she was when in many of our eyes she hadn't matured. Marcia and I had a discussion about this period of time and she was totally unaware of her behavior agreeing it was probably because she was so involved with developing her business.

I seriously believe if she stated, "I am also a breast cancer survivor and this is what I did to get myself back on my feet," only when there were new people in the class, she could move on with the exercises. The constant repetition of the same thing drove some of us crazy. I'm using the plural because it was a topic of discussion when we met in the lobby.

On a personal level the *age thing* really got to me. I'm seventy and I'm still moving. If I stay far enough away from a mirror, I don't see all my wrinkles. If I'm too close to a mirror I do see the sagging chin skin.

Ken sometimes notices me pulling up skin towards my ears.

"What are you doing?"

"I'm making myself look younger."

"Are you planning on having surgery?"

"No, I've had enough. Besides I don't want to look like some female T.V. personalities."

I will accept growing older as gracefully as I can and use my wigs to at least give me an illusion that I'm not ancient.

There was a woman in the class who I'm sure was older than me. Her daughter brought her and she did send out positive vibes. Then she stopped coming. One night Marcia started to tell a story about a seventy year old who was doing an exercise in one of her other classes. Something about her running I believe. Marcia was in total disbelief she could run as fast as she did and keep up with the others in her group. *I thought perhaps a visit to an active adult community was in order.* Seventy year olds do not *lie down and die* if they have a good attitude. They make the most of every day.

The topping on the cake occurred that same evening when we were finishing up the class by standing in a circle with exercise ropes tied together. Kate was on my left and Marcia on my right. Marcia began telling a story about another seventy year old. I was now insulted. I whispered in Kate's ear asking if anyone in the class was older than me. She was in possession of all our medical information but responded with, "I don't know. Why don't you ask them?" It dawned on me quickly it must be part of the privacy laws.

I bluntly admitted to my seventy years.

"Is anyone else my age?" No one was that night but the responses I received were motivating and upbeat.

"I hope I'll be as good as you when I reach your age."

"I want to be like you."

"You're kidding."

"You are my role model."

"I want to emulate you."

"I didn't know you were seventy. You don't look it. You really are doing well." And this was from Marcia. I think I accomplished what I was hoping for. Marcia would no longer bring up age and what we're capable of doing. Perhaps now I could see her in another light.

One night Marcia couldn't make it to class. Kate was doing the program by herself. There was a lighter atmosphere in the room. Over the course of weeks Kate showed me exercises to avoid and a way to substitute them. The class was now up to a point in exercising with those I was to avoid. I felt comfortable enough to say, "I may not be able to do these exercises but I can belly dance."

I didn't realize what a big deal this was. Of course I had to show the group. Kate said it was a fantastic exercise for lymphedema. So here's the seventy year old belly dancing and Marcia is not there to see it. Kate asked if I could show the class at the end of the session. I tried to explain how but no one was able to catch on.

The teacher in me said there had to be a way for the class to learn if this was important for lymphedema. I stayed up a good part of the night and hopefully figured out a way for the women to at least get started. When I went to see Mani the next day Kate had already passed the word around about my belly dancing. Mani wanted to learn. In fact I was trying to teach everyone who came to look. I heard, "Your husband must be having a good time."

Dr. Capp said on my next visit to him "I haven't seen you look this well in years." I'm sure the belly dancing for exercise has plenty to do with it.

The following week someone asked if I could give a repeat lesson. Marcia wanted to know what we were talking about. The other person said Rosalie is teaching us how to belly dance. Our class ended that evening with everyone gathered around me. I showed them how to belly dance incorporating some of the techniques we were doing in class. Deep breathing and control of your stomach muscle is the clue to getting started. Most everyone decided it was better to watch me so they could have a good laugh.

The class at one session started. A woman arrived late looking very upset and on the verge of tears. We were all concerned. Her doctor dismissed her and she was afraid of the *"What do I do now feeling?"* so many of us experience.

I told a joke based on a real incident. A smile appeared on the woman's face. Someone else told a joke. I contributed another one. The woman was laughing. I suggested a laughing party. Marcia said not to have it until she came home from her trip. She wanted to be there. And that was her big moment of change. She identified herself with us and started to speak in a different manner. She was really starting to move on.

We had our laughing party and it was enjoyed by all those who attended. We all contributed food and Kate had some main dishes delivered. I brought some cartoons and passed them around in the beginning to start the proverbial ball rolling.

I asked everyone to come prepared to tell us a funny story that personally happened to them. I made up numbers and everyone drew one from a paper bag. One lady started to get upset. She thought it was a grab bag and hadn't brought a gift. We all heard her sigh of relief when she was told the number referred to our speaking order. People asked for some recipes, others asked for copies of the cartoons and I suggested we write up all the stories and make a booklet out of it. We took a group picture unfortunately with some of us missing.

I admit to hounding several people for their stories and eventually called those who didn't respond. They repeated their funnies over the phone and I typed them up and called them back to confirm what they said. I very quickly drew small pictures under each one. Some of the pages looked empty. It was the best I could do on such short notice. Kate and I were collating the books before class that evening to hand them out to everyone. I heard some excellent feedback.

Marcia started to relate better to all of us and let her hair down. I now believe that was one of the problems. She was caught between her new career and being a cancer survivor herself. She finally found her place.

Cancer and lymphedema have no age discrimination even though it is likely to be more prevalent as we get older. We are all in this together in spite of age, race or religion.

CHAPTER 54

I CAN BREATHE

Throughout the years my doctors new and old were upset about how short my breath was. Taking a deep breath for x-rays was nearly impossible and the tests were often repeated until a tech gave up. Meanwhile I was exposed to additional radiation. I was given all sorts of sprays to put in my mouth or up my nose. Nothing worked. I tried to use a sleep apnea machine without success. My uvula was surgically removed and did nothing. I went to classes for breathing techniques. Nothing worked!

No one ever came up with blockage from all my scar tissue. The closest comment mentioning scar tissue as a problem was the massage therapist in Perrytown.

Mani had a lot of work to do in breaking up all my scar tissue including scar tissue from my spinal laminectomies. It was worth it. I can breathe and Mani took satisfaction with her accomplishment. Learning breathing techniques were successful this time. My lymph system began to work. I have almost forgotten how I used to breathe and am actually unable to do so physically now.

The most remarkable thing of all is how doctors in general do not have a clue or belief in how lymphedema may be the underlying cause of many ailments. Then again many doctors don't recognize lymphedema as a medical condition.

I thought it would be beneficial to inform the woman teaching relaxation at the Cancer Center about scar tissue blockage. I sat in her class every week hearing, "Take a deep breath down to your stomach." My breathing went no farther than my shoulders. *Could she have mistaken the organs in our bodies?* I didn't think so. I heard the same thing for years and knew it was me. We were given the option of closing our eyes but once in a while I would take a sneak peak to see if everyone else's stomachs were moving.

The same thing might be happening to other women as they passed through the facilitator's class. Perhaps if her wording was changed to, "You *should* be able take a deep breath down to your stomach," before the exercise started, it might alert a participant and a question might follow. The facilitator could then suggest checking with your doctor about scar tissue. I decided to mention what happened to me. Unfortunately a woman started a fight with me. I was wrong. Lymphedema has nothing to do with scar tissue.

My well intentioned suggestion went nowhere in the tense atmosphere. After taking so many years to discover my problem this information might have been a clue for others. Additional tests and lung x-rays could be avoided resulting in less radiation. Other people might learn from my experience and this woman blew the whole thing. I was upset and at my next visit to Mani questioned my own ability to help others.

CHAPTER 55

SEVENTIETH BIRTHDAY PARTY

Ben was excited for over a year. He wanted to make me a seventieth birthday party bash. I had my hesitations. I was alive to celebrate my seventh birthday but didn't want to make my own party. If the party was for me, I wanted someone else to make it. I didn't want to contend with fights between family members. It seemed easier to have nothing.

A few of my friends knew of my impending big birthday and felt I should have something. I deserved it. I had been through so much and should celebrate. A friend suggested two separate parties, one for family and one for friends.

Mindy handled the immediate family festivities. Donny decorated their house and I was with my family. I had a lovely evening with everyone all around me. I ignored what was going to upset me and had a wonderful time.

Ben in the meantime was supposed to be setting up the friends' party. My friend convinced me even if there were ten people it would still be a party. We set the date for a Sunday two days before my actual birthday.

Ben made arrangement for my other party in a restaurant near our development. My cousins and friends were invited and I had another lovely day. I decided to cover the entertainment. It was going to be me.

CHAPTER 56

ENTERTAINMENT

I wanted to have bubble blowing using the same type of bubble blower we use in lymphedema exercise class. My goal was to share with relatives and friends one of the things I do in a hospital setting that is actually fun. After looking on the internet and in a craft's store, I discovered it wasn't feasible to invest in a tremendous quantity of bubble blowers. I would never be able to use them up. I asked about purchasing them from the physical therapy department.

I was given nineteen bubble blowers as my seventieth birthday gift. I shared this story with my guests and enjoyed watching their reactions when they each received their own. As soon as one guest realized what he had in his hands the bubble blowing began in earnest. Similar to students in many of my classes the first person didn't follow directions. My instructions were to turn away from the food. Someone decided to cover their food with a napkin and others followed suit. The object of this experience didn't involve giving the food on their plates a bubble bath.

I directed my guests to take a deep breath through their nose and blow out through their mouths. Some people had a problem differentiating between a nose and mouth.

Next I reviewed my life with props saved from my birth. I moved up through the years incorporating my collection in my tale. I usually am very nervous about speaking in front of a group but was determined to forge ahead because it was my birthday. I was going to have fun. The whole presentation turned out to be better than I anticipated. The end of my presentation was about a wonderful and uplifting experience I had at St. Augustus.

I was given a pass for valet parking and asked if I was required to tip. I was told an emphatic no. The service was for patients. Visitors were a different story. One very nice young man helped me the most. I went to the hospital four times a week at the time. One day we had a conversation about art. I remarked about bringing some medium and pad to draw the beautiful floral display growing in front of the hospital entrance. Dino seemed to enjoy speaking to me about my art work.

During this period Cancer Support was having their annual butterfly release. I was asked if I could participate by bringing a matted butterfly picture for an art exhibit.

I made a few small matted butterfly paintings for sale as a donation and a large one for a raffle prize. My painting for the art exhibit was a separate entity. I painted an 8"x10" picture and asked my resident critic Ben to look at it. He wanted me to do something bigger to have the wow factor. I started with an 11"x14" inch work area this time. I did my painting and showed it to Ben. "Yes, that's the one for exhibition." Following directions I matted and covered the painting with plastic and luckily for all of us who participated that we did. Thunderstorms rained down on our art work.

I noticed Dino wasn't there a few days prior to Mother's Day. On the following Tuesday I saw him and asked if he was all right. "I graduated from college, spent Mother's Day with my mom and then it was my birthday." I wished him all sorts of happiness and luck.

I wanted to give him something special. The first butterfly painting I made seemed appropriate. I matted the picture, boxed and wrapped it. I wrote him a congratulatory card stating he now was free to be independent like a butterfly and take off to do great things.

The next day I placed the package on the passenger seat of my car. When I drove up to the valet station he wasn't there. A thought went through my head he might have left for another job and I lost my chance to show him my appreciation not only for helping me out but also for his accomplishment. I left the car with another valet and went to therapy.

On my way out I spotted Dino in the hospital lobby.

"I didn't see you this morning and I have a gift for you."

"A gift for me?" He was genuinely surprised.

He kept repeating, "A gift for me?"

We went outside together and he went to get my car. He always opened the windows to try and let some of the heat escape after sitting in the sun for a long period of time. When he drove up to the valet station I pointed to the gift on the passenger seat.

"It's for you."

Dino still couldn't believe it. I finally convinced him and he stepped out of the car holding the package.

"May I open it?"

"*Of course!* It's yours."

His hands were shaking as he tore off the ribbon and wrapping paper. He opened the box and couldn't believe his eyes.

"Did you paint this?" I nodded yes.

Dino kept repeating over and over how beautiful it was. I asked him to open the card. He was just so happy. Tears were flowing down his face.

"I've never gotten a gift before only m…." He didn't finish the word.

He kept repeating how he loved it and was full of questions.

"How long did it take you to paint? I'm going over to show the painting to my family as soon as I leave work. Can I give you a hug?" I thought it was great making someone so happy.

Dino walked back to the valet station holding the painting in the box as though it were diamonds. I was thrilled I had given someone else so much joy. I decided to make butterflies for all my guests but in a smaller size to finish in time for my party.

Each guest was given a butterfly picture all individually painted and different. I matted the picture and wrapped them in plastic. I personalized a label and signed them with Love, Rosalie.

My guests couldn't wait to get their hands on the butterfly pictures. It was the perfect note to end the party. The birthday cake was almost an afterthought.

People called telling me they had a wonderful time. Two didn't even wait to arrive home. Everyone was surprised about my entertaining "schtick."

Ben was impressed and praised me. I couldn't have asked for a better day and thanked him profusely.

CHAPTER 57

HAIR OR LACK OF IT

Hair is a problem for cancer patients, some for a short term and others like me for the rest of our lives. We have to find a solution we can be happy and live with, is affordable and easy to manage. We have enough to worry about dealing with our medical issues. Hair should not be an added problem. I was given a recommendation for someone by two people. One was a cancer patient.

Human hairpieces are attached to your shaved scalp with glue. The advantage of this method is you have the ability to treat the piece like your own hair. The hairpiece is washed and styled with your own hair, remains on your head until your next appointment and is natural looking.

The downside is a very long list which continued to grow over the years. The costs are excessive and the person I used became very unpleasant, lost her ability to cut and style hair, refused to be accountable for her own errors, was totally irresponsible, made very poor business decisions while leaving me in the lurch numerous times. Unfortunately once my head was shaved I was beholden to her.

Hairpieces are more common for men than woman and therefore more hair dressers are available to males. It is close to an impossible task to find someone who is licensed and capable of working with this method in my area for females.

Unbeknown to me at the time the cancer patient who recommended this hair dresser tapes her piece on every morning and doesn't wash it between visits. This is unacceptable to me. The piece has dirt on it from daily wear and collects pollen when you are outside. If I knew this information from the start, I never would have started with this method.

One of the biggest downsides was my scalp couldn't be checked by my dermatologist. I had to rely on my hairdresser for seeing anything unusual when the hairpiece was re-glued.

I was originally assured my hair would grow back if I decided not to use this method anymore. The old glue would be removed with each visit. Both of these promises proved to be untrue.

The situation became more and more difficult for me. I was caught between a rock and a hard place. When we began the hairdresser convinced me hair was the one thing I would not have to worry about. Yet the opposite was happening.

During one emergency hospitalization electrodes had to be placed on my head. A new headpiece had been attached to my head the day before. Fortunately I had a technician who took her time cutting off the piece without destroying it. My appearance was another matter. I looked like Clara Bell the clown. Adding to my comical look was the thin strands of my own hair sticking out of the sides and back of my head. Five days later one of my doctors gave orders to remove the electrodes.

If I thought my appearance was bad before I was now in strong contention for the clown of the month award. The top of my head was completely bald. I had a hard time looking at myself. I had to do something before visitors came to see me. Besides my head was cold! I made a makeshift hat from a pillowcase and plopped it on my head, then I remembered my hairdresser saying, "I make hospital visits." She couldn't come but had a wig she could loan me. Ben picked it up and I wore it until my next scheduled appointment.

"I've decided to keep the wig as a back-up," I told my hairdresser at my next appointment. "I'll give you a break on the price but the wig needs fitting." She promptly began to cut and sew it. The wig was supposed to be a bargain but I was shocked at the cost. This was not real hair or even new. The charge was excessive, the wig was nothing special and I could have purchased one for less than twelve times the amount. My mistake! I should have asked the price first. It was too late for me to decline. I was later told the wig was made much too small for my head size.

My hospital and doctors' visits were planned around my hairdresser. When she cancelled all my other appointments were thrown off. Her cancellations became very frequent and always an hour or two before I was leaving the house. My hairpieces did not necessarily stay on my head until my next appointment and I was stuck trying to find a solution for what was becoming an unwelcoming embarrassment. Several of my doctors, therapists and my fitter advised me to use a wig permanently yet I couldn't make myself do so. On my hairdressers next to last cancellation with me and her very nasty attitude, I was left reeling. I had to make a change.

I called my fitter Lizzie at the cancer boutique. A beautician who worked with wigs was in her shop and I went to the boutique after the phone call. I brought a small bottle of the glue and a sample of the tape used to reset a hairpiece with me. I knew how to do the whole procedure and perhaps with my instructions the beautician could re-glue my piece.

A volunteer that I knew from Cancer Support, Lizzie and myself went into the beautician's room. Everyone was trying to come up with a solution. The beautician looked at the products I brought with me and heard me describe how to put the piece on. "It's a specialty and I won't even attempt to try it. Why don't you wear a wig? It's so much easier to care for and definitely less expensive." I just wasn't ready to go into a wig. "I know exactly what to look for on the internet and I'll try to find someone to help you." I thanked everyone and left feeling better than when I arrived.

A list was sent over to me with two names and phone numbers on it. I called and wasn't impressed with one of them and the other put me on hold for a half hour. I gave up.

I went for my appointment with my hairdresser and for the very first time had the courage to put her on the defensive. She was definitely surprised by my new demeanor. "Do you realize how many times you've cancelled on me in a short period of time?" She didn't believe it. I repeated all the excuses she gave me. This was absolutely the last time I would put up with her nonsense. I was unable to cope with the stress of dealing with her anymore. She was supposed to make my life easier instead I was being aggravated.

CHAPTER 58

FLORIDA III

Mani checked me out before we left for our next Florida trip. Travelling was much easier this time. Instead of all the bandages I wore a lymphedema glove and a long sleeve compression top. No one bugged me with questions and that helped the whole flying experience. I chose to be patted down rather than go through the x-ray machine and it was done without any fanfare in Newark. I was still checked for gunshot residue.

Ben again deliberately sat on my left hand side to prevent people passing in the aisle with their luggage who continually banged into me. Very few people bring standard size carry-ons on the plane. Most of them take regular size luggage pieces and no one stops them. In addition many males wear big back packs and the women have pocket books on their shoulders the size of suitcases swinging them as they walk by. It is totally irrelevant if they hit someone with their belongings. They couldn't care less.

Our new GPS didn't work again but it did recognize Florida this time around. We went back to our favorite hotel on the East Coast where many of the players on the Mets team and their families stay.

Another one of my grandson's was having his Bar Mitzvah. My hairpiece was re-glued three days before our departure to Florida for our stay of one month. My hairpiece should have remained on my head for our whole trip. An appointment date was made for my hairpiece to be re-glued on our immediate return.

After three days my hairpiece started to loosen and by day five it was totally off my head. Supposedly my piece was double glued. My hairdresser was so involved with her daughter who was sitting in the room with us, she may have forgotten the second coat of glue. Regardless my hairpiece should not have come off in such a short period of time.

I had to deal with the problem at hand immediately. I was extremely upset and left with no choice but to find a wig somewhere. Since I had to solve a new challenge A.S.A.P., I asked Laura the manager of the hotel who is nothing less than wonderful, if she could help me. Her mother died approximately five months before. We sent a condolence card and she was thankful we thought of her.

I was comfortable asking her about a wig and if she knew of a hospital nearby that worked with cancer patients. Not only did she help me but then confided her mother's cause of death was cancer. She would find a place to help me out.

Within fifteen minutes she came back with a phone number to call. "If you need anything else let me know." I was directed to the American Cancer Society and was given the phone number of the closest facility for help. I made arrangements to be there early in the afternoon.

The first wig I tried on was the most attractive and natural looking. Blond and red wigs were in abundance but my choice was perfect for me. At least I would have hair on my head for the rest of our vacation. An appointment was made to come back and have the wig shaped.

Back at the hotel people inquired about my new look. They really liked it.

One couple had an adorable boy who became my *friend* and also a three month old baby girl. The mother and I became as close as people can get in a short span of time and of different ages. She would come down to breakfast and most dinner times with the children. Her husband was a pitcher for the Mets.

The little girl had a twin sister who died the month before. The son repeated every day that his other sister was in Heaven. I was unsure of a way to help comfort Mom who obviously was still quite upset. The only thing that came to my mind was, "You have two beautiful children now. Taking care of them is an honor for the baby who died." She related the situation about her other child to me the first night we met and our first night at the hotel. Perhaps I became an older ear to confide in which she did as the days went by.

When my little friend's mommy saw me at breakfast she asked about my *new* hair. I told her the truth.

"My numerous cancer surgeries and all my medication did a number on my hair."

"My baby was treated with chemo and I know where you are coming from," she said.

I met Joan, a woman who had a mastectomy within the past two years and we related to one another immediately. Joan's husband was part of the film crew for the Mets and they remained in our hotel throughout Ben and my stay. The weather was colder than usual and extremely blustery on this trip. I almost lost my wig several times. Joan gave me a couple of headbands to hold my wig on when it almost disappeared into the Atlantic Ocean.

One of the biggest problems I had regarding my scalp was removal of the glue that held my hairpiece on. I used alcohol but my skin became dry, making my scalp itchy, yet the glue remained. I put a call into the hairdresser. I told her the hairpiece came off.

"What do you use to remove the glue?" I was aware some product was dabbed onto my scalp in a few spots and the glue supposedly was removed. I was willing to purchase anything that would work.

"Use alcohol."

"I'm using alcohol and the glue is not coming off."

"Keep rubbing."

I had a four or five year accumulation of glue on my scalp and was given no other information but to *keep rubbing*.

It took almost a month for me to finally rid my head of the glue residue. My scalp was irritated, red and sore. Bumps were under my skin on the areas of my scalp where the hairpieces had been glued. One bump was much larger than the others. I knew a visit to my dermatologist was a necessity when I returned home.

A few days prior to leaving Florida for home, my hairdresser called. "I need you to come in this afternoon to have your hairpiece re-glued. I know you have your grandson's Bar Mitzvah next week. I have a chance to go to Florida and I want to put the hairpiece back on your head before I go."

"I'm still in Florida," I answered.

"I'm not returning from Florida just to put your hairpiece on."

Our relationship was officially kaput. I would learn to wear and live with a wig.

CHAPTER 59

SMOKE

Our handicapped room was on the fifth floor. No one was above us. The Saturday night after we arrived in Florida, I smelled smoke while in the bathroom and lost my voice. Ben started to smell the smoke as it wafted into the bedroom. I was afraid the hotel might be on fire and was concerned everyone would have to evacuate. I called the front desk. An engineer immediately came up to our room and couldn't tell where the smoke was coming from. "Do you want to change rooms?" There wasn't one available room left in the hotel.

I went into the hallway walking away from our room and eventually my voice returned. I went back to our room sleeping with the door ajar to the hallway for many hours. The next night about the same time the identical problem reoccurred. Smoke was coming down throughout the rooms. I again lost my voice and went down to the hotel desk. The same engineer as the previous night went up to our room. He too was overcome with the smell. We were given a huge suite for the night. The first thing I did was take a shower to wash off the odor of the smoke clinging to my body and clothes.

My voice never returned. Nancy at the front desk encouraged me to use the inhaler I carried with me at all times. Nothing was helping and by Monday morning I was sent to the Urgent Care Center. I was plied with steroid pills, additional inhalers and had a special x-ray taken of my larynx. My test was negative.

Back at the hotel the engineer checked out every possibility for the smoke. He taped up some vents in the ceiling of our suite. Our room was two floors above the one smoking floor. All of the guests on the level directly below us were checked to see if someone had been smoking. I suggested the roof of the building. No one had access to the locked area except for the two with the key and they didn't smoke. The engineer shut the vent entering our room.

Laura had a sit down with me and suggested I go to another hotel not because she wanted me to leave but she was concerned about my health. "I'll hold your room if you want to come back." I declined. The engineer said he turned the main vent in another direction and I was willing to take a chance for another night.

There were no more smoke incidents but I never regained my voice. Apparently everyone was alerted to what happened. Every staff member was concerned about me for the rest of our stay. Conversing with everyone was difficult but everything worked out well.

I did not get better and a few days later went back to the Urgent Care Center. Another doctor said the steroid pills weren't strong enough and gave me a shot of steroids. I was subject to a throat culture which was negative. I went back to the Urgent Care Center one more time and was seen by the same doctor who saw me the second time. He gave me a second shot of steroids which didn't work. I kept mentioning allergies and asthma but perhaps the doctors were themselves at a loss in the way to treat me. My greatest fear of course was cancer and the doctors at the Urgent Care facility had no way of reassuring me that it wasn't. I lived with laryngitis until I saw my own doctor at home.

When we departed the hotel everyone gave us hugs and kisses good-bye. In fact some beach chairs and umbrellas are in their storage room for our next stay. The most interesting thing is on our last day Nancy came up with the conclusion a guest or guests must have been smoking near the vent pipe outside the hotel leading to our suite. That idea really made sense.

We left the hotel in Port St. Lucie and drove over to the west coast of Florida for the rest of our stay. We saw the Yankees play twice and both times had a debacle with our seats. The seats were changed and yet we continue to pay a service fee each time to the ticket sellers for their errors.

Mistakes are made in every area of our lives but medical errors are the most serious of all. My life is a good example of some of the best care and some of the worst and is a prime reason to stay on top of your own health issues.

CHAPTER 60

FLORIDA RESIDUE

My first medical stop when we returned from Florida this time would have to be my internist. My continuing laryngitis had to be checked out. My doctor reminded me of my grandson's Bar Mitzvah and wished me to be there with a voice. She wanted me to see an ENT immediately but I was to have no more steroids. Together we went through several names and a girl in her office called for an appointment with each one of the doctors. Only one ENT was able to see me that afternoon. He was in the same group as another doctor I saw previously.

We headed over to his office and the first question asked was why I wasn't seeing the other doctor? "You were the one with an available appointment." Now that the amenities were over we got down to business. He said the laryngitis may have originally come from an asthmatic attack; it was no longer the case. He wanted to do a test going down my nose and throat. He started going into detail and I realized it was a test I've gone through at least fifty times. I am not exaggerating.

The test only showed spasms in my larynx. The ENT thought it came from GERD. He wanted to give me medication. GERD and medication for it was on my "cheat sheet". *Didn't he read my medications and medical conditions?* I pointed it out to him and he admitted he only gave the sheet a cursory glance. He looked more closely and decided to put me on a small dose of another medication to take at night along with my medication for GERD in the morning. I was to see him in a month. At least I found out my laryngitis wasn't caused by cancer.

I attended the Bar Mitzvah and luncheon afterwards as well as the Friday night meal. I did so with not much of a voice. The prescribed medication did nothing for me but I didn't let the lack of a voice keep me from having a good time and letting my grandson know how proud I was of him.

I was reaching a desperate point again and decided to call the pulmonologist/ allergist on my own. My new one wasn't in but someone in her office agreed to see me the following day. I really like him.

"Are you really seventy?"

"Yes."

"You're very well preserved." I thanked him and told him I would let my mother know when I visited her at the cemetery. Dr. Held read my "cheat sheet."

I brought the test results from the ENT otherwise I would be going through another down my nose and into my throat test. After examining me, Dr. Held gave me a new medicine to try and agreed I should stop using the medication from the ENT. The new medication was a combination of two allergy medications and was working for others. "Come back to see me in a week."

First Dr. Held was going to switch me back to the other new doctor but I only saw her once. She was a replacement for another doctor who had left the practice. I did not want to continue with replacement after replacement. No one would get to know me. I am now officially Dr. Held's patient.

The medication worked and my voice started to return. I have chemical allergies and doctors who do not know me will have to start listening to what I tell them or I will have to find someone else. Dr. Held has now seen me two more times. He says he has other things up his sleeve if I need it. Ben met him and he also was impressed with his very likeable personality.

I was ready to address my head and scalp problems and contacted my favorite dermatologist. Dr. Shui saw me the day I called and examined my head. I had an assortment of conditions. One normally called for a shot of cortisone but we both agreed that was not a solution for me. There was an ointment I could use but Dr. Shui wanted it checked out by my internist. A medication given to me in the past could be applied to all the other areas but one.

The third problem had to be removed by a surgeon. "I'm recommending Dr. Willis. He is a surgeon who is in an adjacent set of offices." Dr. Shui's assistant walked me over to Dr. Willis' office but I had to wait a month for an appointment. Four weeks was a long time to wait to have the lump removed.

I thought about finding another surgeon to have the growth removed at an earlier date. I went on the computer to check Dr. Willis' credentials and they were quite impressive. He was so highly educated and regarded I gave up the thought of looking for someone else.

The best thing I did for myself during this waiting period was to go St. Augustus for my groups which now numbered two. The women who are in the groups have bonded and enjoy being with one another. One woman calls the Monday night group *her girls*. Indeed I think we are all feeling that way. At least we understand one another.

Four weeks went by and I was ready for surgery. I washed what remains of the hair left on my head and put on my wig. I took a formed scarf to fit over my head after surgery. I didn't think a wig would be feasible. Unfortunately neither was a scarf.

My name was called and I followed an assistant into a surgical room. We went over my medications and Dr. Willis walked in. He was a young man wearing bright red hi-top sneakers with silver trim a style boy's wore when I was in elementary school. They certainly made a statement with his conservative blue surgical garments.

Dr. Willis was very pleasant and described the procedure. "Two different types of self-dissolving stitches will be used in the wound. You will be given several shots to numb the area. You can't wear anything on your head for at least five days. I would tell the same thing to my mother," he said.

"May I see the growth?" Dr. Willis must have thought I was nuts.

"Will it be acceptable if I showed the growth to you in a bottle?"

"Sure!"

I had so many internal parts removed from my body this was an opportunity to actually see one. The assistant asked if my husband was in the waiting room and his name. She brought Ben in to give me support and said I was in excellent hands. On a scale of one to ten for surgery this one barely rated a one. My fear was finding out the results of the biopsy. Yet I was getting more consideration than I had with many of my major surgeries and not all of them written about in this book. I suggested Ben take a peek at the doctor's sneakers. He never noticed them.

The doctor spoke to me for a few minutes after my surgery was over and wrote a prescription for a shampoo to be used twice a week. The co-pay for the shampoo was extraordinarily high for a very small bottle. My pharmaceutical statement shows a full cost of almost double the co-pay. Sadly the results do not seem to warrant the cost.

The assistant came over with the vile containing my growth. It is best described as a large pink, clear uncut diamond. I jokingly made the comment it would make a nice necklace. I heard about people making jewelry out of their gall stones.

We had dinner plans and tickets to a show the next night. That was a non-starter though I tried to figure out a way to handle it. The surgeon was most concerned about bacteria and internal bleeding if I moved around. Dr. Willis gave me directions, "Do not do anything except rest." Ben and I ruled out my making dinner.

By the fourth night I was starting to go a little batty and decided to go to my Monday night class at St. Augustus. No one would make fun of me if they saw me wigless. Even if I just sat around and laughed with everyone I would feel better. Ben drove me and I made the correct decision to be there with "*the girls.*"

Five days passed and I called the surgeon's office to see if the results of the biopsy came in. They did not and I was told to try again two days later. My head was still a bit sore and directions said it could take up to three months for the lump to flatten. I was determined to leave the house.

Two days later I again called the doctor's office leaving a message two times. Someone from Dr. Willis' office called later in the day. "Your biopsy is negative." I could again take a very deep breath and smile. There were no tears this time.

My first day out my wig felt too heavy over the surgical area. I put on a jaunty type red beret given to me in Florida by the American Cancer Society. I looked different and believe some people who saw me from our community had no idea who I was. What a difference hair makes even if it isn't your own growth.

CHAPTER 61

SKIN CANCER

Six months after my head lump was taken care of, I noticed something popping out on my nose near my left eye. Unfortunately something much bigger was on the top of my leg. I had to use a mirror to see the whole area but it looked infected and was wet to my touch. A third area stung my back in the shower. I had several doctor appointments during the week including my internist and asked each one about my leg. The problem area fascinated all of the doctors but no one could diagnosis it. I kept the area clean, used an antibiotic and covered the large spot with a bandage. It was time to see Dr. Shui again.

Dr. Shui saw me the day after I called. When she entered the room we discussed all three areas of concern to me. I suggested we start from the top and my nose was examined first. Dr. Shui's reaction to my nose was quite different from my other skin conditions in the past. Her assistant was asked to take pictures of my nose setting off an alarm in my head. "Dr. Willis will need the pictures for location," she stated. Biopsies were taken next and Dr. Shui suspected I probably needed to see the surgeon again.

Dr. Shui looked at my other two areas but her biggest concern was still my nose. Ben had something removed from his face several days before but no pictures were taken. I surmised there was a problem.

The following week someone in the dermatologist' office called and gave me the information for Ben's biopsy. His was negative. I asked about mine. The results hadn't come in yet and would probably take a few more days.

The next day I went for acupuncture and as soon as I entered the house the phone rang. Ben picked it up. I heard him speaking to someone and then he put me on the phone. It was Dr. Shui not an aide or someone from the office. I knew there was trouble. Dr. Shui felt absolutely terrible to have to tell me my biopsy was malignant. I needed surgery. She was going to give me the number of the surgeon and changed her mind. At my request she was going to his office on the other side of the building to try and get me an early appointment. "His receptionist will call you back."

I felt sorry for myself for two minutes. Ben put his arms around me and said, "We'll get through this." I went into the second stage after diagnosis. Taking care of my problem came next.

After two and a half hours no one called. I found the surgeon's number.

"Yes, the doctor spoke to me about you," said the receptionist. I was given an appointment for over five weeks from that day.

"That is unacceptable. I am a cancer patient many times over and this growth came up very quickly."

"I'll put you on a waiting list." I became very bold.

"That is unacceptable." She agreed to put me on the top of the waiting list.

I spoke to Mindy and she told me to call every day for a cancellation. This was something I was planning to do anyway. Early evening I was going to a Susan G. Koman function at St. Augustus. Just before I left the house I called the surgeon's office. I left a message. I still can't believe what I said.

"I'm leaving you my name and phone number and will be hounding you every day for a cancellation."

I arrived at St. Augustus and two of my therapists were there along with a group of women who come to our exercise programs. After warm hugs and kisses I told them what happened. Everyone had the same reaction I did. "With your cancer history, you can't wait five weeks." One of the woman said she would keep calling me as a reminder "to *get on it*" and not to wait.

One of the speakers was from the oncology department and said to contact her if we needed information. During a break I went over to the speaker and she gave me the name of two dermatology offices. "Ask if they have surgeons." That night I thought of calling Tremore and another hospital where I was still being seen for other medical conditions. At seven forty five in the morning the phone rang. There was a cancellation. "Can you come right over?" I quickly got dressed. I didn't want to wake Ben. My plan was to have the surgery and if I couldn't drive home, I would call him to pick me up.

I was about to leave the house and Ben called out to me. He was half a sleep.

"I'll call you if I need you,"

"Sounds like a plan," and he rolled over to go back to sleep. As I was putting on my jacket he called out to me.

"Can you wait five minutes? I'll go with you."

It really was good that I waited for Ben. When the MOHS surgery was over my left eye was closed, I was bandaged up, the stitching pulled up my upper lip and I was swollen all over my face. We spent almost four hours at the surgeon's office. I had to be called in several times until all the cancer was removed.

CHAPTER 62

BILLS

Cancer and lymphedema patients are constantly being billed for one thing or another. Many mistakes are made and my bills are no exception. Try to get a responsible person to help you if you are incapable of taking care of them yourself.

I've been double billed numerous times. My payment has gone to the wrong department in the same facility and my check was not credited to my account. Follow up calls do not necessarily work and then I'm subjected to another bill threatening to send me to collections. Perhaps the medical facilities consider my payment a donation. Tremore suggested I designate on both the back and front of my check the department the check belongs to e.g. radiology, doctor, etc.

One of my wildest experiences was being billed an exorbitant amount of money for a place I didn't recognize. I called the billing department and was informed it was definitely for me. I saw the date of service. I couldn't possibly have been there I was hospitalized. The person insisted I was wrong. He tried to convince me I could be redeemed as he quoted passages from his dominations bible. In the end I would still have to pay or I would be sent to collections. I couldn't believe it. All the prayers and bible quotes were not going to get me out of this improbable situation.

The following week I went to physical therapy and noted the name on the door had changed. It was renamed as the place where I supposedly owed money. I asked my therapist, "Why am I receiving a bill for days I wasn't in physical therapy?" The next day I received an apologetic call, "Your card was placed in someone else's folder during the transfer and you were billed for the other person. I'll straighten everything out." The prayers and biblical passages worked!

There are times I am so frustrated in dealing with some of the people in a billing department I turn the phone over to Ben. No one wants to speak to him unless I give them my formal permission and I end up back on the phone. There have been cases where he too lost his cool with the person on the other end of the line. Many do not speak American English and we are at a loss in understanding what they are saying. They do not understand us either. I recognize the fact we are living in a polyglot society but someone should be on staff that speaks English in an understandable manner.

Bills are often received that are totally unreadable with many columns of charges, credits, etc. but do not make any sense. I may not have majored in math but I am a college graduate plus. I call up for an explanation and the person at the other end doesn't understand the bill either. Why are they working there? Or better yet why aren't the bills simplified?

There was one scenario where I was refused an appointment because a past bill hadn't been paid. After playing Sherlock Holmes I found out that the bill had been paid under my married name. This required an enormous amount of time, numerous phone calls, and a lot of money for postage for all my letters requesting a return receipt to straighten things out. Written complaints to my insurance company, copies of our marriage license, etc. were sent to the hospital. I waited weeks for responses from both places. I needed a copy of the front and back of the cancelled check from the insurance company. It became incumbent on me to prove the bill was paid if I didn't want the hospital to send me to collections and wanted to be seen there again.

After all of the above the check wasn't written by me and therefore the insurance company had to forward a copy of the check. This is exactly what I requested with my first phone call and was denied by the hospital. Eventually I convinced a supervisor from the hospital to directly request a copy of the check from my insurance company. It took months to rectify all of this because someone again didn't look at the name and account number on the check and apply it to the proper place. Meanwhile I was denied an appointment until all of this was resolved.

If you are paid to do a job, do it. Cancer patients may not be up to doing the task I did. Why should we have the additional burden of fixing up someone else's errors and then be insulted by not even being able to get an appointment with our doctor?

I'm going to include those annoying appointment reminders with bills because it inevitably involves your money. You know the ones that say, "The doctor has blocked out time for you and if you don't give us a 24, 48 or 72 hours' notice you will be charged $35.00, $50.00 or $75.00" depending on the doctor.

Some of these calls have involved doctors I didn't even know. How they managed to get my name and phone number is beyond my comprehension. I've received reminders for the right doctor but the wrong date and time. In one case the girls in the office were calling a patient with the same name as mine. The call came in at the very end of the day and was left on my machine. When I tried to call back every one in the office had left. The next morning I had an appointment with another doctor and couldn't call again until the afternoon. The incorrect appointment was for the morning also. Therefore either the right person didn't get the message or I was going to be billed. My phone call netted me the information about another person having my name.

I understand that a doctor doesn't want to be "stood up" but what about a patient who sits in a doctor's waiting room quite literally for hours before they're taken. They can't charge the doctor! Or how about a patient who is on the way to a doctor, has a long distance to travel and when they arrive at the office the staff tells you the doctor didn't come in today. "We were going to call you later." It certainly would have been more considerate to let me know before I left my house, took a few hours ride, paid a toll over a bridge and paid for parking my car. A call after my appointment time is useless. This is not a joke.

A patient's time is valuable also. Many friends and acquaintances say they would not put up with any of the above but as a cancer patient our relationship with our doctors is very important so we tend to be more liberal with inconveniences than others.

CHAPTER 63

WAITING ROOMS

My book would be incomplete if I didn't apply my art education and knowledge to an area surely not covered in medical school at least from my perspective.

I believe doctors consider their office and waiting room décor as an afterthought. Your waiting rooms speak volumes about you and have an effect on your patients. When were your offices last updated and repainted, ten, twenty or thirty years ago? If they haven't been painted in at least five years your office is due for one. A run-down office begs the question, "Are you as a doctor keeping up with your own medical knowledge and newly discovered treatments?"

Certain colors do not belong in your office. Dark browns may have been the in color when your office was last painted but it belongs in your house not on the walls of your waiting room. The color is depressing and not a hopeful emotion for your patients. Grey is another depressing color.

Bright reds, yellows, oranges and purples are poor wall choses as well. They evoke a hyper temperament and your patients' blood pressure may elevate just waiting to see you. Bold stripes and modernistic designs cause anxiety. Black is not the new white and all white is reminiscent of a mental institution with padded cells. Do not even consider neons or chartreuse.

Pale blue, light green and most cool pastels tones relay a feeling of calm and control. A toned down pink is apropos for a gynecologists office. White painted moldings and trim will add to the design and contribute to a sanitary looking area. A small room will look larger and people will not feel confined.

Redo the seat cushions on your chairs in a durable washable fabric. No one likes to sit on seats with numerous stains on them.

Please get rid of those faded old posters. They've lost their color and contribute nothing to the décor. One or two colorful and appropriate sized paintings will give interest to the waiting room.

Another area to consider is lighting. Replace your burned out light bulbs. Remove those dark, dusty and dirty lampshades. Consider replacing them with brighter ceiling lights. At the same time get rid of the old faded and dusty drapery. You need a more modern clean look in your waiting room. Always remember this is an office not your home. Clutter makes small waiting areas even tinier. It is also very doubtful if every item is dusted constantly. Consider how the dust is affecting your patients and staff?

Change your carpet if it is stained, fraying or buckling up and avoid someone tripping over it. The carpet can be replaced with a safer, more durable and inexpensive bamboo or man-made wood floor.

Those dead plants and old small Christmas trees with remnants of decorations should be tossed. Your patients come to you to get well not to die; let the feeling start in your waiting room.

The clothing hooks in some of your offices were screwed into the walls by men over six feet tall as they stood on a ladder. The great majority of your patients are unable to reach them, thereby rendering the hooks absolutely useless.

One area that never ceases to amaze me is the reading material doctors provide for their patients. Why in the world is "Parent" magazine the only thing to read if you're in an office treating seniors? And why do male doctors only consider sport magazines for patients? How about a variety? Not everyone has an electronic reader to bring to your office.

Please replace or repair broken toilet paper holders and paper towel containers in the bathroom. Have someone refill the empty soap bottles. Hire a cleaning company if necessary. Talk to your accountant to see if it's tax deductible. But please do not make your patients bring their own soap, toilet paper and towel when they see you.

Never use a highly perfumed spray or plug-in. If an odor absorber is necessary purchase an odorless one that will not adversely affect your patients. Cancer patients in general are more sensitive to odors. Gilda's Club has signs to avoid perfumes for exactly this reason.

Kudos to those doctors who at least have a water cooler in the waiting room! More kudos to those who keep some snacks on hand. After a wait of several hours a "pep me-up" is often needed. Even if a snack area exists in your building, what good does that do for the patient who is waiting for you in a paper gown?

If you are a doctor and have an emergency, a patient can wait a very long period of time with nothing to do but think about the way your office is decorated and what the office lacks.

IN CONCLUSION

My Aunt Lillian's advice about laughing continues to be an echo in my head as I encounter horrendous or ridiculous circumstances. Frequently joking about a situation comes naturally to me and perhaps those are the Bott genes kicking in. At times my demeanor may be sarcastic at the very stupidity of some encounters or the people I must deal with on various occasions. If sarcasm helps me get through a major dilemma, it's acceptable as far as I'm concerned.

It is also incumbent upon all of us who have been affected and those in the medical profession treating lymphedema of our upper bodies and extremities to insist our condition be recognized as an illness brought on by the treatment of breast cancer. We need advocates.

Everyone in the medical field and patients should be clamoring for insurance companies to pay for our treatment including massages, bandages, machines and compression garments. Medicare pays for medication and shoes for diabetics with no cut-off visits to doctors or hospitals. Why shouldn't lymphedema patients be treated the same way? Lymphedema like diabetes is a lifelong condition that needs continuous treatment.

All major cancer organizations should not only be educating doctors, the public and our government about breast cancer but educating them about lymphedema. Perhaps we will not have to contend with rude people if they are made aware of our condition. The public knows what a crutch is even if they've never used one. Use your advertising ability to help people recognize lymphatic bandages and sleeves. Advertise lymphedema along with breast cancer. TV shows and movies often have a story line about breast cancer. Why not about lymphedema? Lymphedema not only changes our lifestyle but those around us.

I believe it is imperative that we as patients politely inform our doctors if there is a problem in their office. How else will they know? The situation isn't a restaurant where someone can set up cameras to film and record what is going on with their staff.

More than once I've heard friends, doctors and other medical staff say I make them laugh. The ability to laugh at myself is therapeutic. Laughter plays a role in the acceptance of my condition. I can move forward and enjoy the future. Having others laugh at my condition is unacceptable. It's not only insulting and degrading but may touch on very sensitive areas I've spent years trying to forget.

One of my dear friends and I were having an interesting conversation. Lois was depressed. I told her the story of my belly dancing at the class in St. Augustus. After a good laugh she said, "We've had such a long friendship and I didn't know you had a belly dancing talent. What else have I missed?" I promised to let her know as soon as I discover more. I do know cancer and lymphedema are not going to stop me from finding out or laughing. Even writing this book is a new adventure and I laughed recalling many of the episodes in my life. Many horrendous ones are behind me and I'm still alive to write about them.

A main goal of mine was to give you the incentive, motivation and inspiration to move on with your own life and practical hints to achieve a successful outcome. Look to every one of your own encounters as a learning experience. You will be less inclined to make the same errors over again.

Keep your mind in focus about the reason you want to survive and concentrate on it. Your life may depend on this thought by the decisions you make, the tests you may have to endure and ultimately your treatment and recovery. I have not thrown in the towel without a fight. Neither should you. Keep laughing.

ADDITIONAL NOTES
ABOUT THE AUTHOR

Rosalie admits, "My mind doesn't seem to work the same way as many other people I meet who are more traditional in their way of thinking. I tend to be very creative and always look for a solution to problems on a 24/7 basis, often resulting in the loss of much needed sleep."

Rosalie is a survivor of multiple individual cancers. Lymphedema appeared with her first mastectomy in her left hand and wrist almost immediately after her surgery. Additional lymphedema areas were the result of a second mastectomy. All lymphedema sites were exasperated by scar tissue from a nephrectomy, spinal laminectomies and other surgeries resulting in a weight gain and affecting her breathing. Lymphatic massage, the break-up of scarring and an adherence to a certain lifestyle and diet help keep her lymphedema under control.

Rosalie stays very active in the cancer community and participates in on-going exercise and dance programs at St. Augustus. She is a willing participant in sharing her information and giving support to others and is extremely happy she has people to turn to when the role is reversed.

Her husband Ben, a former music teacher and band leader is also creative in his own way. Rosalie and Ben spend many hours a week laughing at what they realize is total nonsense in the world they inhabit.